THE SECOND EMPIRE
AND
ITS DOWNFALL

Flandrin *Versailles*

NAPOLEON III

[*Frontispiece*

The Second Empire
:: *and Its Downfall* ::

The Correspondence of the Emperor Napoleon III
and his Cousin Prince Napoleon, now published
for the first time by ERNEST D'HAUTERIVE
And Translated from the French by - - HERBERT WILSON

Napoléon III, Emperor of the French, 1808-1873.

DC
275.2
N63
1970

WITH TWO ILLUSTRATIONS

719912

LAMAR UNIVERSITY LIBRARY

BOOKS FOR LIBRARIES PRESS
FREEPORT, NEW YORK

First Published 1925
Reprinted 1970

STANDARD BOOK NUMBER:
8369-5464-5

LIBRARY OF CONGRESS CATALOG CARD NUMBER:
74-126266

PRINTED IN THE UNITED STATES OF AMERICA

CONTENTS

	PAGE
Foreword	9

CHAPTER I

Death of Queen Hortense—Arenenberg—The abortive attempt at Boulogne—Captivity of Prince Louis Napoleon at Ham—Prince Napoleon's duel—Financial straits of Prince Louis—Prince Napoleon asks permission to go to Ham—An endeavour to dispose of some articles of value **17**

CHAPTER II

Prince Napoleon in Paris—Petitions to be allowed to go and see his cousin at Ham—A visit to the Tuileries—Situation of Prince Napoleon in Paris—The escape from Ham—Prince Louis in London—Death of Prince Napoleon's brother **31**

CHAPTER III

The Revolution of 1848—Election of Prince Louis as a Deputy—Prince Louis elected President of the Republic—Prince Napoleon and the Spanish Embassy—Prince Napoleon reprimanded by his cousin—Plot against the Prince-President at Marseilles . . **47**

CHAPTER IV

The Crimean War—Prince Napoleon appointed to command a Division—His first beginnings—The situation in Turkey in May 1854—Battle of the Alma; Prince Napoleon awarded the Military Medal—Prince Napoleon returns to Constantinople from the front **59**

CHAPTER V

Return of Prince Napoleon to France—A *brochure* on the conduct of the war—The situation in the Crimea—Birth of the Prince Imperial, 16th March, 1856 . . . . **71**

CHAPTER VI

The Privy Council—Algerian affairs—Prince Napoleon appointed Minister of Algeria and the Colonies—Questions of organisation—Marshal Randon—The Prefecture of Algiers **83**

Contents

CHAPTER VII

Italian affairs—Mission of Prince Napoleon to Varsovie—Newspaper articles—Negotiations with Piedmont—The marriage of Prince Napoleon to the daughter of Victor Emmanuel—French policy as regards Piedmont 101

CHAPTER VIII

Charles Vogt—The *Moniteur* contradicts the reports as to France getting ready for war—Prince Napoleon resigns his position as Minister of Algeria and the Colonies—Is reprimanded by the Emperor Napoleon—Preparing for the war in Italy . . . 113

CHAPTER IX

The Congress—Russia proposes the summoning of a European Congress—The question of Piedmont having a seat on the Board—The Prince's views on the Ministers—The armed watch . . 123

CHAPTER X

The Campaign in Italy—Prince Napoleon in Tuscany—Issues a Proclamation—Commencement of the campaign—The Prince's Corps—March of the 5th Corps—An Armistice—Mission of Prince Napoleon to Verona to the Emperor Francis Joseph—His return to Paris 135

CHAPTER XI

Death of King Jerome—Prince Napoleon at the Palais Royal and at Meudon—The siege of Gaeta—The lawsuit brought by the issue of King Jerome's first marriage in America with Elisabeth Paterson—Prince Napoleon's vague aspirations—The Emperor's advice to him—The question of Rome 152

CHAPTER XII

The Italian Question and Rome—Prince Napoleon's violent speech on the 1st March, 1861, against the Bourbons, and in favour of the Bonapartes—Reply by the Duc d'Aumale—Prince Napoleon and the Grand Mastership of French Freemasons—His quarrel with Prince Murat, former Grand Master—The Roman Question—Another violent speech in the Senate by Prince Napoleon gives grave offence to the Empress Eugénie—Birth of a son to Prince Napoleon 167

Contents

CHAPTER XIII

The Polish insurrection—Prince Napoleon makes a violent speech in the Senate in favour of Poland and attacking Russia; its bad effect; the Emperor reprimands his cousin—The correspondence of Napoleon I—The Polish refugees—The National Archives . . 185

CHAPTER XIV

Prince Napoleon's indiscreet speech at Ajaccio, entailing a public rebuke by the Emperor, published in the *Moniteur* by his command; the Prince's reply, and his resignation from the Privy Council—Subsequent reconciliation between the Emperor and the Prince—Proposals by the Emperor of a form of government on more liberal lines 206

CHAPTER XV

The last years of the Empire—The Pope's appeal to France for support against the threats of the forces of Garibaldi—Defeat of the Garibaldians at Mentana, and the second occupation of Rome by French troops—Incidents of the Elections of May 1869 . . 221

CHAPTER XVI

The Franco-German War of 1870—Prince Napoleon sent on a Mission to the King of Italy to endeavour to gain his active support for France—The disaster at Sedan of General MacMahon's army on 1st September, and the capitulation of the Emperor; the Emperor a captive at Wilhelmshohe—The Empress Eugénie at Chislehurst—Stormy interviews between the Empress and Prince Napoleon—The Emperor at Chislehurst—The forthcoming Elections in France—Death of the Emperor at Chislehurst, 9th January, 1873 234

APPENDIX

NOTE I

"Letter written to the Emperor on the 18th March, 1856, concerning a general amnesty on the occasion of the birth of his son" . . 255

NOTE II

Note for the consideration of the Emperor on the defence of France . 257

NOTE III

Note for the consideration of the Emperor on affairs in Poland . 261

NOTE IV

Note relative to the publication of the correspondence of Napoleon I sent to the Emperor at Compiègne on the 11th November, 1863 . 268

NOTE V

Note on a conversation between the Emperor Napoleon and myself which took place on the 19th June, 1865, at the Tuileries . . 272

NOTE VI

Petition of Prince Napoleon to the Emperor to be given an acting military appointment in the event of war breaking out in 1866 . 276

NOTE VII

Note on the General Elections of 1869 277

NOTE VIII

Note for the consideration of the Emperor relative to the enrolment of the Napoleonic Archives by making a collection of all the letters of Napoleon I 282

NOTE IX

Project of a *Plébiscite* 285

Index 289

The Second Empire and Its Downfall

FOREWORD

LOUIS NAPOLEON, the future Emperor Napoleon III,[1] was fourteen years older than his first cousin Prince Napoleon.[2] Notwithstanding this difference in age, an intimacy was established between them from an early date, and although at times a few clouds drifted over the atmosphere, nothing was ever to break the close connection binding them together. Their friendship, formed in a land of exile in which both passed their childhood and a portion of their youth, was proof against every trial, and endured up to the death of the Emperor.

They were, however, very different in character, and in many points quite contrary to each other.

[1] Charles Louis Napoleon was the third son of Louis, brother of Napoleon I and King of Holland, and of Hortense de Beauharnais. He was born in Paris on the 20th April, 1808, and died in England, at Chislehurst, on the 9th January, 1873.

[2] Prince Napoleon was the son of the youngest brother of Napoleon I, Jerome, King of Westphalia, who married Princess Catherine of Wurtemberg. Three children were born of this marriage :
    1. Jerome Napoleon, born on the 24th August, 1814 ; died on 12th May, 1847.
    2. Mathilde Letitia Wilhelmine, known as Princess Mathilde, born on the 27th May, 1820 ; died on the 2nd January, 1904.
    3. Napoleon Joseph Charles Paul, the subject of the correspondence given in this work with that of the Emperor Napoleon III, born at Trieste on the 9th September, 1822 ; died in Italy on the 18th March, 1891. Generally known by the name of Prince Napoleon, he signed his letters at first " Napoleon Bonaparte," and afterwards " Napoléon (Jérôme)," being careful to put " Jérôme " in parenthesis so as to emphasise that he was the son of King Jerome and that he did not make use of this name, contrary to what many people have thought. In his infancy his mother gave him a nickname by which people sometimes called him afterwards in jest. We find this in the following letters :
    " You will know," wrote Queen Catherine on the 27th January, 1827, to Mlle. de Ferrol, the godchild of King Jerome, " that we have sent Jérôme (her eldest son) to the college at Sienna. This resolve has cost me much, but I am now recompensed by seeing the progress he is making and the satisfaction felt by his superiors at his conduct. Mathilde is now hardly recognisable so much has she changed and improved, and I was saying the other day that I wished you could hear her play the piano so as to have a pleasant surprise. As for *Plompinette*, he is still the dear little fellow you used to know, and his ways perhaps have acquired still more charm."
    On the 13th December, 1828, Queen Catherine wrote to the Comtesse Wonsowich: " My children are growing big. When I announced to him the infidelity of his *belle* [Mlle. Natalie Potocka, whom the young Prince at the age of six called his '*petite femme*'] *Plomplon* coloured up at first, and then, with an air of disdain, said, ' Well ! It's all the same to me ! ' This is a promising beginning, is it not ? Mathilde is delighted with the pretty belt, for which she sends you her best thanks."

Of a meditative and taciturn character, the future Emperor lived in an attitude of expectation of the fulfilment of a dream, which came to be realised. This *doux entêté*, as his mother called him, wore the appearance of irresolution, because he concealed his will. Extremely good-hearted, of a kindness of disposition exaggerated in the head of a State, and of a patience which nothing could wear down, he knew how to wait; and, because he was master of himself, concealed his impressions, reflected at great length, and did not yield to first impulses, he was accused of indecision. People said he was a fatalist. Deep down he trusted in his star, and the event justified this confidence. Greatly swayed by idealism, he sought after the good of humanity in an upright and honest spirit throughout his life. His aims were always elevated, sometimes carried to the point of exaggeration—for this reproach can justly be brought against him of having been too extended in his views, of having possibly pushed his generosity to the realm of Utopia, and of having striven for the happiness and liberty of nations without sufficiently taking into account the consequences that might result therefrom for the future of that nation of which he was the Sovereign.

His cousin, Prince Napoleon, greatly differed from him. Of a liveliness of disposition which he could not always keep down, very intelligent, very discerning, too much given to criticising, very impulsive, and quick to see through things, he applied himself with ardour to everything, but changed frequently the object of his activities. Napoleon III rightly found it necessary to reproach him with a want of perseverance; his impressions were too lively, his ardour too great, to permit him to continue for long upon the same idea. In reality, throughout his life, despite the multiplicity of his enterprises, events never followed each other sufficiently quickly for his liking, and his immense need for activity was ever to remain unsatisfied.

Under an appearance that at first sight sometimes seemed to be hard and selfish the Prince hid an extreme delicacy of mind. If he preserved under every circumstance a frankness in language which was due to his open-heartedness and horror of *banalité*, he liked discussing things that interested him, and welcomed occasions for so doing. His friends, to whom he was always faithful, might say anything they liked to him. He permitted them to contradict him and even remonstrate with him, so long as he felt they were sincere, without their ever being tempted to become familiar. He was fundamentally good at heart, notwithstanding his somewhat cold reserve and occasional appearance of moroseness. Very attractive when he so willed, he knew better than anyone how to charm when he was talking, and side by side with this quality he had terrible fits of ill humour, and used expressions that overwhelmed his hearers when people or things displeased him. In the Tribune his very real eloquence disregarded the usual rules. If in the course of a public debate an opponent raised his voice against him he would turn on him, rate him, and, far from retiring from the contest, seemed to find his natural element in it.

He never varied in his political ideas. He professed under the Empire the same opinions he had held in exile before 1848, and still kept to them later on, when, as the head of a party, he had once again to find a refuge abroad. Deeply attached to liberty, he understood that only a strong power could ensure it without its falling into licence, and that is why he wished to base it on authority. Contrary to the opinion generally held, he was a spiritual man at heart, and by no means an atheist, but by reason of his liberalism he was anti-clerical, not admitting the right of priests to interfere in certain domains. A democrat in his opinions and speeches, he was imperious in his will. Quick, impatient, authoritative, he never learnt how to wait on events. His projects were barely formed before he wished to see them realised. Of an impetuous nature, he was a rebel to all restraint. His was a difficult character, so people said; in reality he possessed *character* in a marked degree. He was an independent. He took no stock of what people said about him. He sought for straightforwardness and simplicity, with an innate horror of the artificial and of all that savoured of the theatrical. His contempt for calumny refused a hearing to malicious gossip, and, as he showed his faults as readily as he concealed his good qualities, he suffered absurd and unjustifiable stories to be invented about him.

If these two Princes appeared to be so different, they had much common ground to draw them to each other. Besides, the opposition existing between two characters does not necessarily keep their natures apart. On the contrary, it would seem that we ought to apply to human friendships that great physical law by which two bodies can only unite completely if they dovetail into each other, and the salients of the one correspond to the openings in the other. In addition, between these two there existed many points of contact, and even certain similarities.

Brought up in the worshipful veneration of the great Emperor, they remained faithful to his memory throughout their lives. Each in his own way always considered he should be the sole inspirer of their conduct, and the ideal to which their every effort must endeavour to attain. They were both impregnated strongly with his ideas, and, even when some dispute seemed to divide them, each brought forward the view he had held in order to explain to the other their reasons for differing. In their admiration for their uncle, Napoleon III had in mind the *Emperor* especially, and Prince Napoleon the *First Consul*.

They held, therefore, the highest idea of the name they bore. They were proud of it with no arrogance or vanity, and considered rather the duties it laid upon them than the glory it reflected. Profoundly patriotic, they gave the first place to the greatness and welfare of France in their conception of these duties, in the absolute conviction that under modern conditions these could only be assured under the *ægis* of the Napoleons. Extremely sincere, they were absolutely loyal, of great generosity of heart and mind, and of an elevation of ideas and sentiments which placed them above the meannesses of any lower conception of life. Let us add that, habituated to hard work from their childhood, they kept up all their life a taste for serious things and study. From the fact of their living in exile and the difficult circumstances of their early youth their characters ripened before the usual time.

Louis Napoleon became attached to his cousin at a very early date. The latter was at school at Carouge, in Switzerland, when his mother, Queen Catherine, died on the 30th November, 1835. King Jerome took him away, and at the request of Queen Hortense sent him to Arenenberg, where he stayed nearly a year, with no other preceptor than the future Emperor. Between this young master of twenty-eight and the pupil of fourteen, drawn together by the memories they held in common, linked by their misfortunes, and lifted up by their hopes, the most affectionate intimacy was soon established. It was like that uniting two brothers, with this shade of difference : that the elder quickly assumed over the younger an authority to which later events were to give another character, but which was always exercised with gentleness and patience, and accepted with gratitude. We shall see in the ensuing pages debates rising between them, differences of opinion dividing them, and even quarrels causing a momentary separation ; but the two cousins never ceased to love, to esteem, and to prove themselves in their affection.

Strengthened in misfortune, their good relations only suffered temporary eclipse in prosperity. It often happened then that Prince Napoleon opposed his cousin in the exercise of his authority, sometimes created difficulties for his government, and even caused him real embarrassment, but never from any ill intention. It was only from sincerity, when he thought his own political conceptions were better for the country than those which he found fault with. On the other hand, as soon as his cousin found himself in a difficult position the Prince forgot it all in order to get close to him again. The faithful supporter of the prisoner at Ham (Louis Napoleon), on the morrow of our country's disasters we shall see him offering to share the captivity of the fallen Emperor. Far from being a follower of success only, he showed himself in a special degree a faithful friend in our evil days.

In order to unfold the nature of this friendship, leaving aside official letters and keeping to those which reveal an intimate character, we have taken in hand the publication of a correspondence which, with very rare exceptions, which we shall notify, has remained unpublished to this day.

We have in mind at the same time another purpose, namely, to make these two Princes more widely known and to assist the historians of the future to raise them to their true perspective.

Foreword

No one, perhaps, has been more attacked, and more unjustly, than these two men. In both cases political passion and, what is worse, religious passion have intermingled. In their lifetime, at the moment of their power, and later, after the fall of the one and during the retirement of the other, they were insulted, calumniated, and belittled with a fury barely extinguished in our own times. Saner views now permit a more impartial judgment to be brought to bear upon them. The reading of these letters, written with no eye to future publication, will assist the unprejudiced historian, more than anything else, to come to a true understanding of their real natures.

These letters are preserved in the archives of the Villa Prangins, in Switzerland, where Prince Napoleon had classified them himself from among many other *dossiers*. Those written by the Emperor are nearly complete.[1] Prince Napoleon was careful to keep any correspondence that might be of interest. He numbered them with his own hand, as a rule noting the day and place where he had received them, and the date on which he had answered them. There are only a very few which are not included in this collection. Almost all of them are written entirely by the Emperor's own hand. Only a very few were dictated, and these bear merely the Emperor's signature.[2] This correspondence extends over a period of thirty-five years, from 1837 to 1872.

Those written by Prince Napoleon, on the other hand, no longer exist in the original. The Emperor made a practice—he mentions this himself in one of his letters—especially during his detention at Ham, of destroying those he received. Perhaps he may have kept a few; these very probably disappeared from the Tuileries after

---

[1] There are in existence a few other letters of the Emperor, relating to special missions entrusted to Prince Napoleon. We shall have occasion to quote from them later on when dealing with these missions.

[2] We have been careful to indicate those which were dictated.

the 4th September. But the archives at Prangins very happily contain the minutes or drafts of a certain number of the letters written by Prince Napoleon to his cousin after 1852. It is these minutes, sometimes written by the Prince himself, sometimes copied by a secretary, which we reproduce in these pages.

Prince Napoleon had certainly considered the possibility of publishing some at least of the letters from the Emperor. A note found among his papers, constituting a preliminary preparation for this, leaves no doubt on the subject. Far from being under any apprehension of going against his intentions by giving this correspondence to the public at the present day, we believe we are really carrying out his wishes, and at the same time are defending his memory against the attacks of which he has been made the object.

If, on reading one or two of these letters, we are tempted at first sight to judge the character of Prince Napoleon to be a difficult one, we cannot prevent ourselves, even though we do not share his way of looking at things, from recognising his good faith and admiring his disinterestedness, which led him to sacrifice the advantages inherent in his position rather than modify his ideas and principles. Nothing, also, gives better proof than these discussions, of the imperturbable patience of Napoleon III, who might have used his authority to put an end to them without any abuse of it. But if he suffered occasionally from the sudden attacks dealt by his cousin against his conduct of the chariot of the State, he knew well his uprightness, admired his quick intelligence, and never placed his devotion in the least doubts.[1]

---

[1] Nearly all these letters have appeared in the *Revue des Deux Mondes* (15th December, 1923, 1st January, 1st February, and 15th March, 1924). In an Appendix we have added some of the notes, written as a rule in great detail, which Prince Napoleon addressed to the Emperor on current questions.

CHAPTER I

Death of Queen Hortense—Arenenberg—The abortive attempt at Boulogne—Captivity of Prince Louis Napoleon at Ham—Prince Napoleon's duel—Financial straits of Prince Louis—Prince Napoleon asks permission to go to Ham—An endeavour to dispose of some articles of value.

AFTER the failure of his attempt at Strasburg (30th October, 1836) Prince Louis Napoleon was expelled from France and set sail for America. But hardly had he reached New York when he heard that his mother was seriously ill in Switzerland. He returned in all haste to Europe and went to Arenenberg, where Queen Hortense expired in his arms a few days afterwards on the 5th October, 1837.

Shortly after her death he wrote to his cousin who was then at Stuttgart.

Arenenberg, 14th October, 1837.

MY DEAR NAPOLEON,[1]—You will have learnt from your brother, to whom I have written, of the fresh misfortune which has just befallen me. I count sufficiently on your friendship to be aware that you share, and have always shared, my moral sufferings.

My mother leaves you in her will a gift of twenty thousand francs, which I am to hand over to you on your attaining your majority, but interest on which at five per cent. I will pay you from to-day. You will let me know where I shall make payable this little revenue, and if you wish to draw it every six months or every year.

Good-bye, my dear Napoleon. It is with pleasure

---

[1] This letter is addressed : " À Son Altesse, le Prince Napoléon de Montfort, à Stuttgard, Wurtemberg." King Jerome, the father of Prince Napoleon, generally bore the name of Prince of Montfort during his exile.

BE

that I write to you, for I love you as a brother, and in moments of isolation of soul like these it is a great consolation to find a heart that will respond.

Again assuring you of my sincere friendship,

Your affectionate cousin and friend,

NAPOLEON LOUIS.

At the end of 1837 Prince Napoleon, then fifteen years old, and to whom France was closed, was sent by his maternal uncle, the King of Wurtemburg, to be a pupil at the military school at Ludwigsburg. From there Prince Louis Napoleon wrote to him:

Arenenberg, 14th July, 1838.

MY DEAR NAPOLEON,[1]—Although I have been a very long time in replying to your letter, you will not doubt, I hope, the pleasure I experienced in receiving your news, for you know I love you as a brother. I was very glad that one of my friends had seen you, and that he was able to appreciate your good qualities. How I should like to be able to see you again, and how I regret the time when we passed our days together here! Arenenberg is so dreary now! I think you are working well and that soon you will make a finished officer. I almost envy you being able to give yourself up to military exercises. They form the body and mind.

Be so good as to send the enclosed letter to your brother, and rest always assured of my sincere friendship.

Your cousin and friend,

NAPOLEON LOUIS.

On the 6th August, 1840, Prince Louis failed at Boulogne in his fresh attempt to seize upon power. He was at once arrested, and on the 9th October, 1840, was

---

[1] The letter is inscribed: "À Son Altesse le Prince Napoléon Bonaparte, à Ludwigsbourg, Wurtemberg."

condemned by the House of Peers to perpetual imprisonment, and incarcerated at Ham, together with his faithful companions General Montholon and Doctor Conneau. There he was destined to remain nearly six years, to the 25th May, 1846. During this long captivity he never lost courage or patience. After a certain interval he was permitted to receive letters, and even visits. He made good use of his long hours of solitude by work. The numerous writings which issued from his pen during this period are there to prove his activity, which was employed unceasingly in the propagation of his ideas and in preparing himself for the *rôle* which he felt he was called upon to play.

We have twenty letters from him written to Prince Napoleon during this period, but, unfortunately, the replies of the latter have been lost. During these years Prince Napoleon had completed his education at Ludwigsbourg, had served for two years on the staff in that place and had left the army of Wurtemburg, the spirit existing in which differed too strongly from his own. He rejoined his father at Florence, with whom he spent a few years, varying this sojourn with journeys to Italy, Spain, and England.

Ham, 11th February, 1841.

MY DEAR NAPOLEON,—I cannot tell you how much pleasure your letter from Florence afforded me. I have never doubted your friendship for me, but it is very sweet, in the position in which I am placed, to receive proof of this. Although it is long since I saw you, your memory has not been effaced in my heart, and I have often taken back my thoughts with pleasure to the times we spent together with my dear mother. To prove to you, my dear friend, how brotherly is my friendship for you, I will tell you that before leaving London,[1] in my wish to

[1] To go to Boulogne.

provide for all eventualities, I made a will leaving to you, as sole heir, all I possess.

I will not speak of my present position; you can well guess what it is. They keep me always in strict seclusion, and the only companionship I have is that of General Montholon and Doctor Conneau. I pass the time in study, in reflecting and hoping. Moreover, I have no regrets for what I have done.

Good-bye, my dear Napoleon. Assuring you of the sincere and brotherly friendship of your cousin and friend,

Napoleon Louis.

Ham, 15th *November*, 1841.

My Dear Napoleon,—Very many thanks for your letter, and the promptness with which you executed my commission. I am sending you a note concerning questions on which I wish to be enlightened.[1] I think this will be difficult.

I have seen in the newspapers that your brother had a fall from his horse at Florence. I trust he has now recovered. When you write to me next you will give me great pleasure if you will tell me of the health of my father,[2] for I have heard nothing about it for a long time. Put your letters in the envelope of M. Noël, notary in Paris, 13 Rue de la Paix. Sent thus they will not be read, and you will be able to give me more details of your life and secret thoughts, which, I am certain, must be closely akin to my own.

I am always busy. Nevertheless, my work on Charlemagne does not make much progress. There is so much research work to do that sometimes I feel discouraged.

---

[1] To this letter, which was addressed to Florence, a note was appended indicating different points which the Prince wished to be made clear in connection with a study on Charlemagne in which he was engaged. He asked particularly if there was in existence "a portrait of Charlemagne other than that preserved in the Monastery of St. Callisto in Rome." This portrait will be referred to again in the following letter.

[2] After being exiled under the Restoration, together with the other members of the Imperial family, King Louis (late King of Holland) had retired to Florence.

Although my sojourn here is not very amusing, my only fear is an amnesty, for here I am in the midst of my fellow-citizens, and from time to time receive visits which give me great pleasure.

Good-bye, my dear Napoleon, with renewed assurances of my sincere friendship.

Your cousin and friend,
NAPOLEON LOUIS.

Ham, 22nd January, 1842.

MY DEAR NAPOLEON,—I have long wished to reply to your letter of the 18th December, but although I am in prison I am always lazy in writing letters; besides, I work so much that that takes up all my time. However, I must tell you, *mon cher ami*, how touched I am by your kind friendship. Although I only knew you when you were a child, and you are a man now, you were always old enough for me to be able to discover all your good and solid qualities, and you well prove to me that I was not mistaken.

Be kind enough to present my respects to your father, and express to him my sincere good wishes for his happiness at the new year.

If Comtesse Camerata[1] is at Florence be good enough to give her the enclosed letter, or send it her where she may happen to be.

Buzolini, unfortunately, is not getting on with the monument to my mother. Tell him that when it is finished I should much like him to exhibit it at some artist's, but only in Paris. I have charged Madame Salvage (with whom, in parenthesis, I am not on very good terms) to urge on this work.[2]

---

[1] Napoléone Elisa Bacciochi, the daughter of Elisa, sister of Napoleon I, born in 1806, died in 1869, married Count Camerata in 1824.

[2] In the end the sculptor, Bar, executed this monument raised by Prince Louis to the memory of his mother. It is in the church at Rueil, where also lies the tomb of Joséphine.

I am much obliged to you for the trouble you have taken over my questions on the history of Charlemagne. After what you tell me I must give up the portrait.

And now, my dear cousin, I have nothing further very interesting to tell you. Here everything is perfectly calm; but it is not more reassuring for that; they still continue to exercise the same surveillance over me, for every day there are seditious cries in the detachment of troops. In addition they change the garrison very often. Every day I receive touching proofs of sympathy, but all that will be of no use so long as the different parties make mutual war upon each other.

Good-bye, my dear friend. May God grant that one day we may be united under the same flag, and that I may be able to prove all the brotherly friendship I have for you.

Your cousin and friend,
N. L.

6th July, 1842.

MY DEAR NAPOLEON,—In a few days you will receive the 215,000 francs I owe you. I am grieved to have made you wait some weeks, but my position is the reason.

I have nothing very interesting to tell you except that a regiment, when passing through here a short while ago, gave evidence of their sympathy for me in so unequivocal a manner that at one moment people thought they were going to carry the citadel by assault. This consoles me for my position, for I am sure that the shade of the Emperor is protecting and blessing me. Ah! how greatly I prefer the sympathy of the people to the homage your sister is going to seek at Neuilly!

Good-bye, my dear Napoleon. Forgive me this indiscretion, but you who have a heart must think of the cruel difference there is between the memories of Arenenberg and those of to-day.

With, etc.,
       Your affectionate cousin and friend,
                      N. L.

Ham Fort, 23rd September, 1843.

MY DEAR NAPOLEON,[1]—Your letter of the 15th, which I have just received, has made me happy, for it is a long time that I have been without news of you, and was wishing to tell you with what interest I have been following all your footsteps during the past year.

Recently I have been wanting to write to you to say how anxiously I was awaiting the result of your duel,[2] when the newspapers arrived to reassure me, and also I did not know where to write to you. You tell me nothing of your state of health; this proves that your wound was nothing of much account. I am very glad of this. Do not worry yourself over what certain bad newspapers have said about you; all those I have read have been in your favour.

You give me great pleasure in proposing to come and see me, and may assure yourself that this would be a real boon to me, but I am afraid they will refuse to let you. You would, perhaps, have first to ask if you might cross France, and make the other request only when you are once there. It is such a long time since we have seen each other, and we should have so many things to relate; and, though I am persuaded that characters such as yours do not change, we should need to see each other

---

[1] Prince Napoleon received this letter at Lucca, on the 3rd October.
[2] Prince Napoleon had just fought a duel with swords with Count De la Roche Pouchin, a general in the service of the Duke of Lucca. The provocation had taken place after an altercation at the theatre in Florence on the 15th October, 1842. Although from that moment the Prince had kept himself always at the disposal of his adversary and had even persistently sought him, the meeting, owing to various circumstances, did not take place before the 5th September, 1843, at Heilbronn in Wurtemberg. In the third round they were both wounded.

again in order to a thorough understanding. I saw Lucien Murat[1] last year and we spoke much about you.

I am not unhappy, for I do not believe my sufferings are without their uses, and I have the conviction of having done my duty, and of being the only one, indeed, of my family who has done so, for I have sacrificed my youth, my fortune, and my life to the triumphing of the cause which we cannot desert without dishonour.

There is no need to repeat what pleasure your letter gave me, for it is so sad in my position not to receive any mark of sympathy from one's family when foreigners and strangers to me are unceasingly prodigal of them! Well, one must resign oneself and be firmly convinced that there is no justice for the conquered.

Good-bye. Present my respects to your father, and accept the renewed assurance of my sincere and unalterable friendship.

Your cousin and friend,
N. L.

Conneau much appreciates your kind remembrance and presents *ses hommages empressés*.

Fort of Ham, 26th December, 1843.

MY DEAR NAPOLEON,[2]—I wish to write you a few lines for the New Year, and to beg you to give me news of yourself more often. It is so sad, in my position, only to receive news of one's family through the newspapers. I have also to beg you to do me a service. I am now in such an unfortunate position that I am trying to sell all I possess. Could you get M. Demidoff[3] to buy a portrait

---

[1] Lucien Murat (1803–78), the second son of Joachim Murat (King of Naples), and of Caroline, the sister of Napoleon I.

[2] This letter was received at Florence on the 3rd January, 1844.

[3] Count Anatole Demidoff married Princess Mathilde, the sister of Prince Napoleon, on the 21st October, 1841. Since her marriage, although living in Italy for the greater part of the time, Princess Mathilde occasionally went to Paris, where she had a *pied-à-terre*.

of the Empress which I have in Paris, painted by Prudhomme,[1] valued at 20,000 francs, and a fine cameo of Augustus found by General Bonaparte in Egypt, which has become historic? Laurent speaks of it in his history of the Emperor illustrated by Horace Vernet. I should like to sell it for 20,000 francs. My mother attached such value to it that she left it to the King of Rome in her first will.

The newspapers say that Countess Camerata is in France. I shall be very sad if she does not come and see me.

Good-bye, my dear Napoleon, with renewed assurances of my sincere and fraternal friendship.

Your cousin and friend,

N. L.

27th July, 1844.

MY DEAR NAPOLEON,[2]—Your letter gave me the greatest pleasure, for it is a real happiness to me to receive the assurance that your friendship has not changed, and that I can always consider you as a brother.

Yesterday I addressed to M. Duchâtel[3] a request conformable with the desire you express and with my own, and I hope we shall receive permission. In any case I asked for an answer of some sort in order to know what to expect. We shall have many things to tell each other, for it is a very long time since fate has separated us, and I experience keenly the need of letting my woes and my hopes overflow into the heart of a real friend.

I beg you will hand to my uncle Jérôme the enclosed

---

[1] This refers to the portrait of Joséphine by Prudhon, not Prudhomme.
[2] Received at Florence 7th August.
[3] Minister of the Interior. Prince Louis had asked him to permit his cousin to come and see him at Ham. This authorisation was never granted.

letter which I have received from that good Ornano,[1] who is in prison at Doullens. It will explain to him the nature of the request which I would ask you to support.

I was very pleased to learn that my little *brochure*[2] had reached you, and that we sympathise in our opinions as in our sentiments.

Good-bye, my dear Napoleon. God grant that we may soon meet again. Meanwhile accept etc.,

Your cousin and friend,

N. L. B.

Ham, 3rd August, 1844.

MY DEAR NAPOLEON,[3]—I have really tears in my eyes while I write to warn you that we must not expect a favourable reply from the Minister. Yesterday I received a very plain refusal. I am told that the Government cannot authorise your journey because the law forbids it.

I confess I am all the more disappointed because I believed they would grant this permission. Well, when one is not the stronger one must submit, and await patiently better times.

With the renewed assurance, my dear Napoleon, of the sincere and tender friendship of your cousin and friend,

NAPOLEON LOUIS.

Ham, 25th October, 1844.

MY DEAR NAPOLEON,[4]—I know that several of your friends are making moves to obtain permission for your

---

[1] Napoleon d'Ornano (1806–59). He took part in the attempt at Boulogne and was condemned to prison by the House of Peers. He was detained at Doullens, also at Persigny.

[2] *De l'Extinction du Pauperisme.*

[3] Prince Napoleon received this letter on the 15th August in Rome.

[4] Received on the 6th November at Florence.

journey to France. I therefore still hope that I shall be able to have the happiness of seeing you again.

To-day I am writing to you to beg you to do me an immense service. You are aware that misfortunes never come singly, and that I have been struck on every side at the same moment. Now I have just received very disheartening news, for it deprives me of my last resources. Everything is not lost entirely, but before a year or two I shall have nothing left. In this extreme case I see no other means of saving myself than to sell all that remains to me, or to try and borrow on it.

Be so kind as to apply to Demidoff on my behalf, and make him the following proposition, either to buy for two hundred thousand francs the articles of which I will give you a list, or to lend me this sum for five years on the same. This is what they consist of:

	FRANCS
1. The talisman of Charlemagne given to the Emperor by the clergy of Aix-la-Chapelle.[1] I estimate its value at	150,000
2. The cameo of Augustus which General Bonaparte found in Egypt among the ruins of Pelusium, valued at	20,000
3. A Gobelin tapestry	20,000
4. A splendid portrait of the Empress, by Prud-homme, valued at	20,000
5. The wash-hand-stand of Louis XIV	5,000
Total	215,000

I should be very grateful to him if he would render me this service, for it would extricate me from cruel embarrassment, for I bear charges, diminishing, it is

---

[1] This cameo of Augustus and Prudhon's portrait of the Empress Joséphine have already been mentioned in the letter of the 26th December, 1843. As regards the talisman of Charlemagne it is a sapphire inside which there is a fragment of the True Cross. It was not sold. Napoleon III gave it to the Empress Eugénie who, in 1919, made a gift of it to the treasures in the Cathedral of Rheims.

true, every day, but which are none the less heavy at the present moment. I beg you, my dear Napoleon, to spare no pains to bring this negotiation to a successful issue, to which I attach such an important value. You can see how cruel is my situation—I who have never thought of money, and have always been happy to give of it in order to oblige others.

In any case send me an answer as soon as possible, for there is nothing worse than uncertainty, and if you do not succeed I must seek elsewhere.

If your brother-in-law is not willing to take the whole lot offer him a portion.

With etc., my dear Napoleon,

N. L.

I have had the pleasure of seeing M. Alexandre Dumas, to whom I talked much about you.

Ham, 2nd December, 1844.

MY DEAR NAPOLEON,[1]—I have received your two letters and send you my best thanks for all the steps you have taken to help me. I hope that one day I shall be able to return you good for good and to give you proofs of my sincere friendship. Do you think our cousin, Comtesse Camerata, could be useful to me at this moment? Write to her, I beg of you, and tell me where she is.

I have read the letters you have written to Prince de Canino,[2] and I can imagine how much the ridiculous pretensions of this person must have irritated my uncle and yourself; but it is impossible to have the correction you speak of made in the French opposition journals, for this special reason, among others, that it is sufficient

---

[1] Prince Napoleon received this letter at Florence on the 11th December.
[2] Charles Lucien Jules Laurent Bonaparte, Prince de Canino (1803–57), the eldest son of Lucien (brother of the Emperor) and of Alexandrine de Bleschamps. *L'Almanach Populaire* of 1845 gives a note—inaccurate as regards certain dates—of all the then existing members of the family of Napoleon I. As regards Lucien it says that this brother of the Emperor, being unwilling to separate from his second wife, received no French title. It was the Pope who conferred upon him the title of Prince de Canino.

to excite universal laughter in France only to mention the name of the *Almanach de Gotha*. I have already anticipated your wish by having inserted in the *Almanach Populaire* of 1845, which I am sending you, a notice of the family wherein each member is put in his right place. This almanac has a circulation in France of 60,000 copies. It is better for our purpose than the *Almanach de Gotha*.

Besides, my influence only extends to the provincial newspapers. And, as a matter of fact, there are twenty of these which are very favourable to me.

I am still hoping that they will give you permission to come and see me. The moment Switzerland is open I will have M. Duchâtel approached by some of my Deputy friends.

Madame Cornu,[1] a woman of high intelligence, and one with whom I have many links, and who was at Venice at the same time as you, would have much liked to see you, but she missed you.

When you next write to me give me news of my father. Tell me how he is, if you see him sometimes, and if you talk to him of me.

I shall be very glad when the monument to my mother is finished. Madame Salvage has the matter in hand, for I gave her the money for it four years ago. I have quarrelled with her, for she has behaved in a most unworthy manner towards me.

With renewed assurances, etc., my dear Napoleon,

Your cousin and friend,

N. L.

28*th December*, 1844.

My dear Napoleon,[2]—I assure you I am greatly touched by the reiterated proofs of friendship which

---

[1] Hortense Lacroix, the wife of Sebastien Cornu the painter. She was the god-daughter of Prince Louis Napoleon, and a distinguished writer.

[2] Prince Napoleon received this letter at Florence on the 6th January, 1845.

you give me, and it is a happiness to me to find in you all the tenderness of a brother. Thank you for having spoken to Comtesse Camerata about the objects I have to sell. If she desires the wash-hand-stand of Louis XIV ask her where she wishes I should send it, and beg her to send what she would like to give for it to my notary, M. Noël, 13 Rue de la Paix, Paris.

I have received from M. Noël the answer that he has had a search made in his study and that he has not found the declaration of which M. de Stolting[1] had spoken to me, but that he will make a search at the Secretariat of State.

How much I regret, my dear Napoleon, not to be able to see you! I should have so much to tell you! But if I must renounce this expectation for the moment, I much hope that our separation will not last for ever.

You will give me much pleasure if you will send me the books you mention, of which I have only heard a very short while ago. With my good wishes for the New Year accept the sincere and solid friendship of your cousin and friend,

NAPOLEON LOUIS.

[1] King Jerome's Secretary.

CHAPTER II

Prince Napoleon in Paris—Petitions to be allowed to go and see his cousin at Ham—A visit to the Tuileries—Situation of Prince Napoleon in Paris—The escape from Ham—Prince Louis in London—Death of Prince Napoleon's brother.

AFTER many fruitless endeavours, on the representations of King Jerome and with the powerful intervention of Comte Duchâtel, Minister of the Interior, Guizot authorised Prince Napoleon to make a provisional sojourn in France, or, more exactly, promised to close his eyes to the journey of the Prince, without granting any written authorisation. At the same time the Government, through the French Minister at Florence, handed to him a passport in the name of Comte de Starberg.

The Prince arrived in Paris on the 16th May, 1845. Two days after, certain persons advised him to call upon Comte Duchâtel, who was specially concerned in the matter. Before going to the Minister the Prince was anxious to know if he should call. The Minister, being forewarned, replied that this step could not fail to embarrass him greatly, since nothing was known officially of the presence of the Prince in Paris. Under these circumstances the Prince kept away.

At the beginning of June he preferred a request to the Minister of the Interior asking whether they would feel disposed to grant him permission to go to Ham and stay a few days with his cousin, whom he had not seen since 1836. The reply was given that this authorisation rested with King Louis Philippe, and that the Ministry would be far from favourable.

Friends counselled the Prince to see the King. He

hesitated, and wished to have his cousin's advice, who, after being made *au courant* with the position verbally, wrote to Prince Napoleon that he approved of the step.[1]

The audience took place on the 9th June at the Tuileries and lasted twenty minutes. The conversation turned principally on Prince Louis, of whom the King spoke first. To the request made by Prince Napoleon that he might go to Ham the King replied that, personally, he would be very favourable to it, but that it was a question that rested with the Ministers.

At the end of a month, not receiving any reply, the Prince wrote again to the Minister of the Interior. On the 9th July his chief secretary came to announce to the Prince that his request had been definitely refused.

The Prince tried in vain to obtain a written reply instead of a merely verbal answer. The Minister obstinately refused to give this. Finally, after numerous discussions, it was agreed that the Minister should send Prince Napoleon an exact statement of the steps taken in connection with this proceeding, and that this document should be regarded as equivalent to a written refusal.[2] Prince Napoleon himself drew up in all their details an account of these negotiations,[3] which, to the great grief of the two cousins, ended in failure, and their separation was to last until after the escape from Ham.

The first impression produced by Prince Napoleon in Parisian society was excellent. "Everyone," Thiers wrote to King Jerome on this occasion, "was struck by his personality, by his resemblance to the most popular figure in modern times, and by what is of greater value —his spirit, tact, and perfect attitude." However, the Government soon took umbrage at his too freely

---

[1] Letter of the 7th June, 1845.
[2] This statement is alluded to by Prince Louis at the beginning of his letter of the 31st July, 1845.
[3] Dated 16th July, 1845.

The Second Empire and Its Downfall

expressed opinions, and especially at his relations with various personages of the democratic party. Scarcely four months after his arrival the Minister presented him with an order to depart. He had to set out again on the road to exile without having fulfilled the principal object of his journey, which had been to see the prisoner at Ham.

During his stay in Paris the latter wrote him the following letters :

22nd May, 1845.

MY DEAR NAPOLEON[1],—I am very happy to hear of your arrival, for I am hoping to be able to see you. Very many thanks for the books you are bringing me. You must go and see that good fellow Félix Desportes, who lives at 6 Rue Lafitte. It will be a great pleasure to him. In a few days I will send M. Joly, a Député, to see you. He will introduce you to M. Courtois, also a Député. M. Vieillard[2] can introduce you to MM. Larabit, Abbattucci, Marie Cambacérès, De Beaumont, etc.

Do not receive anyone whom you do not know, for there are a host of intriguers and spies. Among the latter I will mention Fortins, Burillon, and Paoli, a Corsican.

I hope you will not go to see the King, but I should esteem it quite natural for you to see M. Duchâtel, who is provisionally carrying on the Ministry of Foreign Affairs, in order to thank him for having given you leave (to come to France). This would dispense you from going to see M. Guizot. You could then make a verbal request to M. Duchâtel for permission to come to Ham.

[1] This letter is addressed to : " S. A. le Prince Napoléon, Paris." He received it on the 23rd May.
[2] Narcisse Vieillard (1791-1857), who is often mentioned in this correspondence, was formerly an officer. He had been tutor to the brother of the future Emperor, and after the death of that young Prince (1831) he came back to France, where he entered political life shortly after. A Député, and then Senator, he remained to the end of his days firmly attached to Napoleon III.

CE

I envy your lot in being free in Paris, and, though your heart must often be full, it is something still more to see one's fatherland.

Good-bye, my dear Napoleon. Assuring you of my sentiments of constant and sincere friendship,

Your cousin and friend,

N. L.

If you think it would not compromise you, I should be charmed if you would go and see Colonel Voisin, who is in a home of rest at Passy, and is one of my most faithful and devoted friends.

H., 4th June, 1845.

MY DEAR NAPOLEON,[1]—I hasten to answer your letter of the 2nd, and send this by Bure,[2] my foster-brother and confidential agent.

I think what is best to be done, situated as you are, is to reply to those persons who counsel you to go to the *château*[3] "that you cannot go there before coming here, for people would think doubtless that you were abandoning your cousin and friend in his misfortune." This reply will have the effect, perhaps, of accelerating your obtaining permission, and we shall have in that case time to discuss this visit together.

If you come here you will be able to lodge at the Commandant's, but you will have to obtain from the Minister his authority for this.

Good-bye, *mon cher ami.* I too am longing to embrace you.

Your cousin,

N. L.

[1] This letter, similarly addressed to Paris, was received on the 6th June.
[2] Pierre Jean François Bure (1808–82) became Treasurer-General to the Crown under the Empire.
[3] That is, the Tuileries.

Ham, 7th June, 1845.

MY DEAR NAPOLEON,[1]—I have just seen Visconti, who has explained your position to me. Since you are good enough to ask my advice, I counsel you to accept the invitation of which I have been told and go to the [*château*], with a view to asking permission to come and see me. Taken and explained in this tense, this visit will present fewer inconveniences.

I have heard that the Duchesse de Raguse, who was very intimate with my mother and has seen you, would much like you to go and call. I think you will do well to gratify her wish. You must endeavour to see everybody. La Duchesse de Raguse is in close relationship with the Faubourg Saint-Germain.

Good-bye, my dear Napoleon. Assuring you of my old friendship,

Your cousin and friend,
N. L.

H., 12th June, 1845.

MY DEAR NAPOLEON,[2]—I have received your letter of yesterday, and hope, more than ever now, to have the happiness of seeing you again. I can well understand that it is difficult to tell me in writing the real substance of the conversation of the R[oi] about me, but nevertheless, if permission should still be delayed, I shall be very impatient to know *as nearly as possible* what he said about me. And for this reason : The day before yesterday I received a visit from the Duc d'Istrie,[3] who told me *many things,* and is to return in six or seven days. Now, before his return I should like to compare *les deux versions d'une même pensée.* You will understand very well what I mean by this.—On my side, I

---
[1] Prince Napoleon received this letter in Paris on the 8th June.
[2] This letter is addressed to : " S. A. le Prince Napoléon Bonaparte, Hôtel Demidoff."
[3] Son of Marshal Bessières.

quite understand all that is difficult and even painful as regards your position. I am longing to be able to talk to you of all this with an open heart.

Meanwhile accept etc.,

Your cousin and friend,

N. L.

Ham, 16th July, 1845.

MY DEAR NAPOLEON,[1]—Bure's return to Paris enables me to write at greater length and from a full heart.

I am very sad to see the hope I had long entertained of seeing you again escaping from me, but I have long accustomed myself to every kind of disillusionment. When one enters the arid career of politics one must expect to have to bear every kind of martyrdom and learn how to support it with resignation.

Your position in Paris is very delicate, I know, and it would have been very far from my thoughts to wish to make it still more delicate through egoism. But the true and sincere friendship I bear to you forces me to speak frankly to you. In spite of the skilful manner in which you have conducted yourself, in spite of the reserve you have put upon your words, your presence in Paris is the subject of a host of suppositions which some spread abroad from silliness, some from envy, and others from hatred of all who bear our name. This is due to the fact that a move which is out of the ordinary channels must be explained openly. The public who do not see you and do not talk to you want to know if you have come to Paris to make common cause (like the rest of my relations) with the oppressors or with the oppressed.

It is for this reason that I begged M. Vieillard on his arrival to explain in the newspapers the purpose of your

[1] Received in Paris on the 18th July.

journey, and I much regret that you have thought, with him, that this would be useless. In reality, the moment after you had arrived it was spread about that you had come to claim what is owing to your father, the next day that you had been sent by my family to induce me to commit a cowardly act.

Even if you *had* come to support the demands of my uncle (for which I am far from blaming you, and even consider it to be wholly natural), it was quite suitable to give another purpose in the newspapers.—I am now compelled every day to break every lance in support of you. Three letters lie before me. In one I am told, "Every person attached to the Government openly repeats that the Prince has only come to support the demands of his father."[1] In another that "if your language is extremely correct you show by your actions an indifference which is doing you harm." In the third I am told "the Government, in according hospitality to your cousin, did not grant it without having its own views and calculations. If there be a pitfall, as I fear, I earnestly hope that he will not fall into it."

Here then, put shortly, my dear Napoleon, you have what people are saying. All this has no effect on the friendship I bear to you, and on the high opinion I have of your character, but it leads me at the same time to tell you that it is absolutely necessary for you to make a firm but sober statement in the newspapers when all hope of coming here shall have departed. *It is indispensable*, both for your sake and mine; for me, in order that people may not feel that I am abandoned by all my relations; for you, in order that people may not say that you are playing a very crafty game, and that after having expressed to my friends your friendship for me, and to the republicans your democratic sentiments,

[1] To be allowed to return to France.

you are doing nothing after all but haunt the *salons* of the despised and contemptible men who govern us!

I owed you the truth, my dear Napoleon, and I have told it to you. But be well assured that all that people can tell me will not change in any respect the brotherly friendship I bear you. Alas! you are the only one of my family whom I love as a brother. You are the only one capable of carrying worthily, as I have endeavoured to do, the great name which chance has given us. It is for this reason that everything that concerns you touches me personally, and the criticisms which people bring to my notice are more keenly felt by me than if they had been directed against myself.

Therefore, my dear Napoleon, receive these counsels without ill feeling, and always believe in the sincere friendship of your cousin and friend,

N. L.

Ham, 31st July, 1845.

MY DEAR NAPOLEON,[1]—I have received at the hands of the Government the statement of the successive steps taken by you, and on the following day your letter through another source, and your last reached me the day before yesterday. I need not tell you how greatly I am grieved at the refusal given to you. I read with pleasure the two articles in the *Courrier* and the *Siècle*, and I think they will be sufficient. If I spoke to you about making a public statement, it was because people had told me that that had been your intention. As a general rule, one must not say beforehand that one intends to do a certain thing when you do not mean to do it. Well, my dear Napoleon, I do not doubt in any way your friendship for me, and you are right in thinking that this conviction is a great consolation to me. I am unable

---

[1] This letter is addressed to: "S. A. le Prince Napoléon Bonaparte, à Paris." He received it on the 2nd August.

to make the request you mention, in the first place because it would be of no effect, and finally because I have stated officially that I would never again address any further request to the Government.

I think Madame Vieillard may come and see me. Will you be so good as to put in writing all that you would not care to say to her? You may be sure that, in accordance with my custom, I shall burn your letter after reading it. I should really be very glad to know what you think of my position, both private and political.

Good-bye, my dear Napoleon. With the constant friendship of your friend and affectionate cousin,

N. L.

H., 24th August, 1845.

MY DEAR NAPOLEON,[1]—I take advantage of an opportunity of writing to you, and to thank you for your letter, which I received three or four days ago. From all points of view I regret not having been able to talk to you for a few hours, for there are things which can hardly be put down in writing, which nevertheless it was urgent that you should know. Possibly our way of looking at things is not quite the same, but that matters little. What *is* important is that we should always be united like two brothers, for since we bear the same name we must increase our strength by union. I will not hide from you that several of my friends (who have not seen you, by the way) have regarded your journey to Paris as a misfortune, and your being received at the Tuileries, etc., and that in their zeal they have even sought to report some of your conversations as being hostile to me, but I have withstood this opinion with my whole strength, and replied to them that you had been forced to take steps which were certainly disagreeable, but that you are my

[1] Received in Paris on the 25th August.

best friend, and that the more they praise you and speak well of you the greater I shall be pleased. In reality one must be very stupid to think that a man can separate his cause from the rest of his family, and that by speaking ill of Peter one is benefiting Paul. For my own part, I have never understood jealousy in politics, because I have enough intelligence to know that this sentiment is the greatest hindrance to the realisation of great things. Besides, there is nothing to be done in these days. The nation sleeps, and will still sleep for a long time. Whatever people may say, I took the only means capable of waking it up, for it was only through the army that one could attempt to do anything. I failed very unfortunately. I cannot and will not begin over again, and I await with resignation a better future. And if ever that time should arrive, be firmly persuaded that my first thought and my first desire will be to link closely your destiny and mine.

You have good reason to like and esteem M. Vieillard. He is the most distinguished and virtuous man I know, but is rather a visionary.

Good-bye, my dear Napoleon. My own heart, too, is very full in thinking that you will pass so close to Ham without my being able to see you. With renewed assurances of my sincere friendship,

Your cousin and friend,
N. L.

I have already been informed in writing that the Government has ordered you to leave as soon as possible.

Conneau greatly appreciates your kind remembrance, and begs me to thank you.

Obliged to leave France without having obtained permission to see his cousin, Prince Napoleon returned to his father and brother at Florence, the latter of whom was now seriously ill. He did not remain there continuously, and was often absent. However, he received while stopping there the two following letters:

H., 27th October, 1845.

MY DEAR NAPOLEON,[1]—Many thanks for the friendly letter you have written me, but before replying to it I must let you know all the grief I feel at reading in the newspapers the sad news concerning your brother. I still hope that it is exaggerated. I beg you to give me news of him, and to express to your father all the concern I feel at this fresh misfortune, which I cannot think is beyond repair.

I have not received your long letter, but there is nothing surprising in that, because I have not yet seen M. Vieillard, who is in the country, in Normandy. I have no doubt he will bring it to me when he comes to Ham. Besides, I have written to him to do so.

They are paying not the least attention in Paris to Pierre,[2] and that is conceivable. He said recently to someone, who at once repeated it, "for my part, all I want is a bottle of wine and my sporting dog." And he spoke truly. I have seen him in New York and London. I did what I could to think well of him, but I have never been able to see in him anything but a very mediocre and false man, the worthy son of his mother, and the worthy brother of his brother. He has written me letters which would have touched me if I had not known his character, and I have not replied to the last. They made him come to Paris in order to efface the good effects produced by your presence.[3] The policy of the

---

[1] Received at Florence on the 5th November.
[2] Pierre Napoleon Bonaparte, the fourth son of Lucien (brother of Napoleon I) and of Alexandrine de Bleschamps (1815–81). His eldest brother Charles had taken the title of Prince de Canino after the death of their father in 1840.
[3] In the margin Prince Louis wrote, "You know that M. Joly has broken his leg."

Government is to try to make us lose credit among ourselves.

There is no use counting on our seeing each other again so long as I am at Ham. The Government knows what it has to believe about me, and is not willing that I should be in a position to tell anyone else with my own lips what I have seen and found out.

But everything has an end in this world, and the young have more chances of a future than the old. However, to-day there is nothing else in France but boilers and locomotives to attract attention. It is true they often explode. They have just changed the garrison yesterday. They have sent a regiment from Paris loaded with medals. They have only been here forty-eight hours, and there are already four men in prison for uttering seditious cries!

Good-bye, my dear Napoleon. Never doubt my sincere friendship,

Your cousin and friend, N. L.

Ham, 12th November, 1845.

MY DEAR NAPOLEON,[1]—Just a word to tell you that Conneau, on his return from Paris, where he has been spending a few days, brought me the letter you sent to M. Vieillard for me. It gave me much pleasure. It does honour to your judgment and to your heart, and I will say no more than that I am entirely of your opinion. In spite of my desire to keep a document which I think very important, I have burnt it in order to be faithful to my promise. I wrote to you a few days ago to enquire after your brother. My respects to my uncle, and with my sincere friendship,

Your cousin and friend, N. L. B.

[1] This letter is addressed to: "S. A. le Prince Napoléon, fils du Prince de Montfort, Florence, Italie." It bears the Ham postmark of the 12th November, and that of Florence of the 20th November. Prince Napoleon annotated it, "Found at Florence, 22nd December, 1845."

On the 25th May, 1846, Prince Louis escaped from Ham and took refuge in England. Knowing that his father was very ill at Florence, he asked permission to go to him. The Grand Duke of Tuscany declared that he would not tolerate his presence in his State, and England refused to give him a passport. The Prince, therefore, found himself obliged to remain in London; he was not to leave until after the revolution of 1848.

As soon as Prince Napoleon heard of the happy escape of his cousin he went to join him in London, where he spent several months with him. In 1847 he returned to his father and brother at Florence. The latter, whose state of health was giving increasing anxiety, expired on the 12th May, 1847.

At this time King Jerome addressed a petition to the House of Peers asking for the abrogation of the law of exile in so far as he and his son were concerned. The question was discussed on the 14th June, 1847, and was put back on the 3rd July, 1847, on the Minister promising to take administrative action. A second debate took place in September, when the *Moniteur* announced on the 27th that the Government authorised King Jerome and his son to reside for a short time in France. The two Princes hastened to take advantage of the permission.

London, 28th April, 1847.

MY DEAR NAPOLEON,[1]—I am obliged to you for having given me your news since your arrival at Florence. What you tell me of the health of your brother causes me much grief, and it is very sad to think that neither you nor I have a child. There will be no more Bonapartes except

---

[1] This letter, which was sent by hand, for it bears no postmark, is addressed to: "S. A. le Prince Napoléon, fils du Prince de Montfort." The Prince received it " at Florence on the 14th "—probably the 14th May.

Lucien's bad stock. I should be very glad to marry. From Dresden there has been no further reply. This lady is really extraordinary!

M. Vieillard, who was to have come, has not arrived yet. He has encountered still further difficulties. Joly is to come and spend a few days here, but it is with a view to asking me for money. I could, therefore, well dispense with his visit.

D'Orsay and Prince Wagram tell me much about you. D'Orsay's sister has written to him giving the highest praise to the dignified and reserved conduct of your sister in Paris. Espartero,[1] to all appearances, will not be appointed here, but it is probable he will be recalled. He sends you a thousand messages. There is nothing fresh to report here. The financial crisis still continues, and apprehension exists as regards next year.

You have seen in the newspapers that I have again been obliged to contradict the calumnies of the Government agents. London is a very dreary place since you left. Whether it be due to the festival of Easter or to poverty, I have not been to a single reception. Jenny Lind[2] has arrived, and will make her *début* on Tuesday. They say that her voice is something surprising. Rachel will come at the end of the season. Thank you for your thoughts of me and of my journey to Italy. I will tell you privately that if I get permission I should not be going until about October.

Present my respects to your father, and accept the assurance of my sincere friendship.

Your cousin and friend,
N. L.

---

[1] Formerly Regent of Spain, he had been overthrown in 1843, and since then had been in England. In 1847 he was allowed to return to Spain.

[2] The success of the Swedish singer in London in 1847 was extraordinary.

The Second Empire and Its Downfall

London, 7th June, 1847.

MY DEAR NAPOLEON,[1]—I must ask your pardon for having been so long before telling you how much I am grieved at the death of your brother. Although I have been long expecting it, I have felt a real sorrow, for of the members of our family I only consider your father, his children, and myself to be true Frenchmen. It is therefore doubly painful to see our small numbers diminishing. I will not speak of your father's petition, because I feel that the fact itself of seeing the sole living brother of the Emperor asking to be allowed to have a fatherland is so touching that it would be unprofitable to discuss the style and manner of drawing up the petition.

As regards the escutcheon of the Emperor which is still in Switzerland, I have begged Colonel Dufour[2] to claim it in my name. I shall not retire from this attitude. The laws of the Empire made me the head of the family. These arms should rightly belong to me, and I will not imitate the unbecoming conduct of my uncle Joseph, who was the only one out of all the members of the family to consent to witness the dispersal of heirlooms which could only remain sacred and inviolable by remaining in the possession of one person alone. In a question of relics an equal division is equivalent to complete destruction.

My cousin Marie[3] gave birth to a son a fortnight ago. She begged me to let my Uncle Jerome know how great is her sympathy over the death of your brother, and that she would have written to him had the state of her health permitted.

---

[1] The Prince received this letter at Livorno on the 19th June.
[2] A Swiss officer (1787–1875). He was appointed General shortly afterwards (1847).
[3] Marie Amélie Elisabeth Caroline (1817–88), daughter of the Grand Duke Charles Louis Frederick of Baden (1786–1818) and of Stephanie Louise Adrienne de Beauharnais (1789–1860), who were married on the 8th April, 1806. She married (23rd February, 1843) William Alexander Antony Archibald, Duke of Hamilton and Brandon. The son just born was Charles George Archibald.

I spent eight days in the country during the Ascot races. There are a crowd of Princes here—the Grand Duke Constantine, Prince Oscar, the Prince of Lucca, the Grand Duke of Saxe-Weimar, etc. Jenny Lind has had an extraordinary success. I have no other news of any interest to send you. The French theatre stumbles along on one leg, and everything is feeling the effects of the present crisis and of the dissolution of Parliament, which will come about in the next month or two.

The absurd rumours in connection with Greece which have been spread abroad about me prevent me at present from taking any steps to go to Italy, but we shall see which way things are turning in the autumn. I hope to see you again between now and then. Let me know if you are still thinking of returning to England, so that I can arrange my travelling plans accordingly.

With the renewed assurance of my sincere friendship,
N. L.

Conneau will be in Florence in a month's time. It appears that Charles[1] (Prince of Canino) will be arriving here at the end of the month. He is now in Paris, and is making any amount of fine professions to me beforehand, accompanied by protestations of friendship!

[1] The eldest son of Lucien (1803-57).

CHAPTER III

The Revolution of 1848—Election of Prince Louis as a Deputy—Prince Louis elected President of the Republic—Prince Napoleon and the Spanish Embassy—Prince Napoleon reprimanded by his cousin—Plot against the Prince-President at Marseilles.

ON the 22nd February, 1848, as soon as the news of the events which were taking place in Paris reached London, Prince Louis, yielding to the solicitations of certain adversaries of Louis Philippe, set out for Paris. He arrived on the morrow of the Revolution and went to stay in secrecy at his friend Vieillard's house. His first concern was to apprise the Provisional Government of his presence, and they replied with an order to leave France immediately. With much wisdom the Prince felt that his hour had not yet struck, and returned to England without protest; he remained there till September.

At the elections held in April, while three of his relations, Prince Napoleon, a son of Lucien, and a son of Murat were elected he did not come forward as a candidate. It was not till the beginning of June, at the supplementary elections, that four Departments elected him a Député. This fourfold choice produced considerable stir throughout the country, particularly in Paris. Although alarmed by this Bonapartist agitation which the Prince's friends, more than he himself, had stirred up, the Assembly accepted him as a representative of the people on the 13th June. But in a letter sent from London to the President on the 14th the Prince wrote this sentence which became famous: "If the people impose duties upon me I shall know how to fulfil them."

The excitement in the Assembly was extraordinary.

People thought they saw in these words an indication of an imminent attempt to seize upon power, and severe measures against the new Député only just escaped being put into force. The latter, who was at once informed, calmed all minds by sending in his resignation on the following day, " in order not to give rise to disorder," as he said.

Confident in his destiny, satisfied with the soundings he had just taken, and pursuing the tactics of advance and retirement with adequate adroitness, the future Emperor remained provisionally in his retreat. He knew better than anyone how to wait.

Prince Napoleon, ever impatient and impetuous, and, moreover, having greater liberty of movement, at once threw himself into the *mêlée*. On the 24th February he presented himself at the Hôtel de Ville, and offered his services to the Provisional Government on the 26th. He was elected Député for Corsica almost unanimously, his election was ratified uncontested, and he took his seat among the moderate republicans at first. He entered into politics with all his ardour and with his will thoroughly determined to bring about the triumph of his ideas over which, notwithstanding his youth—he was barely 26—he had reflected maturely during the hard years of exile. From the outstart he gave himself out as a Liberal, and although he made certain reservations on the two attempts made at Strasbourg and Boulogne, he did not abandon his cousin's cause, who wrote him the following letters at about this time.

London, 5th June, 1848.

MY DEAR NAPOLEON,[1]—You ask me what are my intentions and I hasten to reply that from considerations too long to explain to you to-day I have decided not

Received in Paris on the 6th June.

to accept the mandate to represent the people, honourable as it is. I am extremely flattered that people are kind enough to think of me, but in these times of excitement I prefer to remain in the shade.

Assuring you of my sincere friendship,

N. LOUIS B.

London, 16th June, 1848.

MY DEAR NAPOLEON,[1]—You will be perhaps astonished at the resolution I have taken, which is opposed to your way of thinking, but I feel that at this moment, when people are pretending that my quadruple election is an intrigue, I must prove the contrary by submitting to a fresh election if the people so wish. There is no longer any question of personal or private interest in this. Nothing in the world would prevent me taking up my post if I thought it to be my duty. I thank you for what you have said about me. I only regret that you have felt obliged to blame the attempts of Strasbourg and Boulogne. You need not have said anything about them. We shall only be appreciated as our patriotism deserves by keeping completely united in our ideas and sentiments in the eyes of everyone. What would *you* think, and what would people think of me, if in a speech while praising you up I were to say that I regretted that you had paid court to Louis Philippe?

Make certain of this, my dear Napoleon—we must identify ourselves with each other, under pain of coming to grief otherwise.

My tender respects to my uncle, and with my sincere friendship to yourself,

LOUIS NAP. B.

[1] Received in Paris 17th June.

London, 17th July, 1848.

MY DEAR NAPOLEON,—I am truly astonished to learn that the President¹ has not received the letter I addressed to him through the post on the 8th July. I send you another. Put it in an envelope and be good enough to hand it to the President. I wrote to you that I wished to be re-elected, but, truly, everything changes so quickly these days that at the present moment I do not know if this is desirable. Tell me what you think.

I have just received a letter from my uncle Jerome. In order not to multiply correspondence I beg you will tell him that I have already written to Corsica thanking the electors, and that I am asking them in my address to elect General Montholon² instead of me. Whatever may be your opinion of the General, it is advantageous, I think, that this man who was at St. Helena and at Ham should be elected. I sent yesterday a copy of my letter to the Corsican committee in Paris. The address will have the advantage of preventing the success of Louis Lucien's candidature.³ Be so good as to inform my uncle of this, and to explain to him the motives which have caused me to recommend General Montholon. There are some men who have served under the colours that must be adopted, whatever their faults.

With the renewed assurance of my sincere friendship,
L. N.

Try to do for Persigny⁴ what I am doing for Laity⁵. There should be no former enmities in politics.

¹ Cavaignac, President of the Council, and chief of the Executive.
² General de Montholon had accompanied the Emperor Napoleon I to St. Helena, and remained with him till his death. He had also been by the side of Prince Louis at the time of his attempt at Boulogne, and had shared his captivity at Ham.
³ The fifth son of Lucien (brother of Napoleon I) and of Alexandrine de Bleschamps. He was born in 1813, and died in 1891.
⁴ Fialin, called Comte and afterwards Duc de Persigny (1808–72). A friend of Prince Louis from the first, he had taken part in the attempts at Strasbourg and Boulogne, and the important *rôle* he was to play under the Empire is well known.
⁵ He had been one of the accomplices of Prince Louis at Strasbourg, where he was an officer. Under the Empire he became, subsequently, a Prefect and Senator.

25th ——,[1] 1848.

My dear Napoleon,—I have been waiting a long time for the departure of (name illegible) to write to you and thank you for your kind letter. I much regret not having seen you during my stay in Paris, but that was impossible. I have not much to tell you on the events of the day, but I have firmly made up my mind. I am determined not to enter France, nor to accept anything whatsoever, before the Republic is firmly constituted. At the present time I have a word of advice to give you which, I hope, will not offend you; but you, who have so much good sense and tact, ought to thoroughly understand that it is rather unsuitable for you to sign yourself publicly "Napoléon Bonaparte" with no other prefix, for in this way you are signing as the Emperor signed, and are giving no other name to distinguish yourself personally. In addition, no one knows who it is when they see your signature. For myself I always recommend people to call me "Louis N.," in order to distinguish me from my other relations. I should like them to call me Louis Napoleon Nabuchodonosor Bonaparte in order to possess a well-marked personification. Think over this, and you will see I am right. In a word, to sign yourself "N. B." has about it an air of unjustifiable pretension.

Be sure that my friendly relations with you will never change, whatever our divergence in matters of opinion, or rather of conduct.

My respects to my uncle, and my sincere friendship to yourself.

L. N.

On the 17th September, 1848, complementary elections took place in thirteen Departments. This time Prince

---

[1] This letter is dated the 25th November, and is doubtless a slip of the pen. From its contents it must certainly have been written on the 25th July, or the 25th August.

Louis Napoleon offered himself as a candidate, and Paris and four Departments elected him by 300,000 votes. He arrived in Paris on the 24th September, and took his seat in the Assembly on the 26th. At first he preferred to adopt a somewhat self-effacing *rôle*; far from wishing to impose himself upon the Assembly, he sought to reassure it.

At last his hour struck. On the 10th December, 1848, a President of the Republic was to be elected by a *plébiscite*. Out of 7,327,345 votes, 5,434,226 were given for him, 1,448,107 for General Cavaignac, and the remainder for different personages. A few days before the event the Prince had issued a manifesto which was very skilfully drawn up with a view of reassuring the varying categories of citizens.

Notwithstanding this magnificent success, his position could not fail to be a delicate one. He was the man chosen by the country, not by a party. Further, acclaimed as he was by the immense majority of the nation, he set himself at the outset to break down the silent hostility of the politicians. Even within the Cabinet itself which he had called upon Odilon Barrot to form, he was soon to encounter opposition which caused the stir alluded to in the following letter which he wrote to Prince Napoleon on the 28th December. The day before, he had sent to M. de Malleville, Minister of the Interior, a very stiff letter reproaching him for not keeping him *au courant* with the reports transmitted to him by the Prefect of Police, and ordering him to send him thirteen documents which he (Prince Louis) had asked for and which he had refused to communicate; these documents related to the attempts at Strasbourg and Boulogne. This matter was kept secret at first. It was not divulged until M. de Malleville handed in his resignation.

Paris, 28th December, 1848.

My dear Napoleon,—I had thought you to be more logical and more reasonable than you appear to be by your letter.

You allege that I have been wanting in all the ties of friendship with you by not informing you yesterday of what happened at the Council.

The Ministers and myself agreed to keep our difference secret until M. de Malleville's decision should be known. Therefore I had no right to tell you of it yesterday. If it came out, it was through no fault of mine. You see, therefore, that it is very bad taste to be annoyed with me for not having revealed to you what took place in secret at my Council.

I hope, my dear Napoleon, that when you have come to yourself you will realise that questions such as these ought not to make a coolness in our friendship. With, etc.,

Louis N. B.

It was not only from his Ministers that the President was to meet with difficulties; he found them even in his own family, and with the relative he loved most. Prince Napoleon, who, as a matter of fact, had little use for ordinary flatterers, had served his cousin's interests so long as the future remained uncertain, but from the moment he saw him in power he was unable to refrain from criticism, and the President thought it wise to remove him to a distance by entrusting to him the duties of French Ambassador in Spain.

In spite of his new dignity the youthful Ambassador, more desirous of upholding his own ideas than of defending his cousin's interests, had no scruples in speaking of the Government in terms which were somewhat bitter throughout the course of his journey, especially at

Bordeaux. He announced his intention at the same time to become a candidate at the next elections in twenty Departments. The Prince-President was unable to refrain from reprimanding these outbursts of language, and on the 10th April, 1849, wrote him a letter the greater part of which was made public:

Elysée Nat., 10*th April*, 1849.

MY DEAR NAPOLEON,—It is alleged that when passing through Bordeaux you made use of language likely to cause division between people having the best intentions. It is stated that you said that, " dominated by the heads of the reactionary movement I am not following out my own views, and that in my impatience under the yoke I am ready to throw it off, and that with a view to coming to my assistance it is necessary at the next elections to send to the Chamber men who are hostile to my Government rather than adherents of the moderate party." You know me well enough to be aware that I will never submit to the ascendancy of anyone whosoever, and that I shall strive unceasingly to govern in the interests of the masses and not in that of a party. I honour those men who, from their capability and experience, are able to give me good advice. Every day I am receiving the most contrary opinions, but I only obey the dictates of my reason and my heart.

Less than anyone else does it become you to blame a sober policy in me, you who disapproved of my manifesto because it did not accord with all the views of the moderate party. Now this manifesto, from which I have not departed, remains the conscientious expression of my opinions. My first duty was to reassure the country. Well, for the past four months it has remained reassured in an ever increasing degree; every day has its proper task—security first and then ameliorations.

The next elections, I have no doubt, will bring nearer the time for instituting possible reforms by strengthening the Republic with order and moderation. To bring together former parties, to unite and reconcile them, should be the purpose of our efforts. It is the mission attaching to the great name we bear. It will come to nothing if it serves to divide, and not to rally, the supporters of the Government.

From all these motives I cannot approve of your candidature in twenty Departments, for—and ponder this well—there are men desirous of bringing to the Assembly candidates who are hostile to the Government, and of discouraging its devoted partisans by tiring out the people with repeated elections, which will have to be begun all over again.

I hope therefore that for the future you will take all possible pains to enlighten those with whom you have relations as to my real intentions, and that you will be careful not to give credibility by inconsiderate speeches to the absurd calumnies which even go so far here as to allege that sordid interests dominate my policy. Nothing —repeat it in no uncertain tone—will disturb the calmness of my judgment, nor will shake my resolution. Free from all constraint over my mind I shall go forward in the path of honour with my conscience as my guide, and when the time comes for me to relinquish power, if people are able to reproach me for mistakes unhappily inevitable, at least I shall have done what I thought sincerely to be my duty.

With my sincere friendship, my dear Napoleon,

Louis Napoleon.

Write direct to me when you have anything serious to communicate, otherwise, to the Minister.

Prince Napoleon barely did more than enter Madrid. Ill at ease at a Bourbon Court,[1] he was not long in returning to Paris. The President, together with his Ministerial Council, interpreted his departure as a resignation, and relieved him of his functions.

This was the beginning of a coolness between the two cousins which was to separate them from each other for the space of two years.

Elected a member of the Legislative Assembly by Corsica, Prince Napoleon took his seat on the Left benches, which secured for him from that time onward the marked hostility of a portion of the Chambre des Députés and of Parisian Society.

Immediately after the proceedings of the 2nd December, 1851[2], he showed himself to be decidedly hostile to the *coup d'état*, of the preparation of which he had known nothing. Once again he subordinated his personal interests to his ideas, and retired into private life for about a year.

An attempt upon the life of the Prince-President brought about what success had failed to secure, and again drew the two cousins together.

During the month of September 1852, a grand visitation of the Departments of the Midi had been organised in order to feel the pulse of those districts, which were considered to be the most unfavourable to the return of the Empire. It was a complete triumph for Prince Louis Napoleon, who was acclaimed everywhere with shouts of "*Vive l'Empereur.*" However, on the day before his arrival at Marseilles the police seized an infernal

---

[1] The Spanish throne was occupied at that time by Queen Isabella II, the daughter of Ferdinand VII and of Marie Christine of Naples (1830–1904).

[2] The Prince-President caused the heads of the Republican and Monarchical parties to be arrested, and declared the Assembly dissolved. After sternly repressing any indications of a popular rising in Paris, he proceeded to take a *plébiscite*, by which he was elected President for ten years. In the following year the Empire was re-established by the votes of the Senate, and a second *plébiscite* was ratified by that body. (Note by translator.)

The Second Empire and Its Downfall

machine in a house in that city situated on the route which was to be followed by the procession.

As soon as he heard of this abortive plot, Prince Napoleon, forgetting everything that had brought about their coolness, and heeding only the impulses of his heart, wrote to his cousin as follows :

Prince Napoleon to the President of the Republic, Marseilles

Paris, 28th September, 1852.

My dear Louis,—I am writing under the impression produced upon me by the news of the crime against your life that had been planned. All my former feelings of brotherly friendship have been re-awakened as keenly as in the past, and more than ever I appreciate that if politics have been able to separate us my devotion to your person remains the same. Accept now the sincere expression of this.

Friends in adversity, only the good fortune which is pushing you forward has been able to accomplish what misfortune will never do, and my heart goes out to you in the peril you have encountered.

Your soul and mind are too elevated, of this I am sure, to make any party responsible for such an attempt, which will make no change in your calmness and serenity.

With every sentiment of friendship and devotion, my dear Louis,

Napoleon Bonaparte.[1]

The ice—the thin ice—which at the warm contact of these two hearts always really united in spite of everything, was to melt on this occasion as it melted on others and was broken through. The Empire was shortly to

---

[1] It will be noted that in spite of Prince Louis' wish expressed in his letter on p. 51 he signed himself " Napoleon Bonaparte." (Note by translator.)

be re-established, and the future Emperor, conscious of the high intellectual value of his cousin, clung to the feeling of having him near his throne, and to reserving for him a position to which his birth and their affection called him. Therefore, when once the new order of things was established, he made the necessary dispositions to give him the rank of a French Prince of the Imperial House, with the eventual right of succession, together with a seat in the Senate and Council of State, and, a few days later, to confer upon him the rank of General of a Division. Before doing this he wished to put him upon his guard against himself, and previous to the official proclamation of the Empire gave him these somewhat fatherly counsels:

St. Cloud, 6th November, 1852.

MY DEAR COUSIN,—I am writing to tell you to ask my uncle if he would like to come to the Opéra-Comique with me on Tuesday next. I should be very pleased if you also would be of the party. The question is not now only of safeguarding the position, but of establishing a dynasty. I conjure you to pay great attention to what you say, and to hide the disappointment you must have experienced. When one bears our name, and when one is the head of the Government, there are two things that must be done: to satisfy the interests of the most numerous class, and to attach to oneself the upper classes. Since you are not in authority you have only the second of these, to which you must give your careful attention now. Moreover, it is by little trifles that one wins individuals, just as it is only by means of great measures that one can attach the masses to oneself. Measure then your words and count on my friendship.

LOUIS NAPOLEON.

CHAPTER IV

The Crimean War—Prince Napoleon appointed to command a Division—His first beginnings—The situation in Turkey in May 1854—Battle of the Alma; Prince Napoleon awarded the Military Medal—Prince Napoleon returns to Constantinople from the Front.

WE have no letters of the two cousins for a period of two years. It is only at the time of the Crimean War that we recover any trace of their correspondence.

As soon as the expedition was decided upon, Prince Napoleon requested to take part in it. He was entrusted with one of the three Divisions of which the army was composed at first, under the command of Marshal Saint Arnaud; Canrobert and Bosquet commanded the other two Divisions. He left Paris on the 10th April, 1854.

His Division, the 3rd, landed at Gallipoli, was then sent to Constantinople, next to Varna, and finally to the Crimea. At the battle of the Alma on the 20th September it conducted itself in a brave manner under the orders of its Chief, after which, with the rest of the army, it camped under the walls of Sebastopol, where it formed part of the besieging force. Thus only a small portion of the troops forming it were able to take part in the battle of Inkerman (5th November).

The personal part played by the Prince, although it lasted only a short time, was very brilliant.[1] The reports of Marshal Saint Arnaud establish this, and the Military Medal sent to him by the Emperor, far from being merely an act proceeding from kindness, set the seal on the encomiums which the Marshal bestowed on him

[1] We shall have occasion to give detailed accounts of this in a subsequent book.

on the battle-field, when in the face of hell-fire he gained the heights dominating the Alma at the head of his troops. His men, with whom he had lived in the Dobrudska through those appalling days at the beginning, and who had witnessed his bearing during the battle, declared that he "behaved very well under fire."[1]

Unfortunately, at this time the state of his health compelled him to absent himself from the army. Without being actually struck down by cholera, like so many others, he experienced violent attacks of fever at the beginning. The doctors diagnosed "chronic gastro-enteritis complicated by slow fever and diarrhœa, accompanied by a gradual weakening of the principal functions of the body." They prescribed absolute rest and change of air, and the Prince went first to Constantinople.

Operations appeared to be suspended for the winter months, and there seemed to be no likelihood of a resumption of activity before the following spring. Indeed, after the battle of Inkerman it became evident that only a regular siege would be able to open the gates of Sebastopol to the Allies, and that they could not take the town by a *coup de main*, as had been hoped at first. The war would be of long duration. The rigour of the climate forbade any operations on a wide scale. They would have to remain stamping their feet in the same place during long months. It was thought that the army would be

---

[1] See the very interesting journal which a common soldier in the Prince's Division, aged 19, kept from day to day, entitled *La 3e Division de l'Armée d'Orient et le Prince Napoléon*, by Aimé Chartier. We may call to mind the anecdote to the same effect related by one of his faithful friends, Baron Brunet, who had accompanied him on a journey to England. On the 29th March, 1889, the ship in which they were crossing the Channel, the *Comtesse de Flandre*, foundered between Ostend and Dover. The bow was disappearing already beneath the surface. The situation appeared to be desperate. The Prince, who was very calm on the after-part of the vessel, which was sinking gradually, took his companion's hand, and, without raising his voice, said quite simply, and with no apparent emotion, "Here is death coming. Forgive me, my poor Brunet. It is I who have brought you to this." His bravery, as related by those who had seen him in critical situations, was natural, devoid of any pose, and without any stilted language spoken for effect. The doctor who attended him at the close of his life, and was present at the last moments, stated that he had never seen any man die so bravely.

The Second Empire and Its Downfall 61

demobilised, as it were, in winter quarters, after the manner of the wars of the preceding century, when no one took offence at seeing the commanders leaving their troops for the time being, even before the close of hostilities when the unfavourable season rendered impossible the resumption of decisive battles.

A reason of a higher kind drew the Prince to France. He was anxious to place the Emperor *au courant* with the exact situation. Better than anyone else he could tell him the truth, which sovereigns have so much interest and such difficulty in knowing. He was not unaware that Napoleon III at the beginning had not been favourable to the expedition to the Crimea as it was being carried out, and that he had only accepted this solution in self-defence. He would have preferred, himself, to attack the Russians in Circassia by raising up against them the insubordinate races of the Caucasus. When it was decided in August 1854 that the contest should be diverted to the Crimea from the banks of the Danube, the Prince understood the difficulties which would be encountered by an army already greatly enfeebled by disease, contracted in the Dobrudska, and decimated by cholera. Events were not slow in confirming what he had foreseen. It was no longer a question of an expedition lasting for a month, as had been anticipated; it was now a matter of a siege, the duration of which no one could estimate. The war was assuming unlooked-for proportions. It was being waged a long way off, with troops in insufficient numbers which had to be reinforced constantly, far from the supply base, in a country bare of all resources, in a severe climate, before a position which was far stronger than had been suspected, and, lastly, with an enemy disposing of immense resources in men and material. The dilatory beginning had altered profoundly the conditions of the war. If the allied armies were besieging the city, they themselves were held in their camp in a state of siege of a kind by the Russian army of relief. The war had become defensive as much as offensive. The situation could not fail to be critical. A check any day might turn into disaster; we ran the risk of being hurled back into the sea.

This state of affairs did not escape the perspicacity of the Prince, who, on the day following the battle of the Alma, would have liked to see the army established on the heights to the north, and not on the south, with a view to isolating the place completely from the rest of Russia. It was too late now. But if the war was prolonged in the Crimea it was indispensable, in his opinion, to attempt a diversion in force on the western front of Russia, with the complicity of Austria, and by means of this stroke the Prince saw the possible realisation of one of his dreams, namely, the liberation of Poland.

His intimacy with the Emperor certainly permitted him, and even made it a duty, to explain to his cousin the exact state of the armies, the very real dangers threatening them, and the solutions which might hasten the *dénouement*. Dissatisfied with the manner in which the expedition had been conceived, he was still more concerned at the way it was being conducted. Unfortunately, his criticisms were not entirely without some foundation. They might be useful to the sovereign. He could not discuss all these questions by correspondence, and for this reason he determined to return to France, convinced that the war would virtually be suspended for several months.

Without further comment we will give the letters exchanged between the two cousins at this period.

Prince Napoleon to the Emperor[1]
Palais Royal, 25th February, 1854.

SIRE,—At the moment of the outbreak of war I come to beg your Majesty to permit me to take part in the expedition which is preparing.

I do not ask for any important command, nor any distinguishing title; the post which will seem to me to be the most honourable will be that which will bring me closest to the enemy. The uniform which I am so proud to wear imposes duties upon me which I shall be happy to fulfil, and I am determined to win the high place which your affection and my position have given me.

When the nation is taking up her arms, Your Majesty will feel, I hope, that my place is in the midst of her soldiers; and I pray you to allow me to go and take my place among them in order to uphold the rights and honour of France.

Accept, Sire, the expression of every sentiment of respectful attachment from your devoted cousin,
NAPOLEON.

The Emperor to Prince Napoleon[2]
9th May, 1854.

MY DEAR NAPOLEON,—I am taking advantage of Trochu's[3] departure to write you a line to tell you of all the interest I am feeling for your success and prosperity. I hope that you will bear yourself worthily, and to achieve that you have only to follow your own lead, and free yourself from every influence that is not a military one.

I hope that things will go well. I have good news on all sides, and, with God's help, we shall bring the good cause to a triumphant issue. Your father is well. The

---
[1] This letter, of which we do not possess the original, nor any minute, is taken from Bazancourt's work, *L'Expédition de Crimée : l'Armée Française*, Vol. I., p. 14.
[2] The Prince received this letter at Gallipoli on the 23rd May. He replied the next day, but we have not his answer.
[3] Colonel Trochu was then A.D.C. to Marshal Saint Arnaud.

Empress sends you a thousand kind thoughts, and I renew the assurance of my sincere affection.

NAPOLEON.

Prince Napoleon to the Emperor

Constantinople, 20th May, 1854.

SIRE,—I did not write sooner to Your Majesty as I knew that Marshal Saint Arnaud was keeping you *au courant* with every phase of this difficult Eastern affair. I have also kept my father informed very regularly about all I have been doing, finding out and considering, and wished to spare your Majesty's precious time. When the Marshal left the day before yesterday for Varna and Schumla he requested me to supply his place. It seems that the Russians are evacuating the Dobrudska, where they were losing a great number from sickness, and are concentrating round Silistria, which they wish to take possession of. In fulfilment of your orders our troops have occupied Athens. General Baraguay d'Hilliers has received the order recalling him, and leaves to-day. Here there are perpetual intrigues, and I think that Mehemet Ali, the Sultan's brother-in-law (who was formerly a Seraskin[1]), the head of the Turkish party of resistance and the personal enemy of Reschid Pacha, might very possibly come into prominence again, which would disorganise the present Ministry. Sire, this is a very wretched country, and is in a very bad state! I do not know if in the position they occupy *in Europe* the Turks are capabale of *becoming civilised*, but I am convinced of this, that they have no man at their head who is capable of leading them in such a difficult task! The country is drained dry of resources, corruption is everywhere, their regular army in Europe only numbers 80,000 men, and the army in Asia *only*

---

[1] Commander-in-Chief in the Turkish Army.

exists on paper. It is neither paid, clothed, nor fed. There are 20,000 men at Batoum, and 12,000 at Kars, who, in the event of the Russians making an advance, will not be able to hold them back for twenty-four hours. What is saving the country is the excessive prudence of the Russians. With a certain amount of boldness they would be much further advanced.

The Marshal is to draw up his plan with Lord Raglan and Omar Pacha. What is good proof of the extent of their weakness felt by the Turks is their submitting to the authority of the French, and I believe Omar Pacha will place himself under the orders of the Marshal, a thing he would not have done a few months ago.

I, personally, have met with a very good reception here. The Sultan was quite exceptionally friendly. I have much to congratulate myself upon in my relations with the Duke of Cambridge, who is established at Scutari with nearly the whole of the English Army—15,000 *men so far*, with no cavalry.

I believe that the only vulnerable point as regards Russia is *Circassia, and perhaps the Crimea*. It would be necessary to attack them with the aid of the fleet, and there will be certain obstacles, I fear, through *the lack of unity of command*. Effective action is too much split up between the French and English, between Generals and Admirals. It is difficult to work satisfactorily in these conditions. I do not think there is much to be done on the Danube. Both the Russians and ourselves are in sufficient strength to hold each other in check. In either case, the side which attacks will be at a disadvantage. For this reason it is by way of Circassia, by cutting off the army in Georgia and raising the whole country already prepared for this, that we might take advantageous action, with the Black Sea and the fleet as our base of operations. The fleet is fully provided for an operation

E E

of this kind, and they could obtain their supplies at Constantinople. Unfortunately, in this place the Turks are appallingly apathetic. They smoke *and do absolutely nothing.*

The war shows signs of being *long and difficult*, in my opinion. There is absolutely not a word of truth in all the victories and battles announced in our newspapers and telegrams. No encounter between the Turks and Russians has taken place for the last two months. Omar Pacha ran great risks, only to see the Russians take Schumla after they had crossed the Danube. There were only 4,000 Turks in that place, and all the rest were scattered along the length of the Danube. At the present moment the Turks are concentrated round here (Constantinople).

Before leaving, Marshal Saint Arnaud gave orders to our army to make an advance, Canrobert's Division to Adrianople, and Bosquet's to Rodosto. As regards myself, I have been ordered to go by sea to Gallipoli on the 26th, which place I am to leave on the 26th by land with all of my Division that have arrived, and to establish it in a position which I have reconnoitred in front of the Turkish town of Stamboul, between the Sea of Marmora and the Eaux Douces. A third of my troops will be in camp, and the remaining two-thirds in immense barracks. I am leaving the day after to-morrow to begin the movement. Gallipoli is about fifty-five leagues away, and I think I shall require twelve days before returning here. The road from Gallipoli to Rodosto is hardly marked.

Marshal Saint Arnaud reckons on being at Gallipoli on the 26th. I do not think that will be possible. There is already a certain amount of fever among our soldiers at Gallipoli. The country, speaking generally, is rather unhealthy.

Your Majesty will excuse, I trust, the fragmentary

nature of my report. I am very much pressed to be ready for the post, and to get the least thing done so much time is required in this country, on account of the enormous distances, the very difficult means of communication, and the general apathy, so that a very great loss of time is necessitated to obtain scanty results. One never has enough time. May I be allowed, Sire, to include in this letter the expression of all my respects to Her Majesty, the Empress, and accept, Sire, I beg, the homage of profound and respectful attachment with which, I am,
Your Majesty,
Your very devoted Cousin,
NAPOLEON (JEROME).

The Emperor to Prince Napoleon[1]
Biarritz, 23rd July, 1854.

MY DEAR NAPOLEON,—I have not written to you for a long time because I have only had a few small recommendations to make to you, which distance might exaggerate and which, I feel sure, are not required now that your experience from day to day must prove to you how much one gains in one's own, and everyone else's eyes by sincerely performing one's duty. I am pleased with the reports about you that come to me from Marshal Saint Arnaud, and with the satisfactory manner in which you are commanding your Division. It is still very difficult for me to foresee the future, but the farther we go, and the more Austria shows herself to be loyal and sincere, the more does Prussia, on the contrary, turn towards Russia. What fresh complication will that lead to? That is the difficult thing to foresee. In the meantime, I am organising the army as much as possible. The Guards will soon have 800 men on the strength for each battalion. The army at Boulogne has 60,000 infantry.

[1] The Prince received this letter at Therapia on the 15th August, and replied on the 20th.

In the Midi, rendered trying owing to the heat, a camp will be established in September for two Divisions.

The Empress, who is here in order to have the sea bathing, sends you a thousand messages. Accept my sincere affection,

NAPOLEON.

Spain is again in a revolution. It is thought that Espartero may be able to take her fortunes in hand.

The Emperor to Prince Napoleon[1]
St. Cloud, 23rd October, 1854.

MY DEAR NAPOLEON,—I take advantage of the departure of Colonel Renaud to tell you how very happy I have been to learn of your fine bearing at the battle of the Alma. I am sending you the Military Medal in proof of my satisfaction as your sovereign, and of my affection as your cousin. I share very keenly, as you justly think, in all that happens to our army, and I am redoubling my efforts to despatch to the East steamers and reinforcements.

The grandson of Madame Paterson[2] is now out in the East. My uncle was annoyed at his admission (into the army), but there are certain situations which must be accepted, and to show any ill feeling would be extremely impolitic, in my opinion. At the conclusion of the siege I shall hope to see you again in good health, and matured by a few months of rough warfare.

With my sincere affection,
NAPOLEON.

The Empress sends you a thousand messages.

[1] The Prince received this letter at Constantinople on the 12th November. He replied by the letter which follows.

[2] Jerome, the brother of Napoleon I, had been first married in America to Miss Elisabeth Paterson. From this union, which the Emperor (Napoleon I) had refused to regard as legitimate because it had been contracted without his consent, was born in 1805 Jerome Napoleon Bonaparte, who married Susan Gay in 1829. Their son Jerome Bonaparte, who is referred to in the above letter, was born in 1832. Napoleon III permitted his entrance into the French Army as a sub-lieutenant. Later on Madame Paterson will be referred to again. (See text preliminary to the letter of the 18th February, 1861, pp. 158-60.)

The Second Empire and Its Downfall

Prince Napoleon to the Emperor
Constantinople, 14th November, 1854.

SIRE,—Your Majesty's letter, and the Military Medal which Colonel Renaud has handed to me, have made me very happy. This testimony of your satisfaction is a reward which is very dear to me, and the orange ribbon reserved for the brave soldiers of France, which you have deemed me worthy to wear, renders me more proud than could any other distinction.

Your Majesty will have learnt from my father that my health, which is very run down from the hardships I have endured, has obliged me to come to Constantinople to refit. I had the happiness of not leaving my Division until after I had taken part in the glorious battle of Inkerman. Unfortunately, I did not take a very active part in it, my troops being separated and in the second line, a portion of them on the right with the reserve army, and the rest on our left with the besieging force. I only had one battery and two battalions engaged.

The sickness which I have been unable to throw off, and the cessation of operations, which cannot be resumed seriously for some months, render me keenly desirous of returning to France. I hope soon to receive Your Majesty's orders to this effect.

The advanced season, the considerable reinforcements of the enemy, the strength and resources of the position (Sebastopol), which were denied at first, have changed the face of affairs: from being an offensive, our position has become a defensive one, and will so remain until the arrival of very considerable reinforcements. The taking of Sebastopol, which was the object of our expedition, can only come now as the result of a great war against all the Russian forces which are massing in the Crimea. We cannot do much this winter, and operations on a great scale cannot be carried out before the spring. These are my anticipations, Sire, which I beg leave to submit to you, and so far they have been realised.

Will Your Majesty allow me to join Her Majesty, the Empress, in the expression of profound and respectful attachment with which
I am, Your Majesty,
Your very devoted cousin,
NAPOLEON BONAPARTE.

The Emperor to Prince Napoleon[1]
St. Cloud, 23rd November, 1854.

MY DEAR COUSIN,—I have learnt with lively concern that you are ill owing to the hardships of the campaign. I can understand up to a certain point your returning to Constantinople to recover, but I conjure you to go back to the army the moment you are able. Your conduct up till now has rallied all hearts to you. The news arriving from the East has done you infinite good; nevertheless (it is necessary that you know all the truth), if you were to come back now that the situation of the army seems to be more serious, and the object of the expedition has not yet been attained, you would lose in one moment all the fruits of your hardships. In a word, you would be lost irretrievably in the opinion of the public. There cannot be two opinions about that. Already your return to Constantinople has given rise to very bad reports. However, if you are ill, remain in Constantinople till you get better, but let it be known *far and wide that you are returning to the army*, and go back to the army the moment you can.

I hope you will see in this counsel a proof of sincere and enlightened affection.

The Empress sends you a thousand messages, and I embrace you tenderly. NAPOLEON.

[1] The Prince received this letter at Constantinople on the 5th December, and answered it on the 14th. We do not possess his reply.

CHAPTER V

Return of Prince Napoleon to France—A *brochure* on the conduct of the war—The situation in the Crimea—Birth of the Prince Imperial, 16th March, 1856.

NOTWITHSTANDING the advice given in the Emperor's letter, the Prince obtained his recall to France, for the reasons we have briefly indicated. He embarked at Constantinople on the 12th January, 1855. He was very well received by his cousin on his arrival in France, as is seen by the following letter, in which he asked that awards might be bestowed on the officers on his staff:

Prince Napoleon to the Emperor
Paris, 11th February, 1855.

SIRE,—Your Majesty has overwhelmed me with joy in welcoming me on my return to France with a kindly affection which I am conscious I have never ceased to deserve. I should value it most highly if an act of Your Majesty's special favour might add distinguished testimony to the kind reception I have received from you. I keenly desire this on behalf of the brave Division I have had the honour to command, in which I have met with so much good feeling, and on behalf of the army in the east, in which I am sure I have left behind good memories, and, lastly, in order to put an end to the malevolence from which I have suffered so much.

I feel I shall have achieved this if Your Majesty will be graciously pleased to grant to the officers attached to my person, whose faithful service and devotion have never failed me, the following awards.[1] . . .

---
[1] We will not quote the names of these officers, nor the record of their services.

Immediately after Prince Napoleon's return there appeared in Brussels an anonymous *brochure*, which had been announced for some time, on *La Conduite de la Guerre en Orient*. It was a very violent criticism of everything that had been done up to that time in the Crimea. The Emperor had proof subsequently that it was the work of the Hungarian General, Klapka, of whom we shall have occasion to speak later on, and against whom he did not preserve any ill feeling. But at first, giving ear to the reports spread abroad by the malevolence of the public, he believed that it had come from the pen of Prince Napoleon. In one of those rare moments of impatience which we have to note in the sovereign, who at ordinary times was so much master of himself, he wrote the following letter to his cousin in a tone so different from the others that everything in it denotes an official character written with a view to publicity. The Prince replied to it on the same day, and was unable to hide his indignation at this false accusation, which he refuted with a sentence taken from a report by the Prefect of Police, which the Emperor had communicated to him.

The Emperor to Prince Napoleon[1]
Palais des Tuileries, 19th *February*, 1855.

MONSIEUR MON COUSIN,—A *brochure* which has been long announced and which is imbued with ideas which, unfortunately, are your own, has just appeared in Brussels. You will readily understand, I trust, all the gravity of allowing it to be supposed that a lampoon accusing the policy of the Government, the conduct of the war, the honour and merits of the Generals who are dead or are still at grips with the enemy, can have been written or inspired by one who, at present, is the

[1] This letter has probably been already published.

Emperor's most direct heir. There arises, therefore, the absolute necessity that you should issue a flat and official repudiation of this *brochure* and of the ideas therein contained. Otherwise I shall be compelled, to my great regret, to take the severest measures in your regard. It comes to this, that if any General, no matter who he be, allows himself, during a war, to sow disquiet in the minds of the public by exaggerating the difficulties and the losses sustained, and discouragement in the army by anticipating defeat and by belittling the Generals entrusted with the conduct of the war, I should not hesitate for a moment to hand over a General like that to a court-martial, which would perhaps punish him far less severely than would public opinion.

With these words I pray God may have you in His holy and august keeping.

NAPOLEON.

Prince Napoleon to the Emperor
Paris, 19th February, 1855.

SIRE,—Your Majesty's letter arouses profound grief in me. How, Sire, on a mere *on dit*, have you been able to give credit to accusations like these? Even the report you send me proves that the Prefect of Police only sees in them a hostile manœuvre to compromise me. See his last sentence: " The publication of this pamphlet was kept back for one day for the purpose of reprinting 2,000 covers in which there was a printer's error, showing too clearly that Prince Napoleon could not be the author of the *brochure*."

You wish to make me responsible, Sire, for what thousands of men know, say, and write, for what has been proclaimed loudly in the English Parliament, for what a Minister of the Allies has endorsed by resigning ! Under this pretext Your Majesty has written me a letter which I thought you were incapable of writing to me, and one which, indeed, my devotion and my old affection have not deserved. My conduct has been, and is, irreproachable. I did my duty in the army. I left my command on the orders of Your Majesty, and when it was proved to me that there was nothing more for me to do. Since my return to Paris I have exercised the greatest reserve, not in my writings—for I have done absolutely nothing in that connection—but in my private conversations. To you alone, Sire, have I spoken the whole truth upon the false conception of the expedition, the manner in which it has been conducted, and our bad situation in the Crimea. This I have done because I believed I was fulfilling my duty as a Prince, a General, and a citizen, and after Your Majesty had enjoined this upon me in the most positive manner.

I state on my honour that even indirectly I am a complete stranger to a publication which I have only heard of from you.

I do not feel I am called upon to make a retractation of, nor give a *démenti* to, an anonymous writer. This would be to leave a doubt behind, but I have the right, Sire, to ask you for what you yourself have indicated in your letter—a court-martial with the guarantees which the laws accord to the meanest soldier.

If you wish to treat me like any other General, I give you the opportunity. If you feel yourself unable to give me this public satisfaction, and, influenced by your prerogative as head of our dynasty, you are willing to wash our dirty linen in the presence of the family, at least you will recognise my right to demand an enquiry. I must have the proper means to destroy the slightest suspicion.

When the truth, which I call for, shall have been made clear, there will remain, none the less, a deep wound in my heart. This decides me to ask Your Majesty to be good enough to allow me to remain for the future outside *all political or military activity*; my devotion to my country and to Your Majesty will not be diminished thereby, but I feel that I am no longer in a position to be of service to you in the face of the powerful enemies who surround you, and would succeed in separating us, of the prepossessions and suspicions in your own mind, and of the resentment I myself experience.

My conduct in retirement shall be my best justification for the future.

NAPOLEON BONAPARTE.

This severe upbraiding had no bad consequences. The Emperor recognised his error. The two cousins came together again, and the Prince continued to develop in intimate conversations his observations concerning the Crimea. In doing this he was actuated by no fruitless spirit of criticism; he was only carrying out, as he thought, the duty for which he had returned to France. In the month of April, 1855, seeing that the situation was not improving, he thought it might be useful to develop his views in the following letter:

Prince Napoleon to the Emperor

Paris, *April* 1855.

SIRE,—Since my return to France, I have given Your Majesty certain information, which it seemed important you should know, on the struggle taking place in the Crimea between the Allied Powers and Russia. I have thought that, by supplementing what I have been able to tell Your Majesty on a matter I have studied with all the interest I bear in the success of your policy and in the glory of your army, it might be advantageous to place before your eyes, after giving a succinct summary of the present situation, a report as to the means which I think most suitable to bring to a termination the present struggle, with success to your policy—that is, by the real and permanent weakening of the power of Russia.

When in March last Your Majesty, in agreement with England, your Ally, sent out troops to the East, the question to be solved was this: to cover the capital of the Ottoman Empire against every attempt by the Russian Army, and to bring about, by a series of later operations, the evacuation of the Principalities, and the retreat of their (the Russian) army behind the line of the Pruth.

At the end of June this result had been attained without fighting and without effort, through the mere presence of the Allied armies.

After raising the siege of Silistria, the Russians recrossed the left bank of the Danube and began their retreating movement. Austria, at last understanding what were her real interests, announced her intention of supporting openly the Western Powers, and of preventing any future invasion of the Principalities after they had been evacuated. At this moment the wise and firm policy of Your Majesty had obtained a result which I might call almost unexpected. It had placed the Ottoman Empire in a position of safety from an aggression which was keenly agitating the world, and had again placed France, which up till then had been excluded from the European concert, in the influential position she had occupied in the brightest days of her power. Certainly this was to have attained much, and it might have been well, perhaps, before we had abandoned the plan of remaining on the defensive to which this new situation was owing, to have weighed carefully the advantages and disadvantages of waging a war of offence, and especially to have decided upon the point on which it was

The Second Empire and Its Downfall

best to concentrate our first efforts, with the chance of dealing thereby decisive blows. However this may be, towards the middle of July it was proposed to Your Majesty to profit by the presence of your troops in Turkey to put an end to the Eastern question by dealing an important blow to the power of Russia in the Black Sea by the destruction of Sebastopol, and, if necessary the conquest of the Crimea.

You are aware, Sire, of my opinion at that time. While agreeing as to the advantages of such an enterprise in the event of success, I could not but admit that the first act in the war of offence, which it was important to carry through in a glorious and decisive manner, was undertaken under bad conditions, both from the insanitary state of the army and the advanced season. What I feared especially was that this expedition, which had been represented at first as a bold stroke and could not exceed the duration of a month, would degenerate into a war which would carry the theatre of the struggle between Russia and the Allied Powers into the Crimea. Events have only too faithfully verified my apprehensions.

The French Army, which, on disembarking in the Crimea, was composed of four Divisions, representing a mean effective of 25,000 men, now numbers ten Divisions which have necessitated the sending from France of nearly 60,000 men, not including the considerable reinforcements successively received by the four first Divisions. Prodigies of activity and enormous expenses have been required to assemble these forces in the Crimea. Notwithstanding this, what results have been attained after such great efforts? An army condemned to inactivity in front of a citadel it has been besieging vainly for four months, an army enduring hardships with admirable strength and constancy, but which is suffering cruelly from the rigours of the winter, without anything up till now indicating with any reassuring certainty that a resounding success will come to crown so great travail and sacrifice ! I do not wish to enter here in detail into the mistakes and delays which have led to the present situation. I take it that Your Majesty is completely enlightened in this respect. What I am anxious to lay stress upon is the enormous difficulty of continuing a struggle in a theatre 600 leagues from France, without any good intermediate base of operations, and especially without any assured means of retreat in case of a setback. There are abundant proofs of this; it is good policy, just as it is good management, not to risk more than one is able to gain. Now, Sire, we have won striking successes on the Alma and at Inkerman, and these successes have not gained us one step forward; if we had lost one of these battles it would undoubtedly have been the signal of great disasters for us. When a war is carried on at such a distance it is not only at an enormous cost in men and money, but, further, the Government is not in a position to direct it owing to the time required for the interchange of communications. From this fact arises the necessity of entrusting the Commander-in-Chief with extraordinary powers, which is always dangerous, and of leaving to him the absolute direction of events. I feel it to be my duty, Sire, to tell Your Majesty that, in my opinion, no indication has yet revealed a man to whom it would be prudent to give entire control over such great interests.

From the preceding remarks I draw the following conclusions :

One of two things will happen : either the army in the Crimea will obtain a striking success, or it will experience a set-back.

In the first hypothesis two things must be considered : to take advantage of success by concluding as advantageous

The Second Empire and Its Downfall

a peace as possible, or to continue the war. One should not lose sight of the fact that by concluding peace we should break up the formidable combination threatening Russia which it might never be possible to bring together again.

In the second hypothesis it is quite certain that the Allied Powers would not be willing to remain under the blow of defeat, and that the war would be continued on a most vast scale. Now comes in the delicate part of what I have to say to Your Majesty.

In the case of the continuation of the war, great care, as I see it, must be exercised to prevent the Crimea from being made the principal theatre wherein the conflicting interests will be decided. It is at the very heart of Russia that this should be directed. If Your Majesty should do me the honour to consult me in such an eventuality, I should not hesitate to propose to you the immediate organisation of Poland by throwing on this side all the active forces of France and her Allies. A fresh reorganisation such as this, Sire, would correspond with a national desire to which expression has been long given, and would provide us with allies who would be both faithful and useful. It would present an insurmountable barrier between Europe and the pressure of the Russian power. A reconstituted Poland would exercise on the flank of the ceaseless march of Russia towards the East a vigilance both active and efficacious in arresting at an opportune moment any advancing steps she might attempt to make from this side.

I do not disguise from myself all the objections which might be advanced in connection with this reorganisation, but after a careful examination one realises that the difficulties are not very great :

1. As regards the Powers that would participate, Russia is outside the question. Austria would derive

large compensations in the free navigation of the Danube, and, if occasion arose, in a protectorate of the Principalities. And as regards Prussia, her attitude since the beginning of the war, and her almost flagrant hostility, dispense us from taking her into consideration.

2. As to the form of government most suitable for ensuring the future of a reconstituted Poland, I feel certain that every enlightened and intelligent man in that country would accept eagerly what should seem to the Allied Powers to be the best solution.

If, as I do not doubt, a successful war resulted in the consolidation of this state of affairs, Your Majesty would have the glory of having repaired a great political error and a great injustice, and of putting Russia for a long time to come outside the possibility of being a cause of uneasiness to Europe.

NAPOLEON (JEROME).

Meantime Prince Napoleon devoted himself with great energy, and very successfully, to his duties as President of the Imperial Commission of the *Exposition Universelle* of 1855.

At the close of the year he sent his good wishes to his cousin, who replied with the following letter:

1st January, 1856.

MY DEAR NAPOLEON,—I thank you for your letter of yesterday. Be well assured that a word from you, coming from your heart, touches me profoundly, for the most painful feeling I have had for six years was when I felt bound to have doubts of your affection.

With my sincere regards,

NAPOLEON.

The *accouchement* of the Empress was imminent— the Prince Imperial was born on the 16th March, 1856—

and the Emperor wrote to Prince Napoleon the two following letters, one private, and the other official:

11*th March*, 1856.

My dear Napoleon,—I was unable to go and see my uncle to-day, as I was kept by the bedside. I beg you will express to him how *désolé* I am to be unable to offer him in person all the concern I feel at his illness. Happily Ragon[1] has much relieved me this afternoon. I am also writing to you to speak of another matter. As the Empress is about to be confined, two witnesses will be required according to custom, one a relative of the wife (this will be the Duke of Alba[2]), the other a relative of the husband, and I thought naturally of you, as my nearest relation. If you consent, I will send you to-morrow by Fould[3] the official letter enclosed to notify you of my choice.

With my sincere regards,
Your Cousin,
Napoleon.

To His Imperial Highness the Prince Napoleon

My dear Cousin,—The Empress, our very dear Consort, being near the time of her delivery, we have given orders that as soon as she feels the first pangs you be warned to go to the Palace of the Tuileries, to the *salon* reserved for the Princes of the Imperial Family, for the purpose of being introduced into the chamber of the Empress at the time of her *accouchement*. It is our wish that you sign the *acte de naissance* as a witness.

With these presents I pray God, my dear cousin, that He will have you in His holy and august keeping.

[1] Ragon was an officer of Engineers, and orderly officer to Prince Napoleon.
[2] The brother-in-law of the Empress.
[3] Achille Fould, a Minister of State and of the Imperial Household.

Given at the Palace of the Tuileries on the 12th March, 1856.

Yours affectionately,
NAPOLEON.

On the 16th March the Prince Imperial was born. In connection with that event, Prince Napoleon proposed to his cousin, two days after, to grant a wide amnesty to all political prisoners. He dealt at length with the advantages of a measure like this in a note which will be found in the Appendix.

We have no letters passing between the two cousins for a period of nearly twenty months, with the exception of a brief note accompanying the despatch by the Emperor to Prince Napoleon of an allowance made to him on the occasion of the festivities of the 15th August.

The Emperor to Prince Napoleon
St. Cloud, 16th August, 1857.

MY DEAR NAPOLEON,—I am sending you for the 15th August an allowance, which I beg you will accept as a *souvenir* and as a small mark of my sincere regard.

Your cousin and friend,
NAPOLEON.

CHAPTER VI

The Privy Council—Algerian affairs—Prince Napoleon appointed Minister of Algeria and the Colonies—Questions of organisation—Marshal Randon—The Prefecture of Algiers.

TOWARDS the end of the year 1857 the Emperor confided to his cousin his desire to diffuse among the public certain ideas concerning the *rôle* of Turkey. As a result of this conversation Prince Napoleon submitted to the Emperor the scheme of a *brochure*. Although this was approved of in principle, the project was not carried into effect until six months later.[1]

The two cousins had also spoken of a more important matter. The Emperor was desirous of appointing a Regency in case he should die. He was disposed to entrust it officially to the Empress, and thought of constituting a Privy Council at the same time, which would become eventually the Council for the Regency. Although the principle of this step was fully admitted by Prince Napoleon, it aroused his criticism, nevertheless, when it came to choosing the members to form it. He would not sit as a member with certain persons for whom he experienced an aversion he did not conceal. In the end he refused to become a member, and the Council, which was presided over by King Jerome when the Emperor was not present, was made up of Persigny, Baroche, Pélissier, Fould, Morny, Troplong, and Cardinal Morlot.

These two questions, especially the latter, were the occasion for the exchange of several letters.

[1] See Prince Napoleon's letter of June 1858, pp. 93-6.

Prince Napoleon to the Emperor

Paris, November, 1857.

SIRE,—I am sending Your Majesty the scheme of the *brochure* on *Les Turcs en Europe*. I am anxious to know if I have thoroughly understood your ideas, and beg you will be good enough to read it and make any corrections. I made M. Schefer[1] come to see me, and after several modifications I suggest the form I enclose. When it has been approved, it will take five or six weeks to bring out. I await Your Majesty's reply to begin the work.

I have seen M. de Persigny, who at Compiègne suggested to me an idea concerning the *Conseil de l'Empire*, and that is to appoint Cardinal Morlot, the Archbishop of Paris, to be a member of it, and to compose it as follows: My father, the Duc de Malakoff,[2] M. de Persigny, the Cardinal, and myself, with the Minister of State as secretary. I believe the appointment of this Council would be a good one, and useful. I confess that the idea of making a Cardinal a member would not have entered my head, but, taking into consideration the lack of men and several other reasons, I think that this idea deserves to be thought over, and has much to recommend it. If Your Majesty should be willing, as I believe is the case, to limit the number of members to five or six, and to exclude the Ministers and high officers of State, the combination seems to me to be a good one. If this principle be admitted no one will be able to complain, and, to mention names, M. le Comte de Morny will quite naturally find himself outside it, together with MM. Troplong[3] and Baroche,[4] and it would be a pity in every way for this

---

[1] Schefer (1820-98) was First Dragoman at the French Embassy at Constantinople during the Crimean War. He was afterwards Professor of Oriental Languages in Paris, in close touch with Prince Napoleon.

[2] Marshal Pélissier, Duc de Malakoff.

[3] President of the Senate.

[4] President of the Council of State.

person to be in a position to harm you—by his being appointed a member of the Council, which I think would be a very bad appointment, and by preventing you from making appointments to the Council if he was not a member. These are my reasons put briefly and very frankly; briefly, because it would not be profitable to take up your time, and because you see, doubtless, all the grounds in favour of my opinion; frankly, Sire, because, if I am undoubtedly interested in maintaining our dynasty and our cause, I am, however, interested in a less personal manner since the birth of the Prince Imperial, and that permits me, in the interests of your son, to say to you what I should not have cared to say in my own. If it be composed of *devoted and upright* men, few in number, of the same mind, proudly bearing the Napoleonic flag, and ready to sacrifice their lives for the triumph of the cause, this Council will satisfy our friends, will win over those who are undecided, and will frighten our enemies. It will cause no difficulties for you, since it will exercise no direct action.

In the event of your absence or of your meeting with some misfortune, it will be of the greatest advantage to your son, and will ensure the crown for him. Even the present will be strengthened by the confidence inspired for the future. The weak point in our position is that there is nothing firmly stabilised apart from your person. It is necessary, therefore, to make things sure for the future by preparing and organising it, and by showing that this is your wish, of which many are in doubt, and especially by not introducing division, and bad, degenerate elements into a Council which might be called upon to act at critical moments.

I should have much liked to tell this to Your Majesty before my departure from Compiègne, and I venture to write to you now that the Council appears to be made possible by M. de Persigny's idea.

Accept, etc.,

NAPOLEON BONAPARTE.

The Emperor to Prince Napoleon
Compiègne, 11th November, 1857.

MY DEAR NAPOLEON,—I thank you greatly for your letter, which gave me much pleasure, for each time that you afford me proofs of your affection I am profoundly touched. I return the draft, with a few observations. The plan is drawn out well, only we must not omit to make it an entirely religious and civilising question, and in no way an English, French, or Russian matter. We will talk again in Paris about the Privy Council.

With my sincere affection,

NAPOLEON.

Prince Napoleon to the Emperor
Paris, 1st February, 1858.

SIRE,—The Minister of State has just communicated to me the message Your Majesty is sending to the Senate this very day, appointing once for all the Regent and the Regency Council.

The Regency is only the consequence of the Act voted by the Senate in 1856, when I was absent. I do not venture to pass any remarks on it. As regards the Regency Council, Your Majesty, bearing in mind the views expressed in the Act recommended by the Senate, appoints by name my father and myself as being the two Princes of the Imperial Family nearest to the throne with the right of succession, as well as Cardinal Morlot, the Duc de Malakoff, MM. Achille Fould, Troplong, Morny, Baroche, and de Persigny.

I implore Your Majesty not to allow me to consider

these appointments as irrevocable, or to be good enough to permit my name to be excluded therefrom.

My reasons are as follows: the practical abeyance of the Privy Council for the present, and its insignificant importance at any future unhappy time that might arise, to which Your Majesty makes an allusion, since it is only called upon to give advice on four specified points.

I therefore am persuaded I should be weakening your government in no way by not being appointed to the Regency Council. Further, as I have expressed to Your Majesty in the conversations you have been pleased to have with me on this matter, and especially in a letter I wrote to you from Compiègne, I feel that the large number of members in the Council still further weakens its power of action. And lastly, the reason which decides me is its composition. More particularly I find therein the name of a high official with whom I am conscious of being in profound disagreement on almost every question, one who by his acts has manifested under the gravest circumstances his personal hostility to me. I feel that his name can only do harm to the reputation and authority of the Council which, thus composed, instead of being an element of strength and union, would only be a source of weakness to the Regent.

As the appointment by name almost deprives the Crown of the right to change it, there is no other course left to me than to follow the path pointed out to me by my conscience and my honour, by begging Your Majesty to dispense me from taking my seat in a Council thus composed and to save me from having to refuse after your message has been communicated to the Senate.

The very late hour does not permit me to enter into long, lengthy considerations with Your Majesty, nor to expatiate upon all the reasons which have decided me, reasons which I made known several weeks ago, to the

Emperor himself, to the Minister of State, and to M. de Persigny.

I am, etc.,
NAPOLEON (JEROME).

In the meantime the Emperor dissuaded Prince Napoleon from organising an annual dinner to commemorate the battle of the Alma, as he had thought of doing.

Paris, 25th December, 1857.

MY DEAR NAPOLEON,—Since you ask my advice, I will tell you that I do not approve of the idea of an annual official dinner to commemorate a war achievement, for we should be descending to a parody of the famous Waterloo dinner given by the Duke of Wellington. On the other hand, nothing could be simpler than to invite quietly to your house the officers you knew on the field of battle in the East. My advice, therefore, is that you should refrain from inviting any official persons, and avoid all toasts and speeches.

With my sincere regard,
NAPOLEON.

Ever espousing the cause of those who were suffering, or those whom he considered to be the victims of unduly harsh treatment on account of their political opinions, the Prince interceded with the Emperor on behalf of certain individuals imprisoned in Algeria. The Emperor replied with the following letter:

Palais des Tuileries, 1st *April*, 1858.

MY DEAR COUSIN,—Before coming to any decision in regard to the persons you recommend I took steps to obtain information about them. Now there is not one of them who, for serious reasons, is not represented as being very dangerous, nor for whom imprisonment in

The Second Empire and Its Downfall 89

Algeria is too severe a punishment. I regret, once again, to see you being deceived by false information, which prevents my giving you the reply you wish.

With my sincere regard,

NAPOLEON.

On the 5th June, 1858, M. Delangle superseded General Espinasse at the Ministry of the Interior. The Emperor took advantage of this reorganising of the Cabinet to make a study of the status of Algeria, which up to that time had been administered under the authority of the Ministry for War by a military Governor residing at Algiers. His first idea had been to create a special Ministry, and then, after consulting Prince Napoleon, to whom he had it in mind to give this post, he thought of making Algeria into a kind of Vice-Royalty. The question of residence aroused objections on the part of the Prince, who thought it would be indispensable to make a stay in Paris each year of three or four months in order to draw up the budget and to treat of important matters directly with the Emperor.

This divergence of views was the cause of the correspondence which follows. In the end the Emperor came back to his original idea, and on the 24th June, 1858, he created the Ministry of Algeria and the Colonies, the portfolio of which he entrusted to Prince Napoleon. The latter held it until March, 1859.

The Emperor to Prince Napoleon
Fontainebleau, 11th June, 1858.

MY DEAR NAPOLEON,—I have not sent you before to-day my definite decision on the question of the government of Algeria because the subject is sufficiently important to merit considered reflection.

I have made a few indispensable alterations, but the

one to which I attach the most importance is the clause definitely authorising the Lieutenant of the Emperor to remain four months of the year in Paris. To put it plainly, this arrangement, if adopted or even suspected, would destroy the whole system, and would produce the worst effect. How would people understand the transference of all the administration to Algeria if the Minister in charge of that country were to be absent for four months every year? In that case the Minister would be in Paris for a third part of the year, without a seat of administration, and with no intermediary to transmit his orders. It is impossible. If it should be found necessary for the Minister for Algeria to be in Paris, he must remain there, with liberty to go to Algeria for one month each year. Everything depends on the way matters are arranged. If the Minister be established in Paris, and make a visit of a month to Algeria every year, public opinion would think well of him, but if the Lieutenant of the Emperor, after having absorbed practically all the executive powers, were only to leave substitutes in Algeria, and were to come to Paris to amuse himself for four months, people would be reproaching him all the time for being too far away from the Colony.

It is impossible to play with the great concerns entrusted to one, and one must give one's entire devotion to a task or not undertake it.

Therefore, this is my final decision. Either you will accept the conditions which I enclose, and, in that case, you will only come to Paris after obtaining from me leave of absence, which shall never exceed one month except for special reasons, or we will go back to my first idea of creating a Ministry of Algeria and the Colonies in Paris.

Reflect over all this, which is a very serious matter, and give me your answer.

    With my sincere regard,   NAPOLEON.

Prince Napoleon to the Emperor
Paris, 16th June, 1858.

Sire,—I have received the letter[1] Your Majesty was pleased to write to me, together with the decree concerning the government of Algeria.

I have taken a few days, Sire, as you bade me, for reflection. I have embodied my observations in a note copied out in the same form as the project you sent me. I have put at the beginning general considerations on the whole scheme ; next, the decree approved by Your Majesty, which I should like to have signed by you, and, lastly, reasons in support of each of the clauses advocated by me.

I beg, Sire, you will read what I have written with attention ; I feel it to be conclusive. Before sending it I consulted the members of the Commission appointed by you to discuss this question with me, and they were *unanimous* in approving what I have written. Further, they were of opinion that matters in Algeria were suffering from the present uncertainty to such a degree that it is urgent that the Emperor should be pleased, as soon after his return to Paris as possible, to come to a decision either to abandon all attempts at reform in Algeria or to adopt the proposed decree.

On the proposition of the Ministers of Finance and of Public Instruction you are withdrawing from me, Sire, certain powers ; I do not feel this to be just. On the question of the customs I have had a long conversation with M. Gréterin[2], who ended by acknowledging that there were no good reasons against my demands, but that he only feared the moral effect !

Besides this, the question of confidence in me arises when I consider that you were disposed to appoint me

---

[1] The preceding letter from the Emperor.
[2] President of the Special Council of Customs.

Viceroy—that is, to create for me a position far greater than what I consider is indispensable, and to make the separation much more complete, for by appointing me Viceroy you would be constituting a separated Algeria into a kingdom. In referring again to this point of departure, I am unable to understand—I dare to say so—the *petites chicanes* of the Ministers, unless it be from the point of view of their wishing to see the failure of anything which is outside the routine of their administration!

The reasons I submit for the sojourns I shall be forced to make in Paris are an answer, perhaps, to the bad effect Your Majesty might fear of an absence of three or four months fixed in advance. People will see that I have come with a view of discussing affairs with you, of drawing up the budget, and of regulating all the larger questions, and I shall only remain for a time sufficient for these matters; but such personal relations with you, Sire, appear to me to be so indispensable that I cannot even understand the mechanism of the new Government without them; I implore the Emperor to read over carefully my observations on this matter.

I can perform efficaciously my duties as Minister for Algeria only while I am in close contact with you. The system I have proposed is not, perhaps, as simple as you could wish, but the more I reflect over it the more I think it to be the only possible one to harmonise the new organisation with our constitution, our laws, and especially our custom of centralisation and of the intervention of the Emperor in so many details. I shall be very glad to talk over this with Your Majesty for an hour.

Another idea I wish to submit to you, Sire, is to make Randon[1] come here for a few days shortly. He would be able to give excellent advice. This mark of confidence would please him, and he would no longer complain, as he

[1] Governor-General of Algeria.

has been doing, of being quite a stranger to your decisions regarding the country he is governing. And public opinion would then understand why this question has not yet been decided. The foreign newspapers, which are so hostile, say that your Government is powerless to initiate any reform, and that I am asking for absurdities, such as the right to appoint the officers, etc.

If Marshal Randon were summoned by telegram he could be here in five days, and in three days after everything could be finished with, and, I will repeat, this would give a reason, which the public would understand and approve, for the delays hitherto.

See for yourself, Sire, and decide. Be assured, above all, that I am deeply grateful to you for the solicitude you are kind enough to show for my future. You have been a second father to me for a long time, and I too have loved you for long, and been entirely devoted to you—as man more than as Emperor.

When I see you I shall have to talk to you also about information I have received from Italy.

Accept, I beg, etc.,
NAPOLEON (JEROME).

The Emperor to Prince Napoleon
St. Cloud, 20th June, 1858.

MY DEAR COUSIN,—We arrived this evening at St. Cloud, and I wish to see you for luncheon on Tuesday at 11 o'clock.

With my sincere regards,
NAPOLEON.

Prince Napoleon to the Emperor
Paris, June, 1858.

SIRE,—I have the honour to render an account to Your Majesty of what I have done in organising the new Ministry which you have been pleased to entrust to me.

The Commission which we have constituted in agreement with the Ministers of War and of the Navy has concluded its labours; all has been put in order and our work is ready for submission to you for carrying your decree into effect. One question alone has not been able to be decided and is still keeping back the despatch to you of our labours: it concerns the employment of the infantry and marine artillery as Colonial troops. I have nothing but praise for Marshal Vaillant[1]; everything has worked smoothly with him; we have written a despatch, signed by us both, to the Governor-General of Algeria explaining his position to him and defining the method of administration. I regret to say that I have met with a spirit of intractability, barely disguised, in Admiral Hamelin.[2] He has shown himself unwilling to listen to anything or to come to any arrangement. I proposed to him to appoint jointly a commission to examine the question of the marine infantry which is causing the difference between us. He would not have either Marshal Magnan, Marshal Randon, or M. Rouher to preside over it. We spoke about it at the last Council of Ministers without making him budge a step.

We have no other course to take than to beg the Emperor to refer this question of the prerogatives of the Departments of War, the Navy, and of Algeria and the Colonies, to the Council of State, who will submit their opinion to you. I am so sure that I am in the right that I only ask for this question to be studied, which reduces itself to this: the naval troops serving ashore are only for service in the Colonies; they were formed for this purpose in 1838; they do not serve afloat; they are Colonial regiments: as such they ought to be under the

---

[1] Minister for War. [2] Minister of Marine.

authority of the Minister for the Colonies or for War; they cannot remain under the Navy. Already there are quite enough points for the good of the service causing friction between the Navy and the Colonies, without the addition of this one which I fear to be insurmountable. I foresee very great difficulties between Admiral Hamelin and myself in working together. I am determined, on my side, to keep myself always within my rights and to exercise due moderation; but the two services of the Navy and of the Colonies are difficult to separate from each other, and I would ask you, Sire, to give orders for the Council of State to be informed of our dispute.

I have nothing but praise for General Daumas.[1] I think, however, that he will not be able to retain his post; he himself does not wish to do so. There are too many chiefs for Algeria—the Governor, General Daumas, and myself—and that cannot work. I shall have to submit to the Emperor the choice of a new Director, and I am having this under my consideration. Up till now the General has been acting, and has been giving me every assistance. When he gives up his position he would much like to be appointed an A.D.C. to His Majesty. His wish has my support.

M. Fould was to have sent, Sire, an order appointing M. de Chancourtois as Secretary to give effect to my commands. I will put him in charge of my private office. He is a very distinguished mining engineer, attached to M. Elie de Beaumont's course of geology, and was working with me during the exhibition, and accompanied me on my voyage to the North.[2]

I enclose an order authorising the payment to my Ministry of the credits opened with the War Office and Navy which come within my province.

[1] Director of Algerian Affairs at the Ministry for War.
[2] Prince Napoleon made a voyage in the North Sea in 1856.

Work is going on to establish the Ministry at the Palais Royal. In spite of all my energy this will be rather a long process, and the service will suffer until the practical work of settling in is over.

I am busy over your proposed *brochure* on Turkey.[1] I have thought of M. Peyrat, the former Editor in chief of *La Presse*. Although I have not seen him I have ascertained that he would write under his own name a *brochure* in the sense, and with the aim, desired. He is very capable, writes well, and understands the question.

Do you wish me to follow up this project which could be promptly carried out?

How much ought I to give M. Peyrat?

NAPOLEON (JEROME).

The Emperor to Prince Napoleon
Plombières, 6th July, 1858.

MY DEAR NAPOLEON,—I am very pleased with the good dispositions you are manifesting for your new functions, and I have no doubt you will be successful. But I recommend you particularly not to concern yourself at the start over questions of prerogative. You may be sure that if the practical working requires that I should extend them I would not hesitate to do so. The question of the marine infantry is so clear to my eyes that I have written to the Minister of the Navy telling him that I should not consent to their being separated from its Ministry. There are many reasons for this, and one of the strongest in my eyes consists in the lack of unity this would cause in the marines, who have to act in concert with the fleet.

I am entirely of your opinion. You cannot keep

---

[1] This is the *brochure* referred to in the letter from the Prince (November 1857, p. 84) and in that from the Emperor (11th November, 1857, p. 86). Peyrat was then editor of *La Presse*, in which journal he interested himself, especially in foreign policy and religious questions. The *brochure* appeared without the name of the author, under the title *La Turquie devant l'Europe*.

Daumas, but he would not suit me at all as my A.D.C.

I have issued instructions for the speedy installation of your Ministry.

I ask nothing better than to grant the medals which Rouher has requested of me, to take with you on your journey.

I strongly approve of the scheme of the *brochure*, but I prefer that it should bear the name of the author, for I do not wish to be made responsible. I will give P. what he asks if the *brochure* is good. The one that has just appeared on the Principalities is by a master-hand. Do you know who wrote it?

I think your circular is very well drawn up.

With my sincere regards,
NAPOLEON.

Prince Napoleon to the Emperor
Paris, 11*th August*, 1858.

SIRE,—I have the honour to send to Your Majesty a copy of a letter from Marshal Randon informing me that he has handed in his resignation directly to Your Majesty, together with a copy of my reply.

By acting in this manner the Marshal has been guilty of conduct which Your Majesty will appreciate.

The reasons alleged by the Marshal are not correct; I have always held him in the greatest regard, goodwill and entire confidence. It was I who requested Your Majesty to summon him. I have had very long conversations with him on all the important questions concerning Algeria. I asked him to sum up his opinion in writing on all these questions, reserving them for most careful study by myself. The result of our conversations was that there are three courses open:

The suppression of the office of Governor-General and the substitution in his place of a high officer in the Army;

GE

A notable augmentation of his powers, with complete centralisation at Algiers ;

The provisional maintenance of the *status quo*, and reserving any alterations thereto as experience shall dictate.

After what Your Majesty said to me when taking leave of you at St. Cloud, I summoned the Marshal in order to tell him that the Emperor would take the third course, that you wished him to remain Governor-General in his present position, and that I looked to him to return as soon as possible to Algeria.

I accompanied what I said with the most flattering and friendly language, telling him especially that if we must have a Governor-General there no one would be more agreeable to me than he.

The Marshal, with the air of accepting what I said to him, assured me that he would leave at once. A few days ago I was greatly surprised to receive a somewhat obscure and inconclusive letter in which he indicated, nevertheless, his desire that all the public services should be concentrated under his direction in Algeria, that all officials of every grade should only hold communication with me through him, and that the municipal and local budget, amounting to more than ten million francs, should be under his control.

I caused a verbal reply to be given to him by Colonel de Franconière, my first aide-de-camp, and his intimate friend, that his claims appeared to me to be inadmissible, and that I could only submit them to the Emperor when the completed results of the deliberations on the organisation of the government of Algeria should be submitted to you : I caused him to be informed again that for the moment all must remain as it is at present, since this was your decision.

Yesterday I received the letter I am sending you ; the

The Second Empire and Its Downfall

Marshal had not let me know of his decision in any other form. He came to write his name in the book, without wishing to enter my private office, and I have just heard that he left Paris yesterday evening. I find it difficult to explain such behaviour. I trust, Sire, you will approve of my answer.

I make bold to press urgently upon Your Majesty that the Marshal's resignation be accepted. General Renault will be able to act as substitute until your return, when the Emperor will be good enough to make known his wishes to me after an examination of my propositions.

Taking advantage of the permission you have been pleased to grant me, I am hoping to leave to-morrow, the 12th, in order to spend eight days in Switzerland. I shall be back in Paris on the 20th.

As is the practice of several Ministers' current affairs will be despatched by my heads of departments, and I am not having a substitute for so short a time.

I have left the necessary instructions with my private office to forward to me the Emperor's commands, should he send me any. I should feel greatly obliged if his reply to the Marshal might be sent to him through my intermediary.

We have been very pleased to hear of the happy journey of the Emperor and Empress.[1] I hope it will not over-fatigue them.

May it please you to accept, Sire, etc.,

NAPOLEON (JEROME).

The Emperor to Prince Napoleon
Biarritz, 12th September, 1858.

MY DEAR COUSIN,—I have given mature reflection to your proposal as regards the Prefecture of Algiers, and without having any prejudice against the person you

[1] A journey to Cherbourg to meet the Queen of England.

mention I truly think that his appointment would have a very bad effect at the present moment. After you have had the opportunity of doing some good work in Algeria and people are able to judge of your administration, it may be possible for me to make use of the abilities of M. de G. But previous to that his appointment would present grave inconveniences. Those persons who are hostile to you were always saying before you held your new position that if any power were given to you it would only be to the advantage of G. and Bixio.[1] We must not give them any cause to show they were right. The worst thing about these two persons, but especially so in the case of the former, is that they are possessed of no kind of consideration whatsoever, and when one surrounds oneself with people like that, it is always reflected back upon one.

It is true the choice is a difficult one to make, but there are some distinguished men among the Prefects from whom one could select.

With my sincere regard,
NAPOLEON.

[1] Emile de Girardin and Jacques Alexandre Bixio, both of very advanced opinions, were in close touch with Prince Napoleon.

CHAPTER VII

Italian affairs—Mission of Prince Napoleon to Varsovie—Newspaper articles—Negotiations with Piedmont—The marriage of Prince Napoleon to the daughter of Victor Emmanuel—French policy as regards Piedmont.

A RECENT series of articles in the *Revue des Deux Mondes*[1] has given to the public the correspondence of King Victor Emmanuel, Prince Napoleon, and Count Cavour in connection with the preparation and consequences of the Italian war. We therefore feel it to be unprofitable to retrace here the history of these negotiations. With very brief comments thereon we shall content ourselves with giving the letters of the Emperor and Prince Napoleon bearing on these events.

After his famous conversations with Count Cavour at Plombières (21st July, 1858), Napoleon III, fully determined to free Italy from the Austrian yoke some day or other, desired before all things, failing the active help of Russia, at least to make sure of her moral support and benevolent attitude. This question could not be discussed on an official basis. In September, 1858, he summoned Prince Napoleon to Biarritz and commissioned him to proceed immediately to Varsovie, where the Emperor Alexander then happened to be. These negotiations were to remain strictly secret. In order to give a reason for the journey of the Prince to all and sundry, as well as to the Ministers who would have been hostile to it, it was given out as a visit of politeness to the Czar, in return for the interview which the two emperors had had at Stuttgart in the previous year.

[1] In the issues of 1st January, 1st and 15th February, and 15th March, 1923, under the heading " L'Italie Libérée."

In the space of a quick journey to Varsovie[1] and back the Prince accomplished his delicate mission with much tact and ability. His cousin, on his return to give an account of it, was very satisfied with what he had done. Important results were to be expected.

Negotiations, which were still kept very secret, were thus set on foot. The question was to follow them up with the greatest discretion. The Prince could not return to Russia without the risk of arousing attention, and it was indispensable to send to St. Petersburg a man in whom entire confidence could be placed. The Emperor did not know whom to appoint, when Prince Napoleon proposed to him the name of Captain La Roncière Le Noury, of the French Navy, who had been in command of the warship *Reine Hortense*, in which the Prince had carried out his scientific expedition in the North Sea in 1856. The choice seemed to be an excellent one to the Emperor, and he wrote to his cousin :

Sunday, 31st October, 1858.

MY DEAR NAPOLEON,—I am delighted with your *discovery*. Arrange matters so that he leaves shortly. You can bring him to me to-morrow morning.

With my sincere regard,
NAPOLEON.

The Emperor to Prince Napoleon
Thursday, 23rd December, 1858.

MY DEAR NAPOLEON,—I send you the letter for the Emperor Alexander. Read and seal it, and give it to La Roncière. Tell him also that if the treaty is signed I do not wish the date to be inserted, in order that we may not make it public until the events take place. If you

---
[1] We shall publish shortly the account of this mission written by Prince Napoleon himself.

have any observations to make to me, come this evening at 6 o'clock.

With my sincere regard,
NAPOLEON.

The Emperor to Prince Napoleon
Paris, 30th December, 1858.

MY DEAR COUSIN,—I don't know at all what is happening. Up till now you have served me with devotion and intelligence as my intermediary with the Emperor of Russia. I bid you write in my name. I authorise you to use a cipher in dealing with La Roncière, and then, when I give you an order to modify his instructions, you refuse!

This means that you will only serve me as long as it suits you. I confess that this example give me much pain, for what confidence can I have in you in future if when giving you an order I am not sure whether it will be executed? But I will not continue the observations which this incident inspires in me, and will confine myself to requesting you to hand over your cipher to Count Walewski, since in your hands it is only to be used for the purpose of your communications in *so far as it suits you.*

What distresses me grievously is that I see from experience that there are people in whose case a great cause, a great purpose, disappears from their sight the moment they feel themselves wounded in their *amour-propre.*

I still hope that such is not the case with you, and await impatiently any explanation you can give me.

With my sincere regard,
NAPOLEON.

This slight misunderstanding was not continued. La Roncière acquitted himself very well in his mission, and a treaty of benevolent neutrality and diplomatic support was agreed upon between the two sovereigns.

A month previously, while the preparation of events was proceeding thus under cover, *La Presse* had published in its issue of the 23rd November a hostile article against Austria, in which Guéroult spoke openly of the strife which could not fail to break out between that country and Piedmont. Also, on the 27th November, the *Siècle* set forth the advantages to the equilibrium of Europe which "the existence of a great State which should be called Italy" would present.

This was to go too fast. The Emperor requested his cousin to use his personal influence with certain journals in order to counsel greater discretion.

The Emperor to Prince Napoleon
27th November, 1858.

MY DEAR NAPOLEON,—I have received your letter, and readily believe what you tell me so far as you are concerned. What I regret are the articles in *La Presse* and the *Siècle*, for if that kind of thing continues we shall be forced to issue a refutation which will be disagreeable. As far as men are concerned we must not judge them too severely. There are so many people *qui ne nagent que lorsq'on les jette à l'eau*.[1] But if you possess any influence with the Press advise them not to put the trumpet to their mouths when they are unwilling to march. I will see what I can do for M. de (name illegible).

With my sincere regard, NAPOLEON.

I am not surprised at the traveller's delay.[2]

The Press in Paris was not alone in prematurely lifting a corner of the veil beneath which it was convenient to hide matters which had not yet come to a head. At Turin they were showing dangerous impatience which

---
[1] Against these words Prince Napoleon wrote in pencil: "Preparation for the war in Italy known only to the P[rince], and checkmated by the Ministers of whom he complains."
[2] La Roncière.

was explained by the favourable dispositions held at the Tuileries. King Victor Emmanuel II at the receptions of the New Year, after keeping a watch over himself throughout almost the entire ceremonies, let himself be drawn into incautious language at the close. The Emperor was apprehensive of an allusion to this in the speech the King was to make on the 10th January, at the opening of Parliament, the text of which had in the meantime been communicated to him. Although in principle war with Austria had been resolved upon in the mind of Count Cavour, and had been accepted in that of the Emperor, France could only intervene if Piedmont were to be attacked. Contrary to what has been stated by certain historians,[1] the secret treaty which united the *rôle* of the two countries was not signed until the month of January 1859, but Napoleon III felt the imperative necessity of having public opinion on his side both at home and abroad. In order to justify the armed intervention of France it was necessary at all costs that Austria should be the aggressor, and Piedmont the victim. This was why it was important to moderate the ardour of our future ally.

The Emperor to Prince Napoleon
Friday, 7th January, 1859.

MY DEAR NAPOLEON,—I beg you will summon M. Nigra,[2] and tell him to write seriously to Turin in order that they may act with greater restraint. Nothing can succeed without proper sequence and method. Piedmont requires money—well, she can only obtain this by concealing her plans as far as possible. She wishes to have

---

[1] In *L'Empire Libéral* (Vol. III, p. 527) Emile Ollivier thinks that the secret Treaty of Alliance between France and Piedmont was really signed on the 10th December, 1858. Basing our view on the letter of the Emperor of the 26th January, 1859, we are in a position to state that it was ante-dated, and was not concluded definitely until January 1859, while Prince Napoleon was at Turin.

[2] We think it unnecessary to recall the important *rôle* played by the Chevalier Nigra in the negotiations which prepared the war in Italy.

the support of France, and she can only secure this by putting herself in the right in the eyes of public opinion. Now I am greatly distressed at the correspondence from Turin coming to all parts of Europe. Everywhere people are saying : " Piedmont, sure of the support of France, is looking for some pretext to begin war." It is absolutely necessary that they should be more prudent in Turin and if, incidentally, the speech of the King is warlike, it will be impossible to make the loan.

With my sincere regard,
NAPOLEON.

Nothing from St. Petersburg.

On the 13th January Prince Napoleon left for Turin, accompanied by different officers on his Staff and by General Niel, who enjoyed high favour with the Emperor. The object of this journey was not in doubt to anybody. People had been talking of a marriage of the Prince to Princess Clotilde[1] for some time. If it was not yet known that it had been decided upon during the preceding July, after the conversations that had taken place at Plombières people were anticipating this event. No surprise was expressed when the newspapers announced in succession the departure of the Prince, his arrival at Turin, the cordial reception accorded to him, his official betrothal, and marriage, which was celebrated on the 30th January.

The Emperor to Prince Napoleon.[2]

Paris, 15th January, 1859.

MY DEAR COUSIN,—I hope you have arrived in good health at Turin. I am only writing a few words to tell you that I forgot to recommend you to make no promises of the decoration of the Legion of Honour, because the marriage will be an opportunity to bestow a good number.

---

[1] Clotilde Marie Thérèse Louise, born 2nd March, 1843, the daughter of King Victor Emmanuel II and the Archduchess Adelaide of Austria.

[2] The Prince received this at Turin on the 17th January.

La Roncière is arriving to-morrow. The English Minister has written to his Minister in Paris a very hostile despatch concerning the King's speech.

Give my very kind regards to everybody.

With my sincere affection, NAPOLEON.

Paris, 19th January, 1859.

MY DEAR NAPOLEON,[1]—I am awaiting impatiently some details of your stay in Turin. I hope the post will arrive this evening. I send you all the official letters and official requests. As regards the *grand cordon* for Prince Carignan[2] we must reserve this for the day of your marriage, as I wrote to you, for I have nothing else I can bestow upon him.

Misgivings have quieted down here, but I am constantly being displeased with the newspapers. Some say far too much, and others too little.

La Roncière has accomplished his mission very well. We have gained all we could hope for. The Emperor on parting said to him that he gave me his word of honour to do all in his power in my favour, but that he must be left the judge as to ways and the suitable time.

With my sincere regard, NAPOLEON.

The Empress states that it is customary to present a ring at the betrothal, and as she thinks you have not got one she sends you one.

The Emperor to Prince Napoleon at Turin
(Telegram in cipher)

Paris, 23rd *January,* 1859.

I have received the programme. I approve of it, but everyone is struck by the objections arising from such a

---

[1] The Prince received this on the 21st January.
[2] Eugene Emmanuel de Savoie Villefranche, Prince Carignan (1816-88).

precipitate marriage. You must obtain at least a delay of eight days, in order that there may be time to make the necessary preparations. Such haste would give rise to a whole host of comment and danger.

The public mind seeks to connect the marriage with the war; at all costs in the interests of the two countries we must gain a little time for the war, if that is possible. From St. Petersburg and London people are writing in the same sense. I should like the contract of marriage to be put off to the 6th at least. I am especially desirous to know if Piedmont is obliged to go to war this year.

Prince Napoleon to the Emperor
(Telegram partly in cipher)
Turin, Monday, 24th January, 1859.
2 o'clock in the morning.

Received Your Majesty's telegram of the 23rd at 9.35 in the evening on returning from the theatre. The banns were published to-day at the Cathedral after Mass, at which we were present ceremonially, and the marriage was announced for next Sunday. The King, believing that all was settled, and seeing the impatience of General Niel, Prince de la Tour d'Auvergne,[1] and myself for the arrangement of the marriage, exceeded our wishes in hurrying on the conclusion. The Emperor's instructions were to hurry on the marriage as much as possible. On our arrival there were two courses open: a marriage in person, or by proxy. If in person, that would disconnect the marriage from the political question. Count Cavour was in favour of an adjournment, and a marriage by proxy. But my prolonged stay in the Palace is very embarrassing for the King, and my presence here a cause of political excitement. We should be falling into the inconveniences the Emperor is anxious to avoid. A few

[1] French Minister-Plenipotentiary at Turin.

shortcomings in the preparations cannot be put in the balance with such grave interests. As the King wishes to stay for one day at Genoa our arrival in Paris will be deferred to the 3rd.

Let the Emperor be in no anxiety. The note sent yesterday by courier and the treaties which will be despatched to-day by an officer only lay down principles without any particular date. Three months of calm are assured, and the opportunity remains in your hands provided there be no unjustifiable attack on the part of Austria, which is hardly probable.

An adjournment would be deplorable. The King and the Princess would be dissatisfied, I should be taxed with levity, and the Emperor with indecision. In the present state of the question I implore the Emperor to allow me to carry out the programme. To adjourn it would compromise everything. Let the Emperor have confidence in our prudence and in our wish to succeed. Pray reply in the morning before I see the King again. Am in great anxiety.

The Emperor to Prince Napoleon[1]

MY DEAR COUSIN,—I return you the draft of M. de Cavour's circular.[2] I think it is very good. Fould thinks that we should offer a loan for national subscription like the one we have already done. There might be greater chances of success in that way.

Send me by telegraph the names of the persons you suggest for decorations.

Niel tells me of a conversation he had with the King as regards the date. Everything depends on the setting, that is, on the legitimate aspect of the motives. In any case under present circumstances we must allow a certain

---
[1] This letter is not dated. It must have been written on the 25th January, for the Prince received it at Turin on the 27th.
[2] Relative to a loan.

amount of time, for the question has been very badly handled, and public opinion in Europe is rising every day more and more against me, and especially against you, because people believe we want war.

Walewski[1] is not responsible for all the nonsense they are putting into the newspapers. I beg you not to take a dislike to people who are serving me. There is no need for us to create difficulties to no profit.

I am very pleased when you can tell me anything good, and I count always on your judgment and friendly feeling.

With my sincere affection,

NAPOLEON.

The Emperor to Prince Napoleon[2]
Paris, 26th January, 1859.

MY DEAR NAPOLEON,—As I have always communicated with you by telegram and in haste, I have not had the time to congratulate you upon the happy issue of your journey to Turin, and to thank you for the skill you have displayed in all the transactions with which I have commissioned you. Everybody speaks well of the charm and intelligence of your future companion. This makes us very happy, and I hope that this union will bring you good fortune and will have a happy influence over your future. I return you to-day the treaties with my signature[3]; you will bring back to me those signed by the King. There is no other change than the transposition of a sentence, which gives a better effect without altering in any way the general purport. But the point upon which I have laid special stress is the antedating of the Convention with a view to avoid giving any colour to the

---

[1] Minister of Foreign Affairs.
[2] Received at Turin on the 28th January.
[3] This refers to the secret treaty whereby France engaged, in return for the cession of Nice and Savoy, to go to the aid of Piedmont only in case she should be attacked, and to a military convention arising therefrom, which was concluded at Turin between Generals Niel and La Marmora.

assertions of those who repeat everywhere that your marriage is in the nature of a bargain and that it could only be brought about on condition of making a treaty.

As to the question itself I shall always repeat the same thing. We must redouble our carefulness to ensure that Europe shall think we are in the right. The indiscretions being committed are so great that I am receiving news from Rome and Austria reporting that the Duc de Modène, aware that Piedmont wishes to stir up an insurrection within his states, has come to an understanding with Austria and Tuscany to take refuge in Tuscany with his troops when the occasion arises, and to appeal to the Great Powers. The chief difficulty, therefore, is always the same, and I can define it in a few words: if Piedmont has the appearance of seeking an artificial quarrel with Austria, and if I, on my side, have the appearance of approving of her conduct in my desire for war, public opinion in France and in Europe would abandon me, and I should run the risk of having the whole of Europe on my hands. If on the other hand Piedmont should seem to be made a victim while she is justifying her rights, everyone, with my support, would remain neutral. What is to be done then? This: to base the question on some incontestable fact of lawful right, no matter how insignificant it be. For example, if Piedmont (after having made her preparations) has a *lawful right* to protest against the occupation and fortifying of Placentia and presses this point to the utmost, I think, perhaps, she would be placing herself on the surest ground that is possible. In a word, it is in this sense that we must work. I fear that other methods would be *found out*, and that the moment people see an insurrection breaking out at Massa Carrara they will say " *Voici le complot qui se déroule.*" People have already sent me from Florence proclamations made at Massa Carrara.

Well, this is what I was wanting to tell you, in order that you can talk it over thoroughly with the King and Count Cavour.

Tell the King from me how much I appreciate his friendly feeling and his kind behaviour to you. My greatest wish is to prove to him that he may count upon me as his most faithful ally and real friend.

With my sincere and affectionate regard,

NAPOLEON.

I am opening my letter again to tell you that the Empress and all of us think that your wife will be horribly fatigued in coming straight from Marseilles to Paris, and that, in any case, by leaving Marseilles at 6 o'clock in the morning you could be at Fontainebleau at 11 o'clock at night, stay the night there, and come to Paris at about 2 o'clock the following afternoon.

CHAPTER VIII

Charles Vogt—The *Moniteur* contradicts the reports as to France getting ready for war—Prince Napoleon resigns his position as Minister of Algeria and the Colonies—Is reprimanded by the Emperor Napoleon—Preparing for the war in Italy.

NOTWITHSTANDING its brevity, we quote the following letter written by the Emperor to his cousin in order to give a fresh proof of the pains taken by Napoleon III to prepare public opinion for the war which was in prospect.

There was a German professor at the Academy at Geneva, a distinguished naturalist named Charles Vogt, who had been obliged to leave Germany after 1848 on account of his very advanced political ideas. He was a declared enemy of Austria, and a convinced partisan of Italian independence. When he saw the outline of coming events he made a proposition to Prince Napoleon, with whom he was in relations, to direct a propaganda from Geneva with a view to enlightening Germany and to creating a movement in favour of Piedmont. He offered to write a *brochure* and to start a weekly newspaper which should be inspired from Paris, but he recommended that this fact should not be divulged or he would risk losing all influence on liberal Germany.

The Emperor to Prince Napoleon

3rd March, 1859.

MY DEAR NAPOLEON,—I have read the memorandum signed Charles. It is a remarkable document, written with a talent out of the ordinary. I beg you will ask him what he requires to put into execution a plan which I adopt in its entirety, and which I will support with all in my power.

With my sincere regard.
Tell Nigra to come and see me to-morrow morning at half-past nine.

NAPOLEON.

At this point we may add that on the 24th March, 1859, Ferri Pisani, the officer who was so devoted to Prince Napoleon, went to Geneva to find the Professor, came to a definite understanding with him on the subject of this publication, and placed forty thousand francs in his hands. Several months passed by, in the course of which Vogt failed completely in his enterprise. He rapidly lost all credit in Germany, where his efforts had no other result than to provoke a recrudescence of anti-Napoleonic fury. He gave up his project of his own accord, and appears even not to have made use of a credit of fifty thousand francs which Napoleon III had opened for him with M. Mocquard, his own notary. This emerges from the note dictated by the Emperor, which we merely quote in order not to have to return to the subject.

Palais de St. Cloud, 20*th July*, 1859.

MY DEAR COUSIN,—I learn that the fifty thousand francs deposited with M. Mocquard, notary, for M.V.[1] have not been drawn. Please tell me what I am to do with them.

Assuring you of my sincere regard,

NAPOLEON.

The interests of Austria and Piedmont were so profoundly contradictory, the antagonism between these two peoples was so violent, that war in a more or less distant future appeared to be inevitable. England, however, in her desire to play the *rôle* of mediator, redoubled

---

[1] Prince Napoleon completed the name himself, in pencil, and wrote, " Vogt, of Geneva."

her efforts to remove the possibility of this eventuality and sought to win over Prussia and Russia to her views. In France a large party were hostile to the war. An opposition was formed around the Emperor which, though doubtless timid, was nevertheless a real one, and Ministers themselves took a part in it.

In this way Napoleon III was conscious of resistance, both at home and abroad, which forced him to adopt dilatory methods. Neither from the diplomatic point of view, nor materially, were people yet prepared. It was necessary to appease premature alarm. This was the reason for the appearance in the *Moniteur* of a long article written with a view to give a *démenti* to reports of exceptional armaments, and to reassure men's minds. Its effect was considerable. Three days after, another event confirmed this impression: Prince Napoleon, of whose openly favourable dispositions towards Italy no one was unaware, sent in his resignation as Minister for Algeria and the Colonies. People believed he had fallen into disgrace. It was nothing of the kind. We cannot doubt that the Prince knew the secret and real intentions of his cousin, but the hastiness of his character prevented him from lending himself to these combinations, and he could ill put up with the sullen hostility which he encountered from some of his colleagues.

Immediately after reading the article in the *Moniteur* he wrote to the Emperor:

Prince Napoleon to the Emperor
Paris, 5th March, 1859.

Sire,—I beg Your Majesty will allow me to write to you about the general situation, and, consequently, about my own in particular.

For some months past the Emperor has been pursuing a policy which satisfies all those who are animated by generous and patriotic intentions and who love the principles of the Revolution at home, and the upholding of the national dignity abroad. You commanded me to explain and support this policy when I was with the Emperor of Russia at Varsovie, and at Turin in the case of Sardinia.

I have never disguised from myself the difficulties of this great undertaking, but, convinced that this cause was a just one, and that it would meet with the assent of the country, I have devoted myself to it with a zeal which perhaps has been too ardent, but which could only proceed from my devotion to the cause and to your person.

In taking my seat in the Councils of your Government it has not been difficult for me to convince myself that nearly all the Ministers and high officials are opposed to this policy. Their skilfulness has prevented them from combating it openly to your face, but in their private conversations and by their attitude they have made it clear that they are opponents of what you wish to do, and have stirred up against you the reactionaries at home and the greater proportion of public opinion in Germany and England. They have credited you with the most insensate revolutionary schemes. They have said, and made others say, that you wish to overturn everything in Europe for your own personal interests.

In my opinion there were only two lines of conduct which they could honourably follow : either to resign after they had discovered the disquieting lack of agreement existing between the Emperor and his counsellors, or to accept frankly your will and serve you with loyalty. They have followed neither of these two courses. Giving their approval to your face, they thwart, betray, and calumniate you behind your back. There is no need for me to mention the names of those who are at the head of this intrigue ; Your Majesty knows them as well as I do. I had thought that in your desire to follow a different policy Your Majesty would have considered the necessity of appealing to other men of firm views and devotion. Events prove to me that I was mistaken, and that I have understood ill the Emperor's intentions. I feel that I am an incumbrance in your councils.

I think the worst feature in your Government, and what is weakening it, lies in the dissensions at home and the different views held by those directing it. The greater the degree in which authority is strong, and concentrated in the hands of the Emperor, the more indispensable is unity among those who serve him. Well, Sire, it is clear as the light of the sun that this unity does not exist, and what is especially vexatious is that France and Europe know this to be the case. The situation being what it is, I feel I am performing an act of devotion to the Emperor in praying him to relieve me of sitting any longer among the present Ministers.

This decision is a grave one for me who, apart from politics, have been so happy to apply what little intelligence and energy I possess to the solution of the Colonial and Algerian questions which you have been pleased to entrust to me. But I cannot weigh this in the balance with a profound conviction, and the sentiment I feel, that I am rendering you a service by retiring from public affairs.

I will add that the special circumstances of my Ministry have also had their influence on my decision. It is not in the normal condition of the other Ministries. I am in process of organising it. I am trying to institute reforms in it on other lines than the feeble methods which have been followed hitherto. There are hardly any civil servants directly allocated to it, and it is obliged to borrow its officials from all the other administrations. A good understanding and friendly relations and mutual confidence with the other Ministers is more indispensable for it than for any other administration. In the prevailing conditions the Minister for Algeria and the Colonies is powerless to effect any good. I have in opposition against me, not only my colleagues, but the *corps législatif* inspired by its President, in which body a campaign is being prepared against me who can only be defended by the President of the Council of State, himself hostile to most of the measures I have submitted to the Emperor for his approval.

The struggle is too unequal. It would weary the Emperor and weaken his Government even if from feelings of goodwill and personal kindness the Emperor should wish to support me while retaining the same counsellors.

I know what joy among my enemies and what calumnies of every kind the appointment of another Minister for Algeria and the Colonies will excite. They will point at my headstrong and irresponsible mind, my lack of perseverance and judgment, my difficult character. I submit beforehand with philosophy to anything that will be said. What I am determined to safeguard are the loyalty and uprightness of my convictions, and my devotion to Your Majesty.

To continue to sit by the side of colleagues with whom I have the misfortune to disagree on most points of policy at home and abroad, and who, in my opinion, are ill-serving the Emperor and France, would be bad conduct to which I ought not to commit myself. I think it would be better to have a Government of a kind I do not approve, but one which is united, than bickerings within.

When I have left the Council of Ministers unity on fundamental questions will be established quite by itself.

Through the reports spread far and wide by my adversaries concerning my well-known opinions, people credit me with an influence Your Majesty, better than anyone, is aware is not real. I have never done anything but carry out your commands as well as it has been given me to understand them. You are desirous of calming public opinion at the present time, of strengthening our interests, and of satisfying the reactionaries at home and in Europe, by retaining those men who sit in your councils; nothing will be better able to accomplish these ends than replacing me. The Bourse will rise, and you will be congratulated from every side. As regards myself, I make this sacrifice with no bitterness as I understand the political needs. I surrender my portfolio and my part in public affairs without regrets, provided that your esteem, your confidence, and your heart remain to me.

The Emperor to Prince Napoleon[1]

Paris, 5th March, 1859.

My dear Napoleon,—I was much surprised at your letter and only wish to tell you to-day that you are right in counting on my confidence as well as my affection, but as regards the root of the matter we must talk this over together, for I can find no good reason nor pretext for this sudden resolution. One ought not to put one's *amour-propre* before one's duty in the affairs of life, and in truth I do not understand what can have been the motive for your determination. The general considerations which you advance are not quite accurate, and have not all the weight in my Government that you attach to them.

In conclusion I shall be greatly grieved if you do not go back upon this unexpected resolve. Come to-morrow at 9 o'clock. We will talk it over together.

Ever with my sincere regard,

Napoleon.

[1] The Prince wrote in pencil on the margin of this letter: "Resignation of the Prince from the Ministry of Algeria, not being able to get on with the other Ministers."

The Emperor to Prince Napoleon
Paris, 10th March, 1859.

MY DEAR NAPOLEON,—I write to you to-day after mature reflection to give you some advice as a friend which, if it bear fruit, should have a deciding influence on your destiny. You know how much I have loved you from your earliest years, how much your interests are linked with my own—well, listen, I implore you, to the words of advice I wish to give you for your general good. If you follow them you may acquire a great influence in the country. If you neglect them you will do harm to me, with no benefit to yourself.

You hold, I believe, very national opinions; I share them. You have much intelligence and general knowledge, but you do not possess sufficient tact in your conduct, or restraint in what you say. Do you want to be a politician, upholding my authority and strengthening the throne, or only a clever man, sceptical, laughing at everything and sticking to nothing? If you want to be a politician it is absolutely necessary to rule over your conduct and measure your words, for without this politics are out of the question. Confidence does not impose itself; it has to be won. Now what confidence can I myself repose in you if I am not certain of your discretion, if bad advice or false reports are able to have direct influence on your conduct, or if one can no longer discuss things secretly in your presence? Only during the last two days see all that has come to my knowledge:

1. All our conversation with Chasseloup-Laubat[1] which we three held together was known on the very same day, although neither he nor I mentioned a word of it. 2. The Treaty with Sardinia is secret from all the world, and only I had the right to speak of it, yet you mentioned

---

[1] Was a member of the Council for the Colonies at the Ministry for Algeria, and on the 24th March succeeded to the portfolio which Prince Napoleon had resigned.

it to Benedetti[1] who was completely ignorant of it.
3. Finally, yesterday M. Persigny said that you had told him that on the day the article in the *Moniteur* appeared I wrote to Count Cavour contradicting the article point by point. You are aware, nevertheless, that this is not true. Read the article in this day's *Times* and consider the effect it must have.

What do you expect people to think of all this, and what advantage can you derive from it! Without the proper spirit in one's conduct, and reserve in one's speech, one can never succeed in anything. Men who have least judgment so far as they themselves are concerned judge others very well, nevertheless, and when people see a man in a high position openly explaining to all and sundry dangerous notions and projects which could only be brought to a successful issue in secret, they conclude that a man like this has nothing serious in him; and by divulging his plans to no purpose he renders them impossible of fulfilment.

I am expressing myself at some length upon this subject because I feel that it is of the highest importance for you, for me, and for the whole country. I implore you, therefore, to pay scrupulous attention to your words, for everything you say is immediately retailed, amplified, and distorted.

I have told you all that has been in my mind. Profit by it. Ever with my sincere regard,   NAPOLEON.

As is shown in a note by the Prince the latter attributed these reproaches made by the Emperor to "*cancans inventés par les autres ministres*," and to the unfavourable disposition of the Empress towards himself. The Emperor, whose reprimands still retained a somewhat paternal tone, does not appear ever to have kept up any

---
[1] Political Director at the Ministry for Foreign Affairs.

feelings of annoyance in regard to his cousin, whose good offices during the months that followed he was to employ more than ever in the preparation of the great Italian movement.

In the letters that follow we see Napoleon III requesting the Prince to continue to busy himself in the various negotiations on foot, among others with the project formed by Klapka, the Hungarian General, to stir up a rising of his compatriots against Austria.

The Emperor to Prince Napoleon

12th March, 1859.

MY DEAR NAPOLEON,—Would you send Nigra to me this evening at nine-thirty. If you see V,[1] ask him what means there are to put his plan into execution. I was much struck by his memorandum.

Gl. K.[2] can always correspond with you, for you are not serving as my intermediary as Minister for Algeria but as my cousin and friend.

I think the reply of Count Cavour to England on the enrolling (of troops) is very good. I will have an enquiry made by the Prefect of Police, but that will not be easy.

With my sincere regard, NAPOLEON.

18th March, 1859.

MY DEAR NAPOLEON,—I had no time to answer you yesterday. I was writing to tell you that I received M. Alessandri the day before yesterday, and arranged an interview between him and the War Minister, who will consign 10,000 rifles to him for Prince Couza.[3] I can do no more at the moment.

With my sincere regard, NAPOLEON.

[1] Vogt. See the Emperor's letter of the 3rd March, 1859, pp. 113–14.
[2] The Hungarian General Klapka (1820–92).
[3] Elected Prince of Moldavia on the 17th January, 1859, he was to become shortly afterwards the ruler of Wallachia. He was a declared partisan of the union of the Principalities.

CHAPTER IX

The Congress—Russia proposes the summoning of a European Congress—The question of Piedmont having a seat on the Board—The Prince's views on the Ministers—The armed watch.

THE situation was becoming more acute day by day. In Germany hostility against Napoleon III, secretly stirred up by England, showed itself more and more threatening, when suddenly a *coup de théâtre* took place. Russia, usurping the part of mediator which England up till then had been claiming for herself alone, proposed to submit the differences to a congress in which the five great powers should take part—France, England, Austria, Russia, and Prussia. While in principle respecting the Treaties of 1815 the discussions were to bear upon four precisely defined points. But two preliminary conditions were not long in making very difficult the carrying into execution of this project for safeguarding peace: on the one hand Piedmont was not invited to be represented at these conferences in the course of which her fate was to be decided, and, on the other, Austria laid down the proviso that before any discussion Piedmont must disarm.

Prince Napoleon had constituted himself, as it were, the advocate of Piedmont. Together with his cousin he was firmly convinced of the desirability, in the interests of the security of France and the balance of power in Europe, of creating an independent and powerful country on the other side of the Alps, which would be capable of counterbalancing the action of her neighbour. In reality this was nothing else but a return under another form to the old French policy of Richelieu—namely, that of humbling the House of Austria.

And foreseeing from the outset that these conditions would be turned against his *protégée* the Prince was unable to refrain from taking up her defence with an ardour which we have seen expressed in his correspondence with Count Cavour[1] and which may be found in the following letters:

The Emperor to Prince Napoleon
19th March, 1859.

MY DEAR NAPOLEON,—This is a résumé of my conversation with Kisseleff[2] : Russia made the proposal of the congress in order to be of use to France and Piedmont. The result should be the isolation of Austria.

Into this fresh Congress, composed of the five Great Powers, it was impossible to admit Sardinia.

That would mean making Sardinia a sixth Great Power.

If, together with Turkey, she took part in the last Congress, it was because she was a *partie belligérante*. If it were desired to have a Congress in Italy we should have to admit all the Italian sovereigns. But when it is a question of discussing a matter of European interest with the Great Powers alone it is impossible to make an exception by admitting any other.

I must confess that this argument is so logical that there is no need for me to refute it.

Assuring you of my sincere regard,

NAPOLEON.

Prince Napoleon to the Emperor
Paris, 22nd March, 1859.

SIRE,—I open the *Moniteur* and see that the Congress is announced therein, also its composition, and with such precipitation that the replies from London, Berlin, and Vienna have not even arrived, and before the bare

---

[1] "L'Italie Libérée," *Revue des Deux Mondes.*
[2] Russian Ambassador in Paris.

observations of Piedmont have been heard! And yet they have been telegraphed and the mail should arrive this very day! This was announced officially to the Ministry for Foreign Affairs by the Sardinian Minister. You have been willing to act before hearing the reasons advanced by unhappy Italy to be admitted to a conference in which her fate is to be decided without her participation, and against her!

When the soldiers of Piedmont were found worthy to take part by the side of these Great Powers during the Crimean War, King Victor Emmanuel had the honour of being allowed to spend the blood and money of his people in favour of these same Great Powers who to-day show him the door on a purely Italian question, while Austria, his enemy and an Italian power, is admitted, and while precedents are against this procedure, as is easy to prove. And this very grave decision is taken before she has been heard, in the determination to listen to nothing from her! Sire, have you calculated the effect of this action in all its bearings?

It means the reconstituting of the Holy Alliance against the different nations;

It means the punishment of the Italian race;

It means the despotism of the strong over the weak;

It means the determination to decide for, that is to condemn to death, Italy without even hearing her representatives;

It means the tearing up of the Treaty with Piedmont, the promises made and the hopes given to her, and the abandonment of the plans drawn up together and concerted with her.

This will bring you to lead an expedition against Piedmont from Rome. It means precipitating an explosion in Italy.

I foresee what will happen as clearly as I see the sun.

Either M. de Cavour will resign and my father-in-law abdicate after giving an explanation to the world of the motives underlying these acts, or Sardinia will protest against the Congress, and nobly resist its decisions with her arms if she does not accept them, and immolate herself.

This will mean one more nation sacrificed, and a great cause lost.

No illusions can be made in this respect.

And all this without even being certain of the cohesion of the five Great Powers. England will be much hurt at this publication, which has been made before her official reply to the proposal of Russia, and will feel humiliated at this breach of the understanding with her.

Neither will Austria be satisfied.

Everybody will be upset, except Russia.

If, Sire, you have reckoned upon what will happen and the consequences, I deplore it, but there is nothing I can say. If you are creating illusions for yourself, events will undeceive you before a week is over.

You did not wait to see the effect of M. Granier de Cassagnac's first article. That too is grave in another way.

For those who have served you in the policy of progress, emancipation, and nationality which you had taken in hand, nothing remains but to withdraw and forget and consume their grief in silence.

With, etc., NAPOLEON (JEROME).

The Emperor to Prince Napoleon[1]
Palais des Tuileries, 22nd March, 1859.

MY DEAR COUSIN,—The circumstances in which we are placed are sufficiently difficult to necessitate an examination of them calmly and without passion. Now I do not

---

[1] This letter was dictated by the Emperor, who merely signed it. According to a telegram sent the same day by the Prince to Count Cavour, the two cousins had an interview in the course of the day.

at all share your opinion in regard to the consequences of the Congress. We must unfortunately in this world bear the pain of the mistakes we have committed. If Piedmont had not been guilty of regrettable indiscretions I should not find myself in my present position of having the whole of Europe against me, and of being unable to help Italy except by seeking means to create a division among my enemies. The Congress is the only means left to me. I cannot impose my wishes on all the Powers without having at least the appearance of reason. Now the only thing possible to-day is a Congress of the five Great Powers, with, or without, the addition of the Italian Princes.

What is more essential than the composition of the Congress is to know what is to be discussed at it. My thoughts are concerned principally with this point. I am under no illusions as to the difficulties arising from all sides. Although Piedmont and myself wish for the same thing our conduct at the moment is diametrically opposed. In order to divide my enemies and to secure the neutrality of a portion of Europe, I must give clear testimony of my moderation and my desire for conciliation. The Government of Piedmont, on the contrary, with a view to maintain her position and to uphold her influence over men's minds, must foster the hope of war. From this attitude naturally arise inevitable misunderstandings, but it is necessary for each side to act a little in its own interests and for mutual confidence to remain the same.

I have read over again all Walewski's despatches, and have seen nothing to find fault with. As regards the announcement in the *Moniteur*, this was indispensable, since the newspapers had already been speaking about it, and the acceptance of all the Powers had arrived, although not officially.

I received Count Cavour's letter this morning. I

shall reply in the same sense, recommending the greatest discretion, as I do to you.

With my sincere regard,   NAPOLEON.

The Emperor to Prince Napoleon
Tuesday, 22nd March, 1859.

MY DEAR COUSIN,—People are raising up many bogeys for nothing. Walewski has just told me that it had always been intended in the last resort to call in the interested parties as is always done. It appears that in London, Holland has also been included, but he is going to propose that the Italian Princes shall be represented as soon as [three words illegible] send their deputies.

With, etc.,   N.

This same day, 23rd March, 1859.

MY DEAR COUSIN,—Please tell M. Nigra to come this evening to the Tuileries at 9.30.

With, etc.,   NAPOLEON.

24th March, 1859.

MY DEAR COUSIN,—I had already pledged myself in regard to M. Chasseloup-Laubat, and his appointment[1] will be announced on Saturday.

With, etc.,   NAPOLEON.

Cavour has left for Paris.

25th March, 1859.

MY DEAR NAPOLEON,—If you desire to be just and to weigh well my position you will allow that I cannot act in any other way than I am doing. I am *désolé* at the effect produced in Piedmont, but really people cannot be angry with me for trying to disunite all Europe in a coalition against me! "*La passion fait sentir,*" says

---

[1] As Minister of Algeria and the Colonies.

Montesquieu, "*mais jamais voir.*" In truth I find that in Piedmont they feel keenly, as men of courage, but do not see!

I hope to be able to convince M. de Cavour of the difficulty of my position.

With, etc., NAPOLEON.

I should be very glad to have a talk with you if you will come at about 2 o'clock.

2nd April, 1859.

MY DEAR COUSIN,—We are expecting every day the reply from St. Petersburg in order to convene the Conference. The Ministerial crisis in London will possibly retard still further a decision.

With, etc., N.

9th April, 1859.

MY DEAR NAPOLEON,—Will you reply to the King that I shall come to a decision to-morrow and will inform you of it, and that in the meantime I will make choice of an officer to send to him?

With, etc., NAPOLEON.

The Emperor to Prince Napoleon[1]

19th April, 1859.

MY DEAR NAPOLEON,—I have had the explanation of Cavour's telegram. La Tour d'Auvergne mistook a personal remark of Walewski for an official telegram. But Count Cavour has already replied officially that he will accept the principle of disarmament if he is admitted to the Congress. As England agrees, the chances of war are diminishing for the present. If Count Cavour thinks it possible to have Tuscany as an ally I should ask for nothing better.

With, etc., N.

[1] This letter was quoted by Prince Napoleon in the telegram he sent the same day to Count Cavour (" L'Italie Libérée.")

19*th April*, 1859.

MY DEAR NAPOLEON,[1]—La Tour d'Auvergne writes that Cavour is very much discouraged. I beg you to write to him and tell him from me not to lose heart, and that everything may yet take a favourable turn. I can say no more, for the political aspect changes its colour three times a day.

With, etc., N.

Prince Napoleon to the Emperor
Paris, Wednesday, 20*th April*, 1859.

SIRE,—I wrote yesterday,[2] as you desired, to Count Cavour for the purpose of explaining to him the action of Prince de la Tour d'Auvergne, and I will write again to him this morning with a view to combating his discouragement, as commanded by you yesterday evening.

I am under no illusions, however, as to the results of all that is taking place. The article in the *Moniteur*[3] indicates a concession on the part of France the question of which has not arisen, namely, the putting into effect of the disarmament immediately after the Congress; I was under the impression that only the principle of disarmament was contemplated, and the putting it into effect to be subsequently arranged. What the *Moniteur* said yesterday changes the question. Further, what do you wish the King and his Minister at Turin to think of an explanation which tells them that M. Walewski has two forms of language, one the expression of his *personal views*, and the other the expression of your Minister, while this *nuance* is so subtle that even Prince de la Tour d'Auvergne misinterpreted it? One can say all this, but it is difficult to be convincing with arguments such as

---

[1] Quoted in " L'Italie Libérée." [2] See "L'Italie Libérée." [3] Of the 19th April.

these. Well, what is to happen? This: that, surrounded by very grave circumstances one can have no further confidence in oneself nor in one's friends; that one is doubtful of everything and everybody; hence arises discouragement!

To what can this systematic equivocation in regard to all questions lead?

I can understand such action as applied to an adversary (Austria), to doubtful friends (Russia and England), to neutrals (Germany), but as applied to Piedmont, the advance guard of our own country and of your friends, this I do not understand.

Your Ministers serve your person, but not your policy. Everybody feels this, and knows it. Thus it happens that there is nowhere any confidence or any heart, that everyone is dissatisfied and distrustful—the partisans of peace at any price because you do not afford them enough assurance; the opponents of the cause you have embraced, because they see you surrounded by divided and hostile agents who repeat this and prove it on every occasion! Thus you labour under the disadvantages of two policies. Your Majesty is very contemptuous of men; you think there is very little difference between the services an imbecile can render you and a man of talent, between a reactionary and a patriot, a Jew and a man of integrity, and instinctively you use those at hand. Well, Sire, this is very dangerous! You cannot do everything by yourself, and your wishes are unceasingly betrayed in their execution. Look at your Ministers; they are not in agreement with you on scarcely one single point.

M. Fould is a well-filled, self-satisfied man. He desires the enjoyment of his material interests, and the *status quo* at home and abroad.

M. Walewski merely carries on the work of his former

chief, Guizot. He wishes to bring to naught the cause of Italy, and has no higher dreams than a good understanding with all the despots of Europe, in the ranks of whom he desires to have you accepted ; further, he is timorous.

M. le Maréchal Vaillant is more of a patriot, but he is old, sceptical, mocks at everything, believes in nothing, and washes his hands of everything that may happen.

M. Delangle has no political sense. He is a moderate, and all his antecedents and his surroundings are purely Orleanist. He brings no driving force into his Ministry.

Admiral Hamelin is more than hide-bound. He carries out his instructions without the least intelligence.

M. Magne is most narrow-minded as a Minister : his *physique* is a good counterpart of his mental equipment. He is a good first-class clerk, at 12,000 francs a year. All he thinks of is to keep everything in its place, to avoid all progress, and, above all, to find posts for his relatives.

M. Baroche is a lawyer without any convictions, who would accept any brief offered him, and who tolerates his son in the Orleanist camp while he is drawing his salary from you.

The above constitute the principal machinery of your acting Government. What can you do with instruments like these? How can you surmount the present crisis with them? Add to this that these men without distinction are outworn, looked down upon, and detested as much as it is possible to be by every shade of opinion. Behold the kind of crew you have in a ship on a stormy sea !

All this can only lead to vexatious results. As to holding any definite opinion day by day on the different points of policy which changes so often, as Your Majesty says in your letter, I find that to be impossible, and I do not venture upon it. To arrive at that it would be necessary to know the smallest details, and to follow all its phases; a telegram, a phrase, a word is capable of changing everything. These reflections are suggested to me by my heart, which is yours, and by the difficulties of the present and the dangers of the future. I am not afraid, but I foresee.

Accept, etc., NAPOLEON BONAPARTE.

The Emperor to Prince Napoleon
20th *April*, 1859.

MY DEAR NAPOLEON,—I return your letters, which are curious. You can tell Count Cavour that I will support him as regards not authorising volunteers. England has sent her proposals to Vienna. If she (Vienna) has refused we shall know it to-morrow, and then we shall have either peace or war.

With, etc., NAPOLEON.

21st *April*, 1859.

MY DEAR COUSIN,—The news from Vienna is for war. I have just given the orders to place all the army on a war footing.

With, etc., N.

22nd *April*, 1859.

MY DEAR COUSIN,—I send you the reply to make to Turin. As regards your letters of recrimination and microscopic investigation circumstances are sufficiently grave to avoid putting little personal animosities in the place of the great interests of the country. The men are not perfect, but where are others to be found? Will Girardin and Bixio[1] aid me in saving France? Let each only occupy himself in performing well what is entrusted to him, and not concern himself with anything else, and all will go well.

With my sincere regard, NAPOLEON.

[1] An allusion to the friendship of Prince Napoleon for these two persons. See p. 100

24th April, 1859.

To Count Cavour—very confidential and not to be divulged at Turin: Orders have been given for the entry of the French troops by way of Suza and Genoa.

NAPOLEON.

24th April, 1859.[1]

You can reply to Count Cavour that Marshal Canrobert has orders to do everything he may think reasonable to come to the aid of Turin. N.

At the moment when France was about to engage in this war with Austria Prince Napoleon, with his habitual perspicacity, was looking at our eastern frontier, and was asking himself with anxiety what would be the attitude of Prussia, especially if our arms met with reverses in Italy. In a note which will be found in the Appendix, p. 257, he felt it to be his duty to lay before the Emperor both his fears for the near future and the urgent measures which it was indispensable to take at once for the defence of France.

[1] The Prince received this letter at two o'clock in the afternoon, and at once telegraphed it to Count Cavour (" L'Italie Libérée.")

CHAPTER X

The Campaign in Italy—Prince Napoleon in Tuscany—Issues a Proclamation—Commencement of the campaign—The Prince's Corps—March of the 5th Corps—An Armistice—Mission of Prince Napoleon to Verona to the Emperor Francis Joseph—His return to Paris.

SEVERAL letters from the Emperor contained in this chapter have been quoted by Alfredo Comandini in his work *Il Principe Napoléone nel Risorgimento Italiano*, which has appeared recently in Italy. It has, however, seemed to us of interest to reproduce them, for they form an important contribution to the history of the relations of the two cousins during the campaign in Italy.

The war in Italy had begun.

The French Army was divided into four corps, in addition to the guard. Shortly afterwards a fifth corps was created out of the Divisions under Generals Uhrich and Autemarre, to the command of which Prince Napoleon was appointed. Nearly all the troops composing it came from Africa. At first the Prince had to remain at Genoa for the purpose of completing there the organisation of this Corps as and when its component parts arrived. Then, on the 17th May, after the overtures made to the Emperor by two emissaries from Tuscany, he received orders to transfer provisionally Autemarre's Division to the Army, to embark for Livorno and proceed to Florence with Uhrich's Division, for the purpose of fulfilling a mission which was both political and military. Without mixing in any of the interior affairs of Tuscany, his instructions were to prevent disorders from taking place, to keep that country in alliance with us, to organise her forces, to incorporate the command of these with that of his own troops, and to cover himself by advanced posts against any movement by the Austrians.

We may add to this anticipation of subsequent events that the Prince acquitted himself satisfactorily in this delicate *rôle*.

The Emperor to Prince Napoleon[1]
Alexandria, 17th May, 1859.

MY DEAR COUSIN,—I have seen to-day Marquis Lajatico and M. Salvagnoli.[2] They spoke to me of the state of Tuscany, which we absolutely must keep within our control, and which threatens to turn over to Socialism. I have even decided, partly from political and partly from military considerations, to send you to Florence with Uhrich's Division by way of Livorno. This Division, the first battalions of which should arrive at Genoa to-day, will not land, but will proceed straight to Livorno. As soon as you know that a brigade has disembarked at Livorno, you could go there and take it to Florence. I would send you artillery and everything necessary to the proper composition of this division. As regards Autemarre's Division, I will keep it until I have thrown back the Austrians beyond the Tessino, and then I will send it to you to make up your own army corps. The sudden appearance of an armed force at Florence, the strength of which will not be known, and which we must even exaggerate, will produce a great effect, and will compel the Austrians to divide their forces. You will concern yourself with assisting[3] the organisation of the Tuscan troops. You will take command of all the French and Tuscan troops, and will place advanced posts

[1] Letter quoted by Comandini.
[2] The Marquis de Lajatico (1805–59) and Vincent Salvagnoli (1802–61) had come to ask the Emperor to land a body of troops for the purpose of safeguarding the territory of Tuscany against invasion by the Austrians.
[3] The Emperor first wrote "*tu t'occuperas à organiser.*" He put his pen through the word "*organiser*," and substituted "*favoriser l'organisation.*"

on the routes to Modena and Bologna. Acknowledge the receipt of this letter, and give orders for the whole of Uhrich's Division to proceed straight to Livorno instead of landing at Genoa. You will take care that there is no confusion, and that those who should land at Genoa are not sent to Livorno.

With my sincere regard,   NAPOLEON.

You can take the *Reine Hortense*, which will bring you to Livorno.

Alexandria, 20th May, 1859.

MY DEAR COUSIN,[1]—I return you the Proclamation,[2] in which I have made several changes. First, I have effaced the name of the King of Sardinia in the first line

[1] Quoted by Comandini. It was dictated, and only signed by the Emperor.
[2] The Proclamation drawn up by Prince Napoleon for the people of Tuscany, which he issued on his arrival at Livorno on the 23rd May. It has already been reproduced in several works, notably in Bazancourt's *La Campagne d'Italie en* 1859. It may be of interest to give the text proposed by Prince Napoleon side by side with the actual text as corrected by the Emperor.

Original Text	*Text as Corrected by the Emperor*
Inhabitants of Central Italy.	Inhabitants of Tuscany !
The Emperor and the King of Sardinia send me to your country at the request of your representatives in order to support in your midst the War of Italian Independence against our common enemies.	The Emperor sends me to your country at the request of your representatives in order to support in your midst the war against our enemies, the oppressors of Italy.
My mission is exclusively a military one; it is not for me to concern myself with your government, and I shall not do so. What France desires is to give you your Fatherland ! She is looking for no other reward for her sacrifices than the triumph of a sacred cause, of a free and strong people, and of a strong and grateful Ally.	My mission is exclusively a military one; it is not for me to concern myself with your internal organisation, and I shall not do so. Napoleon III has declared that he has only one ambition, to accomplish the triumph of the sacred cause of freeing a nation, and that he will never be influenced by family interests.
Content with her power, not desiring any increase of territory, which could not add to her true greatness, despising any petty family interests, she uses her arms solely in the service of justice and civilisation. If God shall have them under His protection, Italy will be at liberty after the victory to establish herself in freedom, and will enter the European family, giving guarantees to maintain order and the equilibrium.	He has said that, content with her power, the sole aim of France is to have on her frontiers a friendly people who will owe their regeneration to him. If God shall have us under His protection, and give us the victory, Italy will be free to establish herself and, counted henceforth among the nations, will strengthen the equilibrium of Europe.
Rest firmly convinced that no sacrifices are too great when Liberty and Independence are the reward, and show to Europe that you are worthy to be free by your discipline and your moderation as much as by your energy.	Rest firmly convinced that no sacrifices are too great when Independence is to be the reward of our efforts, and show to the world by your union and your moderation, as much as by your energy, that you are worthy to be free.
NAPOLEON (JEROME).	The Prince, Commander-in-Chief of the 5th Corps of the Army of Italy. NAPOLEON (JEROME).

because I cannot admit that you are under his orders. I desire also that the proclamation be addressed to Tuscany alone to prevent it being supposed that it is addressed to the Papal States. Lastly I have deleted the word " *liberté,*" which is used too often. I have repeated the words I said because you must remember the principle that only the sovereign can speak officially in the name of France. I think your letter to the Minister at Florence is very good, and I count on your intelligence and your friendship not to exceed the limits I have laid down for you.

Bear well in mind that the mission I am entrusting to you is one of the highest importance, and that you have it in your power to make a very great reputation for yourself if you act with great discernment, above all, if at every moment you are deeply penetrated with this truth that you must do nothing which I should not do myself. I sent you Walewski's telegram because it was interesting *à propos* of Russia. I am really vexed that you take any notice of tittle-tattle and calumnies like those aimed at the triumvirate. As soon as you are able I think you must despatch a French brigade with the Tuscan troops in the direction of Modena.

Assuring you of my sincere regard,

NAPOLEON.

The Emperor to Prince Napoleon[1]
Alexandria, 25th May, 1859.

MY DEAR NAPOLEON,—I saw the King yesterday, who came to show me a letter from M. Buoncampagni[2] telling him that the conjunction of Tuscany with Piedmont must not be entertained in any manner whatsoever, and in this connection he said to me that he was vexed that I had agreed to tell you to act in this sense.

[1] The Prince received this letter at Livorno on the 27th May.
[2] Commissioner of the King of Sardinia at Florence.

I answered him that this was not the case at all, and that on the contrary, I had enjoined you not to take any part in the internal affairs of the country, but I have received news to-day that you have made M. Farini promise to support this cause. I repeat my injunctions that you do nothing.

I have received your letter of the 24th May. I think the Tuscan contingent is very feeble. They were talking of such a large number of volunteers. I will write to the Minister for War for the battery and 1,200 rifles.[1] I approve of the dispositions you have made; you can send the gun-boats to Toulon.

Assuring you of my sincere regard,

NAPOLEON.

I enjoin upon you to be always very respectful in your language towards the Pope, and full of consideration for the Duchess of Parma,[2] just because she is a Bourbon.

Alexandria, 26th May, 1859.

MY DEAR NAPOLEON,[3]—I am taking advantage of the departure of Rasponi[4] to write you a few words. I am going to take the field on the 1st June. As I have changed my plans, I am leaving here for the moment Autemarre's Division, and I think I shall be able to despatch it to you at Genoa within ten or twelve days. Thence it will proceed by sea or land; you will decide this in accordance with the means at your disposal for sending it by sea. I am very anxious that you should threaten Modena, and perhaps take possession of it, if we are by then over the Tessino. Your arrival at Florence

---

[1] These rifles were to be used in arming the Bersaglieri.
[2] Louise Marie Thérèse (1819–64), the daughter of the Duc de Berry and sister of the Comte de Chambord. Her husband, Duke Charles III, died in 1854, and since that date she had been carrying on the Regency in the name of her son, Robert I, born 1848.
[3] Quoted by Comandini. Received at Livorno on the 27th May.
[4] Count Joachim Rasponi of Ravenna (1828–77). His mother, Louise Julie Caroline, was the daughter of Joachim Murat, King of Naples.

has alarmed the diplomatic world, but I am much counting on your prudent conduct to reassure those who are not hostile to us.

With my sincere regard,
NAPOLEON.

Alexandria, 28th May, 1859.

MY DEAR COUSIN,[1]—The news I am receiving is not at all in accordance with the reports you have received concerning the arrival in the Duchies of General Wimpffen's[2] army. I shall advance, I hope, on Monday, leaving Autemarre's Division to guard Tortona and Alexandria. After I have crossed the Tessino I think the Austrians will retire, and in that case, as I shall have no need of it, I will send it back to you. The cavalry regiments[3] are *en route* for Genoa. It was impossible for me to send them by train owing to the pressure on the railway.

I have received very good news from Russia. The Emperor continues to behave very loyally towards me. It has been hinted to me that you might play a very fine part in bringing about the return of the son of the Grand Duke, and making him agree to a constitution and an alliance with Piedmont. As far as I am concerned I should in no way be opposed to such an arrangement, if it were possible in the present state of men's minds. You must be the judge of this.

With my sincere regard,
NAPOLEON.

P.S.—I will send you twenty thousand francs of *fonds secrets* on the first opportunity.

---

[1] Quoted by Comandini. It was dictated by the Emperor, who signed it. The Prince received it at Livorno on the 30th May.
[2] Field-Marshal François de Wimpffen, in command of the 1st Austrian Army in Italy.
[3] The 6th and 8th Hussars of Lapérouse's Brigade.

PRINCE NAPOLEON

[p. 140

Vercelli, 1st June, 1859.

MY DEAR COUSIN,[1]—I have received your letters and have seen Franconière.[2] I can well imagine your position is a difficult one, but these are the points we must keep firmly in view :

1. To respect the neutrality of the Papal States so long as we are without *certain* proof that the Austrians are violating it.

2. I am going to try to establish by diplomatic means that this neutrality *has* been violated.

3. Your offensive against Modena and Ferrara cannot serve me until we have advanced towards the Adda or the Mincio. Until then we must confine ourselves to making things difficult for the Austrians and to endeavouring to place them in the wrong with the Holy Father. Certainly I should much like to be able to occupy Bologna with our troops, but if I were to take the initiative I should put the whole of Catholic Europe against me. We must, therefore, be patient.

Two *belles affaires* have taken place.[3] Your regiment of Zouaves proved very serviceable. It captured six guns, and killed a great number of Austrians.

I am leaving to-day for Novara.

I do not understand in what respect I have wounded the King of Wurtemberg.

With, etc., NAPOLEON.

The Emperor to Prince Napoleon (Telegram in cipher)
Alexandria, 4th June, 1859.

Do not count upon Autemarre's Division for the moment. I am unable to despatch it to you by sea. You will have it later on by land.

[1] Quoted by Comandini. The Prince received it at Florence at 2.30 in the afternoon of the 3rd June.
[2] Colonel de Franconnière, 1st A.D.C. to the Prince, who had been instructed by him to deliver a detailed account of the situation to the Emperor.
[3] The two engagements at Palestro, on the 30th and 31st May. It was in the second that the 3rd Zouaves distinguished themselves.

Telegram : The Emperor to the Prince, at Florence

General Headquarters at San Martino,
5th June, 1859.

I will send you Autemarre's Division as soon as possible.

I have won a great battle over the enemy.[1] We have taken three guns, two standards, 7,000 prisoners, and placed 20,000 Austrians *hors de combat.*

Telegram : The Emperor to Prince Napoleon, Florence

San Martino, *5th June,* 10.10 *at night.*

Send to Toulon all the ships at Livorno ; we require them.

The Emperor to Prince Napoleon, Florence
(Telegram, partly in cipher)[2]

Milan, 10*th June.*

You must conform to the general exigencies. You will have again, I hope, your second division at *Placentia.* But we insist on your leaving *two thousand French troops at Florence.* We have won a fresh success at Melegnano.

The Emperor to Prince Napoleon, Florence

Milan, 10*th June,* 1859.

In all probability *Placentia will shortly be evacuated.* In that case I will send to you there *Autemarre's* division, *which is at Pavia.* Tell me if you can *come to Placentia with your troops.*

---

[1] The battle of Magenta.
[2] This and the two following telegrams are quoted by Comandini. The words italicised were in cipher.

The Emperor to Prince Napoleon, Florence

Milan, 11th June, 1859.

General d'*Autemarre* will not be *at Placentia* with all his division *before the day after to-morrow.* As regards your question, you must be the judge of that. Everything depends upon *the position of the Austrians.* Put yourself in communication with *Autemarre,* but my purpose is to recall *all his troops* to Lodi and to make him join up.

Milan, 12th June, 1859.

MY DEAR COUSIN,[1]—As the Austrian Army is concentrating on the Mincio, I intend to assemble all my forces there.

On the 13th Autemarre's division, with his regiment of Lancers and two batteries, will be at Placentia.

My aim is that you should reassemble the whole of your force in that town, in order to effect a junction with me as soon as possible. As I am not on the spot, I leave to you the choice of means and the route to follow.

Therefore endeavour to make the greatest haste possible.

Act in the way you intend as regards the garrison in Florence. It was Count Cavour who came to implore me to leave there 2,000 French troops.

The telegraph will, I hope, be restored as far as Pavia, and I shall then be able to correspond freely. In any case, I will send you orders to Placentia.

With, etc., NAPOLEON.

Cassano, 14th June, 1859.

MY DEAR COUSIN,[2]—You already know that the Austrians have evacuated not only the entire right bank of the Po, but also Cremona and Pizzighettone.

[1] Quoted by Comandini. The Prince received it at Florence on the 14th.
[2] The Prince received this letter at Lucca on the 16th June, and replied on the following day.

I repeat very urgently my previous orders.

The 5th Corps must rejoin me as soon as possible. As we shall be on the Chieze in four days, the 5th Corps therefore can effect a junction with me by crossing the Po at Cremona on ferry-boats and by following the great road from Cremona to Brescia.

General d'Autemarre is at Placentia to-day, and I place him again under your command. It will be his and your duty to find out, in accordance with the resources of the country and the position of the enemy, whether he should proceed to rejoin you at Cremona by the right or the left bank, crossing the Adda at Pizzighettone or below.

When passing through Modena, Reggio, and Parma endeavour to establish in those cities energetic provisional Governors, and try to collect at Cremona a large amount of stores by commandeering any existing resources along the whole of the right bank of the Po.

I am awaiting news from you with impatience, and send you my sincere regard.

NAPOLEON.

Brescia, 18th June, 1859.

MY DEAR COUSIN,[1]—I hope that the arrival of Colonel Reille and the news of the rapid evacuation by the Austrians will have hastened your march. Now I am no longer awaiting you at Pavia, Placentia, or Cremona, but at Piadena, crossing at Casal Maggiore or Bresello.

You can see that in the event of my having a battle on the Mincio, how impatient I am for the arrival of your forces. I cannot conceive how it is you are so long in starting. I am giving orders to Autemarre to go to Cremona, so that the junction can be made with the utmost rapidity.

---

[1] This letter was dictated and only signed by the Emperor. The Prince received it at Massa at three in the afternoon of the 19th June.

Brescia, 21st June, 1859.

MY DEAR COUSIN,[1]—I have received your letter of the 19th June. I think, all things considered, it is more prudent to assemble your force at Cremona than at Casal Maggiore. Nevertheless, I will write to you again before the 26th or 27th, since, unfortunately, you cannot come before then. The Austrians have evacuated the strong positions of Lonato and Castiglione, and are making a decided retirement behind the Mincio.

With my sincere regard,
NAPOLEON.

The Emperor to Prince Napoleon, at Parma[2]

Volta, 29th June, 1859, 11.45 p.m.

According to my information *there is no need to fear a sortie by the Austrians from Mantua.*

Volta, 30th June, 1859.

MY DEAR COUSIN,[3]—I am waiting for you with twofold impatience, for, apart from the pleasure of seeing you again, you will greatly reinforce my army. All our information agrees in reporting that there are no more than 7,000 men in Mantua, and that the entire Austrian Army is behind the Adige.

I beg you, therefore, to arrive as soon as possible, taking the shortest route from Piadena to Goito. You can take other routes more to the left for your artillery and baggage. However, you must march in military order—that is, each column in the following disposition:

1. A cavalry squadron for taking observations;
2. A quarter company of engineers;
3. Two guns without caissons;

---

[1] Dictated, and signed by the Emperor.
[2] Telegram; the words italicised in cipher.
[3] The Prince received this letter at Casal Maggiore on the 30th June, at four o'clock, and replied verbally next day. A portion is reproduced in Bazancourt's work as having been telegraphed by the Emperor.

4. Two regiments of infantry.
The rest of the battery, and convoy of mules.
With, etc.,

NAPOLEON.

Tell me exactly the day and the hour when you will arrive at Goito. You must avoid the great heat of the day.

Valeggio, 3rd July, 1859.

MY DEAR COUSIN,[1]—I have decided to draw up my lines closer, as they were too extended, and to confine myself, so long as Peschiera is not taken, to a line of defence extending parallel with the Mincio from Castelnovo to Pozzolo. Your troops, instead of proceeding to-morrow to Villafranca, will establish themselves to the right of Valeggio, parallel with the route from Valeggio to Marengo, in a position which will have to be reconnoitred first so as to find water in the proximity. You will place the advanced posts on the Roverbella side. You will have your headquarters at Valeggio.
With, etc.,

NAPOLEON.

Valeggio, 3rd July, 1859.

MY DEAR COUSIN,—When I say a thing I am sure of it; not only is there a bridge at Pozzolo, at a place called Molini della Volta, but there are two, and I have crossed over them. I have had a third made this very day a little higher up. General Bourbaki[2] has carried out exactly the orders he received.

Assuring you of my sincere regard,

NAPOLEON.

[1] This, and the two following letters, were dictated, and merely signed by the Emperor.
[2] Bourbaki's Division (3rd and 4th Corps) handed over his entrenched position to Uhrich's Division.

Valeggio, 4th July, 1859.

MY DEAR COUSIN,[1]—I am really angry that on the first day of your arrival you begin by not carrying out punctually the orders you have received.

After what had been arranged between us I was firmly counting on Uhrich's Division being in their appointed position on the left bank of the Mincio this morning, and on this understanding I had withdrawn the guard from the bridge of boats, which would become unnecessary. You see how important it is in war to carry out punctually orders received.

I was firmly counting on having this morning a division on my right covering my bridges and my cavalry, and now there is not a man there.

You will therefore cause your first division to start to-morrow morning at three o'clock; the second will leave at six. You need leave at Goito till the arrival of the Tuscan Division only a General and one regiment, which will rejoin you later, with a view to placing the Tuscans *au courant* with the position at Goito. You will leave at Goito your two companies of engineers to work at the bridge-head and to throw the bridges already prepared over the Mincio. I have given orders that the Tuscan forces shall be provided for by the Quartermaster-General. I leave you also for the moment in command of General Desvaux's division of cavalry, which should remain where it is and continue to make *reconnaissances* in the same directions as before. As regards your General Headquarters, your Chief of Staff appears to have expressed your wish that it should be at Pozzolo. I do not find any objection to this. But, nevertheless, I think it would be better that you should be at Valeggio.

With renewed assurances of my sincere regard,

NAPOLEON.

[1] Only the signature to this letter is in the Emperor's hand.

After the victory of Solferino, in face of the reports coming from Germany, and fearing the hostility of neutrals, and disturbed, moreover, by the state of health of the army, Napoleon III took the step on the 6th July of proposing an armistice to Francis Joseph, which was signed on the 8th. The two sovereigns met at Villafranca on the morning of the 11th July, and for one hour discussed the general conditions of peace, without putting anything into writing. On the same day, after talking these over with the King of Sardinia and Prince Napoleon, Napoleon III entrusted to his cousin the delicate mission of going to the Emperor of Austria and of settling with him the terms defining the preliminaries of peace, and of obtaining his signature thereto. The interview took place at Verona, and at 10 o'clock at night the Prince brought to the Imperial Headquarters the preliminaries signed by Francis Joseph.[1]

Next day Napoleon III signed them in his turn. On the 16th July he left Italy, and arrived at St. Cloud on the 17th.

The definite Treaty of Peace was to be drawn up in a neutral country, at Zurich. In view of this the Emperor requested the following information from his cousin:

The Emperor to Prince Napoleon
St. Cloud, 24th July, 1859.

MY DEAR COUSIN,[2]—In view of the negotiations to be opened at Zurich I think it will be very useful to me to be well posted on what passed between you and the Emperor of Austria at Verona. I beg you will give me an exact account of all your conversations. For what you said in my name naturally possesses great

---
[1] An account of this mission, written by Prince Napoleon, appeared in the *Revue des Deux Mondes* (1st August, 1909) under the title: " Les Préliminaires de la Paix, 11th July, 1859, Journal de ma mission à Vérone auprès de l'Empereur d'Autriche."
[2] Received in Paris by the Prince, 25th July.

importance. As for example, if you said, as I believe, that I would never consent to an armed intervention in the Duchies, this view, if expressed on that occasion, would amount to a protest.

With, etc., NAPOLEON.

The French army had begun to return to France, with the exception, however, of five Divisions, which the Emperor deemed it prudent to leave provisionally in Italy. The 5th Corps, therefore, remained there intact at first. Instead of interpreting this measure in the light of a favour, Prince Napoleon was offended at the thought that the regiments which had been placed under his command would not take part in the great military ceremony which had been prepared for the 14th August to welcome the return to Paris of the army which had fought in Italy.

The troops were to march through the streets of the city on that day, and pass before the Column in the Place Vendôme. Tribunes had been erected in the square. One of them, in which the Empress was to take her place, was close to the Ministry of Justice, in which the sovereign would take up his position during the march past. Princess Clotilde had been invited to be present at the ceremony in this tribune, but Prince Napoleon declared that she would not appear, and that he himself would not be by his cousin's side.

In order to explain why the 5th Corps, detained in Italy, would not take part in the march past, a special notice appeared in the *Moniteur* on the 14th August.

The Emperor to Prince Napoleon
St. Cloud, 2nd August, 1859.

MY DEAR NAPOLEON,—I thank you for your written account. I think it very well done. I have recommended to Bourqueney's[1] attention the question of the Hungarians, and I think that their demobilisation will entail no difficulties. As I wish to leave five Divisions in Italy, I have decided to keep there the whole of the 5th Corps. It is a favour I am conferring on them, and one which, in my opinion, should compensate them for the disappointment of spending a day in Paris.

With my sincere regard,
NAPOLEON.

Tuileries, 13th August, 1859.

MY DEAR COUSIN,—I will begin by doing justice to you, and by saying in no uncertain fashion that you did nothing in Italy that was not in obedience to my orders, and that you carried out with zeal and intelligence the missions I entrusted to you. But as to your general conduct, I am unable to conceal from you that you incessantly paralyse all the good I desire for you by a false conception of *amour-propre*. For example, you hand in your resignation in a newspaper article.[1] At Vareggio you were within an ace of abandoning the command of your corps. And to-day, because I did not wish to break up the 5th Corps owing to the exigencies of the service, here you are seeing in this a cause of offence, and desirous of making the crowd (which does not understand the inner workings of things) believe that I am dissatisfied with you. Further, the daughter of the King of Sardinia, on a question of *amour-propre*, will not be present at the entry of the troops which fought in order to give Lombardy to her father. What will the public think of that! You must see things in the right light. There are circumstances to be regretted, I know, but you

---

[1] Baron de Bourqueney, French Ambassador in Vienna before the war, was appointed to represent France in the Zurich negotiations. As regards the question of the Hungarians, see the paragraph preceding the letter of the 1st September, 1859, p. 151.

[2] An allusion to the resignation of the Prince from the Ministry of Algeria and the Colonies.

must not aggravate them. I therefore count upon you to be at the Tuileries at 8.30 to-morrow morning, and upon Clotilde to be at the Ministry of Justice at 9.30.
With, etc.,
NAPOLEON.

The notice regarding the 5th Corps will appear to-morrow morning.

During the war a Hungarian legion had been organised to go to the assistance of Piedmont. At the time of the armistice it already numbered more than 5,000 soldiers, all Austrian subjects. In the peace preliminaries Napoleon III stipulated for a complete amnesty for those desirous of returning to their country. The question now was to have this clause respected by those negotiating at Zurich. In spite of the engagements entered into by M. de Rechberg, Minister for Foreign Affairs at Vienna, there was apprehension lest Austria should evade her promises and institute various punitive measures. This was the fear of Kossuth, the former head of the Hungarian revolution, who profited by his relations with Prince Napoleon to beg him to intervene in favour of his compatriots.

The Emperor to Prince Napoleon[1]
Saint Sauveur, 1st September, 1859.

MY DEAR NAPOLEON,—I did not reply to you before because I was awaiting the news from Zurich. To-day I have received advice from De Bourqueney that he has M. le Comte de Rechberg's written promise that the Hungarian soldiers forming the legion will be returned to their homes. Be good enough to inform Kossuth.
With, etc., NAPOLEON.

[1] This letter was dictated. Only the signature is in the Emperor's handwriting.

CHAPTER XI

Death of King Jerome—Prince Napoleon at the Palais Royal and at Meudon—The siege of Gaeta—The lawsuit brought by the issue of King Jerome's first marriage in America with Elisabeth Paterson—Prince Napoleon's vague aspirations—The Emperor's advice to him—The question of Rome.

FOR some months King Jerome, who was nearly seventy-six years old, had been feeling his strength decline. At the beginning of the summer of 1860 he went into residence on his estate at Villegenis, Seine et Oise. He died there on the 24th June in the arms of his son and daughter.

Prince Napoleon to the Emperor[1]
(Telegram)

Villegenis, 23rd June, 1860, 9.45 *p.m.*

M. Rayer[2] has arrived, and issues the following *bulletin* :

" The condition of S. A. I. is the gravest possible."

Only the Emperor can be the judge of what he will do. In any case, the Empress must not come and be present at the dreadful grief of our family.

My father is almost unconscious, but it is impossible to say when the fatal moment will arrive.

NAPOLEON (JEROME).

Telegram from the Emperor to Prince Napoleon at Villegenis

Fontainebleau, 24*th June,* 1860.

The Empress and myself hasten to offer you at once our entire sympathy in your sorrow.

[1] Telegram sent to Fontainebleau.   [2] The doctor (1793-1867).

The Emperor to Prince Napoleon
Fontainebleau, 25th June, 1860.

MY DEAR COUSIN,—You can have no doubt of the grief I feel in thinking that the last brother of the Emperor is now no more. I share very keenly in your just and poignant regrets, and hasten to assure you that this sad event cannot but tighten closer the bonds of affection which have united us since our earliest years. M. Fould will confer with you as regards the honours to be rendered to your father, and I beg you will express to Mathilde from me my keen sympathy.

With renewed assurances of my sincere regard,

NAPOLEON.

After the death of King Jerome the Emperor placed at the disposal of Prince Napoleon, who was already installed in a portion of the Palais Royal, the Château of Meudon and the apartments in the Palais Royal which the dead King had been occupying. But at the same time the Emperor thought that it would be possible to curtail the expenditure on the upkeep of these two palaces. This was not the view of the Prince.

Prince Napoleon to the Emperor
Paris, Friday, 20th July, 1860.

SIRE,—Monsieur Fould has informed me of the orders you have given him concerning my residence. Colonel de Franconière was unable to make any observations, as the Minister added that he held a *mandat impératif*. Under these circumstances there was nothing else for me to do than to inform the Minister of State that I was unable to accept the dispositions indicated by the Emperor, and that I should prefer to go and live either at my private house or at some house that I would rent. I only asked to be given till the 1st September, to allow me the time necessary to effect such a radical change in my position.

I shall not present myself before Your Majesty to make a complaint. I only beg you will allow me to explain in the note I enclose the reasons for my decision and that of my wife, since the Emperor has not summoned me, and has therefore not permitted me to present them to him verbally. I hope the Emperor will not blame me, circumstanced as I am, for leaving the Palais Royal.

The Emperor to Prince Napoleon
21st July, 1860.

MY DEAR COUSIN,—Clotilde delivered to me yesterday your memorandum. After what she told me I do not understand how you can distort my intentions, and that a mere matter of estimating expenditure can make you entertain doubts of my regard. I have made no change in my intentions towards you. I have told you that I give my consent to letting you have the Palais Royal and Meudon on conditions analogous to those existing in the time of my Uncle, and I hold to it. It is only therefore a question of figures. You allege that the Palais Royal will cost as much in up-keep, in heating and lighting, for one establishment as for two. That does not seem to me to be correct. Besides, I am going to have the figures looked through again.

Assuring you of my sincere regard, NAPOLEON.

The Emperor to Prince Napoleon[1]
Palais de St. Cloud, 25th July, 1860.

MY DEAR COUSIN,—I send you the exact details of what the Palais Royal and that of Meudon cost in the

---

[1] This letter was dictated, and only the signature is in the Emperor's handwriting. Two memoranda were appended, showing the details of the expenditure on each of these palaces. M. Fould was Minister of the Emperor's Household, and M. Alphonse Gauthier was the general secretary of this Ministry.

time of my Uncle. As regards Meudon, I do not find any change necessary, but for the Palais Royal I find there is a reduction to be made of about 47,000 francs. For the military service of the two palaces we must reckon on a sum of about 43,000 francs. This would make, therefore, a reduction of 90,000 francs.

As the two palaces together were costing 418,000 francs by taking off 90,000 francs there remain 328,000 francs I had thought that still further reductions in the *personne* might be made, and on that account the allocation c 300,000 francs for the two palaces had seemed to me to l sufficient. But, since you hold a contrary opinion, i beg you will appoint someone to discuss the figures with M. Fould or M. Gauthier, in order that this matter may be settled quickly.

As regards the apartments I wished to reserve for myself, I give them up willingly to you, for if in any exceptional case I might require to lodge a foreign Prince in them, you would place no objection in the way.

Assuring you, etc.,   NAPOLEON.

We need not relate the death-struggle of the Bourbon dynasty at Naples during the year 1860. We have only to recall that the King, François II (under the threats of Garibaldi, who at the instigation of Count Cavour, had stirred up a rebellion in Sicily and had conquered it), had abandoned his capital and fled to Gaeta, where he was soon after besieged by Piedmont.

Like many other Frenchmen, Napoleon III was moved by the misfortunes of this youthful sovereign, who was paying for the mistakes accumulated by his ancestors. He determined, therefore, whatever the consequences might be, to keep open the port of Gaeta, by means of which the King, in the event of a definite overthrow, might be able to effect his escape and find safety on

board the French ships. This is what happened five
months later, on the 13th February, 1861, after a siege
during which the French squadron systematically prevented a blockade by sea.

The Emperor to Prince Napoleon
St. Cloud, 26th September, 1860.

My dear Cousin,—Admiral de Tinan[1] has orders
to prevent by every means, even by the employment of
force, any blockade and *any attacks* by sea on Gaeta. To
leave open an exit by sea is indeed the least I can do for
the King of Naples, who has followed my advice, though
tardily.

The attack on Gaeta by the King of Piedmont is an
enormity, and can only compromise the future of Italy.
I have already done very great service to Piedmont by
hindering or retarding Austrian or Spanish intervention
by my attitude, but I cannot join my policy with that of
a Government which faithlessly and disloyally tramples
under foot the rights demanded by justice and equity.

With, etc.,

Napoleon.

At the end of 1860 we find the two following short
notes, which demonstrate the good terms on which the
two cousins were living.

The Emperor to Prince Napoleon
Compiègne, 30th November, 1860.

My dear Cousin,—I was hoping to go and see you
and Clotilde before my departure, but I have been so
much occupied that I have not had time to do so. As
soon as I return I will call at the Palais Royal. I see
no objection to your going to Switzerland.

Assuring you, etc., Napoleon.

---

[1] Admiral Le Barbier de Tinan (1803-76).

Tuesday, 4th December, 1860.

MY DEAR COUSIN,—Emile Augier is to come and see me to-morrow to read me his play.[1] I should have liked to ask you and Clotilde to come and dine, but I do not know whether you would care to meet Walewiski and his wife. Tell me frankly if that is distasteful to you.
With, etc.,
NAPOLEON.

Throughout the period preceding the campaign in Italy and during the war itself, Prince Napoleon's energy found ample material in which to occupy itself. But when calm had returned during the ensuing months the Prince came to the conclusion that his duties as a Senator were not sufficiently important, and regretted not having a more imposing *rôle* to play. Carried away by his imagination, he went so far on one occasion as to ask himself if he would not find this outlet in the newly formed monarchy of his father-in-law. It was a mere caprice, which his cousin had no difficulty in making him put out of his mind when he disclosed it to him.

Just at the time when he was passing through this crisis the Prince experienced annoyance at seeing the memory of his father mixed up in a lawsuit which he was obliged to defend in his own name and in that of Princess Mathilde.

We may remember that when he was only nineteen years old King Jerome, in the course of a visit to America, had married on the 23rd December, 1803, Miss Elisabeth Paterson,[2] the daughter of a rich merchant in Baltimore. When the young couple wished to return to France in 1805 Napoleon I, who had just assumed the Imperial Crown, declared the marriage which had been contracted

---
[1] *Les Effrontés*, which was presented for the first time at the Théâtre Français on the 10th January, 1861.
[2] We find this name written sometimes with one " t," sometimes with two. See the letter from the Emperor of the 23rd October, 1854, p. 68.

without his consent to be null and void, and forbade the young woman to land in France, Jerome was obliged to submit to the all-powerful will of his brother.

Miss Paterson first took refuge in London, where, on the 7th July, 1805, she gave birth to a son, who was given the name of Jerome Napoleon Bonaparte. She returned afterwards with him to Baltimore.

Jerome Napoleon Bonaparte married an American in his turn, Miss Suzanne Gay.

One of their sons, Jerome Bonaparte, born in 1832, came to France after the Empire had been restored again, and was admitted into the French Army.

After the death of King Jerome Miss Paterson (Elisabeth) and her son demanded the legitimation of the marriage contracted in 1803, the right of Jerome Napoleon to bear the name of Bonaparte, and to share in the right of succession.

On the 15th February, 1861, the Court of First Instance non-suited their demands. They appealed on the 28th March, and on the 1st July the court confirmed the first decision.

Prince Napoleon to the Emperor
Palais Royal, Monday, 18th February, 1861.

SIR,—Your Majesty expressed yesterday the wish to have the exact text of the conclusions arrived at by the Public Ministry in the *affaire Paterson*. I have the honour to send to Your Majesty the shorthand copy of the hearing. I have marked the passages which seem to be reprehensible, in order to assist the Emperor to come to a judgment.

I should like, Sire, to return again to my idea of a plan of travel which you seem to disapprove of. The following are my motives. Your Majesty is always very good and kind to me, but since the death of my

Father I have become convinced that I have no political future in France to hope for. My position wears the appearance of being a very agreeable one, but it does not satisfy me, because I am doing nothing imposed upon me by the name I bear, because I am vegetating in a life of idleness, which is humiliating to me, because, in a word, I can do nothing to win renown and a place in history that should be personal to me. A lawsuit just brought against the memory of my Father has pained me keenly. I experience a need to quit the *milieu* in which I am, and an absence of some weeks has become a necessity to me.

Where can I go? The most natural thing seems to me to take my wife to her family, whom she has not seen since her marriage, but, as regards myself, I should get tired of Turin after a few days, and I might be a source of inconvenience to my father-in-law. I should like, therefore, to leave Clotilde there, and utilise a few weeks in gaining knowledge. A great transformation is taking place in Italy. One can only know a country well by seeing it. Hence my first idea is to visit the whole of Italy. I have given up Rome and Venice as I understand the difficulties to which a visit to these two places might give rise. I shall much regret to be obliged to visit the other provinces in the kingdom of my father-in-law. Foreseeing that my arrival in Naples and Sicily might arouse certain susceptibilities in the eyes of the Italian Government, I have ascertained that they do not find any objection to it, and would even view it with pleasure. Therefore this could provoke nothing more than a few newspaper articles and a certain amount of tittle-tattle of no great importance among the diplomatists. I should establish the purely scientific purpose of my journey by taking with me one or two of my friends who are members of the *Institut*, with a view to making a better study of the antiquities of mighty Greece and Sicily, with which I am not acquainted and shall never be able to see under more favourable circumstances. Further, I will confess frankly to Your Majesty that I should like to be in a position to form a judgment whether, if all hope of bearing worthily my name in France were to be taken from me, I might possibly be able to create a position for myself in Italy, either in peace or war. My father-in-law's Government wants men. It would still be serving the Napoleonic and liberal cause to work at the building up of Italian unity, which you alone have rendered possible. It is a vague desire. I catch glimpses of the difficulties, but it is worth my taking the trouble to make them my occupation.

You should have no difficulty, Sire, in understanding the motives I am putting before you, and, I hope, in approving them. I feel not the least bitterness, but much dullness! If, notwithstanding my arguments, I am unable to obtain your consent, I will ask your permission, Sire, to take my wife to her family, and to be allowed at least to visit Egypt and the Archipelago, only touching at the coast of Southern Italy for a few days. Will the Emperor allow me to come and learn his decision, for it is indispensable for me to fix my plans and arrange my affairs accordingly?

May it please you, etc.,

NAPOLEON (JEROME).

The Emperor to Prince Napoleon
Paris, 19*th February*, 1861.

MY DEAR NAPOLEON,—Politics in these days are sufficiently complicated to prevent my wishing to render them more confused. Your journey to Turin and Egypt has nothing extraordinary about it, but the same does not appear to hold good if you go to Naples and Sicily, I therefore oppose this formally, for it could not fail to create great difficulties for me, without doing you any good.

With regard to your wish to create a position for yourself in Italy, I confess that I do not understand an idea of such a kind. Your position in France is a very firm one, and it only depends upon yourself to make it better. You know all my regard for you, and are aware that I should be happy to give you some occupation which might bring to light all your abilities, but you will allow me to tell you that to win success continuity of mind and perseverance are necessary. Without these indispensable qualities one arrives at nothing, notwithstanding any mental capacity one may possess. Your past is here to prove the truth of what I state.

You behaved well in the Crimea, but lack of perseverance caused you to lose all the benefits you might have derived from the campaign. You had a certain amount of success while at the Ministry for Algeria, but the same failing caused you to lose all the benefits of your labour. To-day, without any known reason or motive, you would like to find an occupation in Italy! But you do not understand that in that case you would lose your entire position in France! And then there is your civil allowance to start with, for you should understand that the country does not pay a Prince an income of a million francs for him to go and spend it in another country. Even a simple legionary is obliged to spend his 250 francs pay in France! I am much distressed to see that with such excellent qualities your mind feeds itself on impossible fancies, and turns these same good qualities to your detriment. Just think of it! Here is a Prince who has spent twenty years in exile, and who, after regaining his fatherland

and his position, wants to return to exile of his own
accord! In very truth that is unreasonable. I hope
you will think over this, and you may count always
on my sincere regard.

Napoleon.

Prince Napoleon to the Emperor
Paris, this same day, 19th February, 1861.

Sire,—You are severe towards me. If I go to Turin
or to Egypt, I could put in for a few days at Naples and
Sicily, as I have requested, or is your veto to touch at
any point whatsoever on the coast other than at Genoa
absolute?

If I have thought in a vague way and quite secretly of
creating for myself a position in the Government of the
kingdom of Italy, I have weighed the consequences well,
and have considered that my civil allowance and my
advantages as a French Prince would be taken from me.
That would be a grievous and painful change, but
possibly a laudable one, for me to make—from a rich and
high, but humiliating, position to one that would be
modest, difficult, struggling, but more glorious, maybe,
and more worthy of my name. I have spoken of it to
Your Majesty as a mere idea running through my wish to
pass a little time in Italy, because I have absolute confidence in you! I call to mind a deep saying you uttered
to me when in exile in England, which I made a note of:
" There is no position possible for us in France except
power or prison."

The Paterson lawsuit is going to begin over again.
Jerome is appealing. If Your Majesty wishes to give an
open expression of your dissatisfaction to the father and
the son whose cause is pleaded jointly to-day, you would
have to place this young man in the alternative of having
to separate his suit from that of his father's by using the

name of Comte de Sartène, or of your stopping his pension and retiring him from active employment. But I have spoken at too great length, Sire, about my affairs.

I am struck by the graveness of the Roman question,[1] and by the necessity to prepare some solution. The unified Italian Parliament is going to hurry on events. I am informed of what it intends to do. You will have to decide for, or against, the temporal power of the *Pope in Rome*. It might not, perhaps, be impossible, by using energy and skill, to force the Pope to decide, and to be beforehand as regards the action of the Parliament. The moment is a favourable one owing to the want of money felt by the Court of Rome. This is one of the reasons which might make it give way. Tell the Pope: "*Arrange the matter with the King of Italy: I wish it*; failing this, I shall make a treaty with Victor Emmanuel providing that your personal security shall be safeguarded and that your independence and spiritual authority shall suffer no diminution, and I will evacuate the territory of St. Peter, handing it over to the Italian soldiers after I have obtained my guarantees. The situation of Papal Rome being guarded by Frenchmen against Italians cannot continue, and I will not have the Italian Parliament imposing its own solution upon France, or compelling her to enter into a struggle with Italy."

By an exercise of great power we might, perhaps, succeed in making him give way, or else we might settle the affairs of the Papacy in spite of the Pope.

Really, the position of your soldiers in Rome will become as false as was that of your fleet at Gaeta. France has the appearance of an offended husband whom his wife sends out to take a walk, who never follows his advice and succeeds in compromising him for a bad cause in spite of himself, and in spite of his real friends. To know

[1] See the paragraph preceding the letter of the 16th October, 1861, p. 176.

how to wait is a great virtue in politics, always on the condition that when the right time comes vigorous action comes too. Within a few weeks, Sire, you may be compromised for the sake of the Pope, whom you blame, and in the eyes of the Italian nation through its representatives. This will mean a second expedition to Rome; the great cause of Italy, of liberty, of French interests, and of the changing of the map of Europe to our advantage, will be spoilt for the sake of an obstinate old man, and a feeble clerical party who would have you assassinated if they could.

Pardon my frankness. Notwithstanding my resolve to retire into myself and to keep out of all that does not concern me, my love for my country, and the devotion and affection I have had for the Emperor since my early boyhood, overflow when I find myself in opposition to Your Majesty.

May it please you, etc.,

NAPOLEON (JEROME).

The Emperor to Prince Napoleon
Paris, 22nd February, 1861.

MY DEAR COUSIN,—I am not severe towards you; quite the contrary. You will always find me just and affectionate, but I owe you the truth when you go astray. One cannot change one's fate at will. Anything you endeavour to take up outside your own country will do you harm instead of good. In France you hold the position which all Princes of the Blood have always held. Your position is similar to that held by the Duc de Berry and Charles X in the time of Louis XVIII. It is similar to that occupied during the reign of the last King of England by all his brothers—the Duke of Sussex, the Duke of York, and the Duke of Cumberland before he became King of Hanover.

You are a General of Division, a Senator, and a Councillor of State. In a time of peace what more can you want? It all amounts to this: You say, "*My position is not very honourable so long as I am not a Minister.*" Now this is a dilemma which I am unable to admit, because Princes must not be Ministers.

As regards your journey to Italy, I completely disapprove of it at the present time. You can only be strong and popular by appearing to all as a support, and not as a source of embarrassment, to me. Now, to go to Turin when I have no Minister there, and to have the air of wishing to fish in troubled waters, will only serve to create many diplomatic difficulties, without being advantageous in any way to your own personal consideration or to any chances you may foresee in the future.

I will therefore sum the matter up by telling you frankly that I am unable to give my consent to your journey to Italy under present circumstances.

With, etc.,

NAPOLEON.

Prince Napoleon to the Emperor
Palais Royal, 22nd February, 1861.

SIRE,—I thank Your Majesty for your frankness. I will not go to Italy, nor to Turin, nor anywhere else, since you do not wish it. From what the Emperor has written to me, I see that I have explained my position badly. I had greatly wished to be at the head of the Navy, believing that I might be able to make a name for myself and render some service. Inasmuch as the entire organisation of France since 1815 has been in the hands of Ministers, I thought that in order to do any good I ought to have some ministerial authority. Your Majesty has thought otherwise. I gave up the thought several months ago, and am not thinking about it any more. Confidence is not a thing one can impose. I do not possess yours for this post, and under our constitution a Minister can do nothing without the absolute confidence of his sovereign.

What humiliates me is to be an entire stranger to the Government, and to witness the most important affairs of the Empire being decided by men of no greater merit, possibly, than myself; it is the feeling that I am not, and shall never be, anything in the political world of France. I had thought of an acting command in the Army, that of the Imperial Guard, for example; of a mission to take possession of Savoy, or of being admitted to your counsels, as was my late father. But, I will repeat, I abandon these projects completely, and Your Majesty shall never hear me speak of them again. What I desire above everything is at least to be no cause of embarrassment or of annoyance to you.

If I go to Egypt or the East direct from Marseilles, Your Majesty, doubtless, will find no inconvenience in this, as a journey of this kind could not give rise to any political difficulties. My wife will remain here.[1]

May it please you, Sire, etc.,

NAPOLEON (JEROME).

[1] The Prince deferred his travels for some months.

CHAPTER XII

The Italian question and Rome—Prince Napoleon's violent speech on the 1st March, 1861, against the Bourbons, and in favour of the Bonapartes—Reply by the Duc d'Aumale—Prince Napoleon and the Grand Mastership of French Freemasons—His quarrel with Prince Murat, former Grand Master—The Roman Question—Another violent speech in the Senate by Prince Napoleon gives grave offence to the Empress Eugénie—Birth of a son to Prince Napoleon.

THE Italian question continued to dominate French politics. It was a very delicate matter. The Emperor found himself placed between the anvil and the hammer. Piedmont did not pardon us the occupation of Rome by our troops, which was the only effective obstacle to the realisation of her ambitions. The Clerical Party in France reproached the Emperor for not having acted with sufficient energy to safeguard the Temporal Power of the Pope. This question gave rise to a heated debate in the Senate.

On the 28th February, 1861, the Assembly had begun the debate on the address to be presented to Napoleon III. Several Senators, notably M. de la Rochejaquelin, had defended the sovereignty of the Holy Father. Next day, on the 1st March, Prince Napoleon mounted the tribune, and made a speech which has remained famous. With a violence which was entirely unrestrained he attacked the Temporal Power, took certain Royalists to task, made a withering onslaught on all the Bourbons in Spain, Italy, and France, and uttered a resounding *apologia* on the Bonapartes. For over three hours he displayed undeniable eloquence, although it exceeded all the recognised rules. His oratorical success was considerable. The Emperor congratulated him on the following day. How came the letter he wrote to him on this occasion, which we reproduce, to be divulged? We do not know. But the Emperor did not conceal his annoyance over the indiscretion.

This violent diatribe against the Bourbons was not to everyone's taste. The animosity against the Prince felt by certain persons in France redoubled. From where he was living in exile the Duc d'Aumale took it in hand to refute this speech. Under his signature there appeared at the beginning of April a *brochure* entitled *Lettre sur l'histoire de France*. It was a justification of his family, and, at the same time, a very lively attack on the Bonapartes, and on Prince Napoleon in particular. The Government ordered the *brochure* to be seized. Prince Napoleon, on the other hand, who liked nothing better than a dispute, and did not shrink from opposition, insisted upon the authorisation of its free circulation. For a moment it was thought the two Princes would come to blows, but a duel would have added no arguments on a question of history to this dispute between two members of rival families.

The Emperor to Prince Napoleon
Paris, 2nd March, 1861.

MY DEAR NAPOLEON,[1]—Although not sharing all your opinions, I desire, nevertheless, to congratulate you on the immense success you obtained yesterday in the Senate. There are some patriotic sentiments so well expressed in your speech that I make a point of telling you how happy I am over it.

With, etc.,

NAPOLEON.

[1] This letter has been published before.

Paris, 7th March, 1861.

MY DEAR COUSIN,—I am greatly annoyed to see the letter I wrote to you appearing in the newspapers. One has no right to publish a letter written to one without the permission of the writer. It is all the more disagreeable to me as it will have to make me more circumspect in my relations with you. Nevertheless, accept my sincere regard.   NAPOLEON.

Thursday, 7th March, 1861.

MY DEAR COUSIN,—Your explanations satisfy me. I think it is quite natural you should have spoken about my letter, but as I wrote to you quite alone in my study, I cannot understand how it came to be reproduced, as I mentioned it to no one. Anyhow, as it is nothing but an involuntary indiscretion, I shall no longer be angry with you.

With, etc.,   NAPOLEON.

Prince Napoleon to the Emperor[1]
Palais Royal, Sunday, 14*th April,* 1861.

SIRE,—The Duc d'Aumale has published a *brochure* in reply to a speech I made a few weeks ago in the Senate. The Public Prosecutor has pronounced this to be a misdemeanour committed against the laws of the Empire and an attack upon your Government. Acting in the public interests, he has seized and brought this publication to the notice of the Courts of Justice.

It was his duty to do so.

Yesterday I saw the Minister of the Interior with a view to begging him to put a stop to an exceptional situation by an exceptional measure, and to allow policy to supersede justice.

I have been attacked in the *brochure* by the Prince of

[1] This letter has been already made public.

Orleans. This is a further reason for pressing my point before your Majesty in order to stop the proceedings. Suppression is no answer. I implore you, Sire, to allow to the reply of M. le Duc d'Aumale free circulation, in the certainty that the patriotism of France will judge the pamphlet as it deserves, and that the good sense of the people will estimate at its real value this *soi-disant* historical lecture which is nothing more than an Orleanist manifesto.

Veuillez agréer, Sire, l'hommage du profond et respectueux attachement avec lequel je suis,
De Votre Majesté,
Le très dévoué Cousin,
NAPOLEON (JÉRÔME).

The Emperor to Prince Napoleon
Palais des Tuileries, 16th April, 1861.

MY DEAR NAPOLEON,—In the position in which you are placed by the *brochure* of the Duc d'Aumale, the following is, I think, the best attitude for you to adopt:

" Go to Belgium and write to the Duc d'Aumale that you were not attacking either him or the younger branch in your speech; that he, on the contrary, has taken exception to it with marked intention against you personally; that it will be an easy matter for you to refute the facts he alleges against you, and that you can only consider his *brochure* in the light of a challenge; that, being unwilling that his exile should place a barrier between you, you have gone into a neutral country, there to await his reply."

This move will put an end to the reports and calumnies now being spread about in Paris, and will make you take up an excellent attitude which is my dearest wish, for you know all the affection I bear to you.

NAPOLEON.

Paris, 18th April, 1861.

My dear Napoleon,—I will reply very frankly to your letter. I gave you what I thought to be good advice in your own interests. You think it is bad advice. I have nothing more to say. You are mistaken as regards the hatred you think the Empress bears to you. She is very quick in her impressions, but has always shown very friendly sentiments towards you. While regretting your decision, neither our relations nor my affection for you shall change.

Napoleon.

23rd April, 1861.

My dear Napoleon,—You have analysed our conversation of yesterday very well. Nevertheless, make Count Cavour quite understand in a postscript that my proposals so far form only the basis of a Treaty which it will be necessary to examine thoroughly in connection with all the obstacles.

With, etc., Napoleon.

30th April, 1861.

My dear Napoleon,—I return you Count Cavour's letter. Although it is urgent to take up some position as regards Rome, I always hesitate to enter into definite relations with a Government which is at the mercy of a freak like Garibaldi, can do nothing in the way of organisation at Naples, and can keep secret no negotiations whatsoever *for a fortnight.*

I do not see any objections to your going to Switzerland.

With, etc., Napoleon.

Very shortly afterwards another affair very nearly brought Prince Napoleon and Prince Murat[1] to blows.

[1] Napoleon Lucien Charles Murat (1803–78), the second son of Joachim (King of Naples) and of Caroline.

The latter, who was Grand Master of the *Grand Orient* in France, had spoken in the Senate in favour of the maintenance of the Temporal Power of the Pope. The Lodges did not forgive him for this attitude, and he was obliged to resign. The Freemasons asked Prince Napoleon to come forward as a candidate to succeed him. From this resulted a clash of opinions which nearly resulted in a duel. Being apprised of what was happening, the Emperor put an absolute veto to an encounter, and it could not take place.

Feeling ran high in the Lodges. In the meantime the Grand Orient nominated Prince Napoleon as Grand Master at a meeting held on the 23rd May, 1861. His nomination had already been voted when on the same day a decree issued by the Prefect of Police was sent to the Grand Orient to the effect that " the election of a Grand Master of the Masonic Order would give rise to an agitation of a kind to endanger public security," and forbidding them to proceed with this election before the following October. The Prince protested against this intrusion of the Government into Masonic affairs, but, nevertheless, he had to give way. We may add that a few months later the Emperor nominated by decree Marshal Magnan to be Grand Master of French Freemasonry.

The Emperor to Prince Napoleon

21st *May*, 1861.

My dear Napoleon,—As I am desirous of putting an end to the unfortunate affair which has occupied us this week, I have required from Murat the withdrawal of his letter. Now that this has been done we must likewise put an end to the occasion of the dispute, which is the Grand Mastership. I therefore desire you will withdraw your candidature. Murat will likewise resign

and will leave the election (a word illegible). Persigny will have spoken to you about it yesterday.
With, etc.,
NAPOLEON.

Prince Napoleon to the Emperor
Palais Royal, 24th May, 1861.

SIRE,—The election of the Grand Master of the Freemasons should have taken place on the 20th May.[1]

Without exerting any influence on my part, and without my taking any steps to obtain their votes, the Freemasons of France decided to nominate me.

I said that I would accept their votes only on the very eve of the election, and under circumstances which you know made it a duty to me. In acting thus I was influenced especially by the feeling of being useful to the country and the dynasty.

I will not remind Your Majesty of the dissensions which have taken place upon this subject in our family. You have recognised that right, moderation, and energy have been on my side. Yet you have intervened as head of our family, and have even intimated to me an order of arrest at the hands of the Prefect of Police. This *affaire d'honneur* between Prince Murat and myself should have been allowed to take place.

The election of a Grand Master has been marked by the most unheard-of and illegal threats of violence. Notwithstanding these, the Masons have shown themselves to be as determined as they are moderate. They have manifested their wishes in spite of material interference. They nominated me Grand Master by a written and signed vote. Further, they confirmed this vote in the lawful place of their meetings with all the due formalities, and I was nominated unanimously by those present by 91

[1] It was deferred until the 23rd May.

votes out of 140. Those who did not vote for me abstained from voting, or were absent, and not one vote was cast for any other candidate.

It is in circumstances like these, when all had been finished, that the Prefect of Police took action by adjourning the election for six months. This action, the grounds for which were based on disturbances which never took place, is illegal from every point of view. The Prefect of Police has no authority to concern himself with the internal proceedings of the Masons. There is no shadow of reason to justify this intervention.

I am lawfully the Grand Master of French Freemasonry; in point of fact there is another Grand Master whose authority is upheld by your police.

The choice of two things only is left to me: either to take note of the violence which has been done to Freemasonry, and to defend its rights by every means offered by the law—I should certainly follow this line of conduct if I was not Your Majesty's cousin, and a French Prince, and a member of the Imperial Dynasty—or to subordinate my rights as a Mason to those pertaining to me as a Prince and as your relative.

Faithful as I always shall be to the devotion and obedience I owe to your person, in spite of the injustice that has been done to me, in spite of your intervention, which has displeased me from every point of view—an intervention which Your Majesty has thought fit to bring to bear against me while refraining from taking action against my adversaries—I desire to put an end to this dispute.

I have not yielded to any consideration which is foreign to it. I obtained the support of the immense majority of the Masons. To-day I am shattered by an act of your will and power. Deeply pained by the conduct His Majesty has thought fit to pursue towards me his friend from boyhood, his friend during evil days, whom he practically brought up in exile, I give way, as nothing can make me determine to resist him. I have the honour to present my resignation as Grand Master to His Majesty, since he has made himself the *de facto* arbiter of Freemasonry.

The Emperor will be pleased, I hope, to give me leave, at some time I shall think fitting, to acquaint him with the steps I have taken, without entering into the details, and with the reasons which have actuated them in regard to the Masons who elected me. I owe them this explanation of my conduct.

May it please you, etc.,

NAPOLEON (JEROME).

The Emperor to Prince Napoleon

28*th May*, 1861.

MY DEAR COUSIN,[1]—I have written to Murat that I absolutely forbid him to fight you, and that he is to express to you his regret for the improper letter he wrote you. I impose upon you the same veto. It is quite impossible for scandals like this to take place in my family.

With, etc., NAPOLEON.

Prince Napoleon spent the summer of 1861 outside France. On the 2nd June he left for a visit to America and Africa. He returned on the 10th October. During his absence the Italian question had become singularly involved. The soul of the movement, Count Cavour, had died on the 6th June. His successor, Ricasoli, had continued his policy with greater boldness and less tact. On the 27th June the Emperor, yielding to the urgent entreaties made to him, recognised the young

---

[1] Contrary to his custom, the Emperor did not employ the *tu* to his cousin in this letter, which leads us to suppose that it was written with the idea of its being made public.

kingdom of Italy, which included the whole with the exception of Rome and Venice, but at the same time he kept our troops in the Holy City, thus opposing an insurmountable barrier to the ambitions of Piedmont. On his side the Pope refused to be persuaded to commit moral suicide, and repelled the combinations entered into to snatch from him a portion of his sovereignty. Napoleon III would certainly have gladly seized upon any opportunity which would have allowed him to withdraw honourably our troops from Rome; but, for the moment, to have taken away our flag would have stirred up Catholic opinion against him, and this he was obliged to take into account. He did not cease to preach patience.

In order to find a way out of the *impasse* in which she was struggling, Piedmont, a prey to interior agitations, harassed by the critical state of affairs which still remained unsettled, disturbed over her dilapidated finances, torn asunder by the brigandage rampant in the Neapolitan provinces, and threatened with anarchy, turned to Paris for a solution of the problem. At Turin the sympathies of Prince Napoleon were well known; as soon as he returned he was made the object of the most pressing solicitations on the part of his father-in-law, Ricasoli, and Rattazzi, the President of the Parliament of Piedmont. He referred the matter to his cousin.

Prince Napoleon to the Emperor
16*th October*, 1861.

SIRE,—As I have been absent from Paris for four and a half months, I have written to no one in Italy, yet, since my return, ten days ago, my father-in-law has written two letters to my wife, and M. Rattazzi has come to see me, and, lastly, M. Ricasoli has just written me a letter which I am sending to Your Majesty.

I do not know what reply to make to all these communications. My bond of relationship with the King, the friendship which united me to Count Cavour, my well-known sympathies with the cause of Italy, and even the inclinations of Your Majesty in the first beginnings of the Italian affair, have connected me with the politics of the two countries. Does the Emperor wish that these relations, which are wholly official, should continue? And does he give me his permission to continue to transmit to him the information I receive? Or should I let it be understood in Italy that, since I am outside politics, I can no longer act as a link between the Emperor and Italy? This will depend, Sire, on the answer it shall please you to give me. But I must know it.

The Italian Government finds itself in a difficult situation, facing an *impasse* and a time-limit. Their Parliament is about to assemble. It will have to define its policy. It can only do this by knowing frankly what are the intentions of the Emperor, more especially as concerns Rome. However perplexing the truth may be for him, he ought to know it, and take up a definite position. Failing this, he will be attacked by the reactionaries who are conspiring under the protection of the French flag in Rome, will be urged on by the advanced party, and will come to grief, and anarchy will be re-established in Italy. Dire confusion will ensue, in which chance alone will play any part. I do not think it would compromise you if my father-in-law and his Government should wish to know clearly what are your intentions. I think this is the consequence forced upon them by the presence of our troops in Rome, which fact constitutes you the arbiter of all that shall happen in Italy and of any arrangement between the Papacy and Italy. It seems to me that up till now the

Italian Government has known better what you do not wish than what you do. It is in order to clarify the situation that my father-in-law and MM. Ricasoli and Rattazzi have applied to me, thinking that you would prefer a confidential explanation. I do not know if this suits His Majesty, and I beg he will give me his views as to how I should reply.

I write to Your Majesty, as your absence[1] prevents my asking you by word of mouth what should be my line of conduct. I do not doubt that Your Majesty understands that I have no wish to seem to be meddling with what does not concern me, but that my relationship, position, and antecedents in connection with the Italian Question compel me to tell them politely: "*Leave me alone*," or "Accept what services I can render to *France and Italy* by acting as an official intermediary in my position as the Emperor's cousin and the King's son-in-law."

If Your Majesty opposes no objection, I will leave on Thursday, the 24th, for the country, for the centre of France.

May it please you, Sire, etc.,

NAPOLEON (JEROME).

The Emperor to Prince Napoleon[2]

Paris, 22nd October, 1861.

MY DEAR NAPOLEON,—I ask nothing better than that you should act as intermediary in regard to the demands and wishes of your father-in-law.

I have seen Rattazzi this morning, and repeated to him what I have always said; namely, that in spite of my desire not to go contrary to the wishes of the Italian people, I shall not leave Rome until I can do so without

---

[1] The Emperor was still at Biarritz. He returned shortly after, passing through Paris on his way to make a stay at Compiègne.

[2] This letter was published by Comandini.

doing violence to my antecedents and promises. In other words, I shall not withdraw my troops until I can do so honourably in regard to my country and Europe. To bring this about we must therefore wait for either a favourable opportunity or a clear-cut compromise on the part of the King of Italy with the Pope.

I see no objection to your journey, and renew the expression of my sincere regard. NAPOLEON.

At the time of the outbreak of the war in Italy, Klapka, the Hungarian General, had proposed to the Emperor through Prince Napoleon a complete plan to stir up a rising of Hungary against Austria. Napoleon III had been attracted by the idea, had discussed it with Klapka, and had handed to him 50,000 francs. The latter had left at once for Jassy, but, as peace had come too soon, his projects were brought to naught. He then returned to Geneva. Before this mad escapade he had held the appointment there of director of the Banque Générale Suisse, and had charge of its interests in London and Constantinople. His proceedings at Jassy had interrupted his work, and he was greatly embarrassed. He wrote to the Prince, who advocated his cause with the Emperor.

The Emperor to Prince Napoleon
Paris, 13th December, 1861.

MY DEAR NAPOLEON,—I have not replied to you sooner because, unfortunately, the state of my finances is not very prosperous, and I have to limit my expenditure as far as I possibly can. However, it is essential to come to the aid of an honourable man. I therefore send you 38,000 francs.[1] I have been unable to entertain your proposal because the Minister of Finance has

---
[1] The Prince transmitted this sum to Klapka, and sent the receipt to the Emperor on the 22nd December.

elaborated an entire scheme, and one must not discourage him now by an enquiry which, I fear, would not be of much value.

The Empress and I have been feeling rather indisposed; had this not been the case, we should have come to see Clotilde.

With, etc.,   NAPOLEON.

The debate on the Address afforded another opportunity to Prince Napoleon in 1862 to make a speech in the Senate which provoked wide comment. On the 22nd February, replying to MM. de Ségur and de la Rochejaquelin, he stood up hotly for the ideas of the Revolution, made an attack on his opponents, demanded complete liberty for the Press, and ended by advocating the principle of heredity resting on the will of the people, in opposition to the principle of heredity by divine right as understood by the Royalists. He used very biting terms, and of set purpose made them very aggressive. The violent tone of this speech was not well received at the Tuileries, especially by the Empress, who was not favourably disposed to her cousin, and her *entourage* interpreted certain sentences as being aimed at her.

The Prince explained himself afterwards from the tribune of the Senate, and the misunderstanding was dissipated, but not without leaving some trace of it behind.

The Emperor to Prince Napoleon
Paris, 23rd February, 1862.

MY DEAR NAPOLEON,—I cannot help regretting keenly your speech of yesterday. Moderation and calmness are the first requisites in anyone wishing to persuade; and attacks against persons and entire classes are always impolitic. Since you quote the Emperor, you must accept his entire system. Now the Emperor truly thought that a society overthrown, and divided up by opposing parties, could not be re-formed by enthroning liberty, and especially the liberty of the Press. He wished to rally all upright men, whatever their antecedents may have been. Now, to proclaim unlimited liberty and to re-awaken memories of our civil disputes is certainly not following the Emperor's precepts. Your speech will do harm to my Government and to yourself. On the one hand people will think that I share your ideas of hatred of a bygone period, and on the other they will feel that from ambitious views you are making out yourself to be ultra-liberal. I admit that you have not the same opinions as I have, but, in order to give vent to them, all the more is it requisite that they should be surrounded by so great moderation that they could not fall foul of anyone. Now you have had the faculty of falling foul of persons most devoted to you. I must repeat this to you, and I keenly deplore it. I am told you mean to speak against the salt tax and against the clergy. I hope you will do nothing of the sort, for I wish to calm people's minds and prevent an explosion of violent sentiments which hinder the ordered march of my Government and of my policy. The more any exaggerated tendency is shown in any one direction the greater is the degree of opposition in any steps I may take. It must be so.

I have thought it well to show my disapproval to you, because you must get it thoroughly into your head that, the more you present the appearance of separating yourself from me, the less influence will you have in the country. Certainly you may find a few flatterers and may meet with interested applause, but you will lay no solid foundations.

I have spoken frankly to you, and renew the assurance of my sincere regard. NAPOLEON.

24th February, 1862.

MY DEAR NAPOLEON,—Since I last saw you I have found the Empress so much up in arms against you, because people have made her feel that the words you spoke about heredity were an attack on the rights of her son, that I must request you not to come this evening because an explanation in public would be very disagreeable.

With, etc.,   NAPOLEON.

Paris, 25th February, 1862.

MY DEAR NAPOLEON,—Nothwithstanding the articles in the newspapers it is clear your speech has produced a bad effect; you saw yesterday the capital M. de Boissy made out of it. I think it to be indispensable that you should yourself rectify to-day the double meaning of your words.

I should have asked nothing better than to see you to-day, but I prefer that there should be no meeting, since your officers repeat in my *salon* that your speeches are concerted with me beforehand.

With, etc.,   NAPOLEON.

26th February, 1862.

MY DEAR NAPOLEON,—I was very pleased with your words in the Senate yesterday. I think they were of great advantage both for you and me. The Empress begs me to tell you that if she is hasty in her first impressions, *like you are*, she cherishes no animosity and is always disposed to do you justice.

I hope that matters will now be *couleur de rose* again, more especially if well-meaning apostles do not take it upon themselves to blow up the fire again.

With, etc.,   NAPOLEON.

The Prince was to experience shortly a great joy. At the end of March, 1862, the official announcement of the pregnancy of Princess Clotilde was made, and on the 18th July she gave birth to her eldest son, Prince Napoleon Victor Jerome Frederic. His godfather was Victor Emmanuel II, the King of Italy, and his godmother Queen Sophie, daughter of King William I of Wurtemberg, and the husband of William III, King of Holland.

The Emperor to Prince Napoleon
27th March, 1862.

MY DEAR NAPOLEON,—It is the Minister of State who should announce in the *Moniteur* (in terms similar to those used in the case of Empress), the pregnancy of Clotilde.
With, etc.,
NAPOLEON.

The Emperor to Prince Napoleon, Paris
(Telegram)
Vichy, 18*th July*, 1862.

I approve of the names you wish to give to your son, but think that as the Queen of Holland is a Protestant she cannot be the godmother. I did not write to you, as I thought that the *accouchement* would not be till August.

Compiègne, 6*th November*, 1862.

MY DEAR COUSIN,—We were very uneasy for a moment on knowing that you were on the sea in such vile weather, and we are glad to hear of your arrival on the coast of Brittany. I see no objection to your going to Switzerland. Give Clotilde many kind messages from me. I know your son is going on well, and I congratulate you.
With, etc.,
NAPOLEON.

Compiègne, 24th November, 1862.

MY DEAR NAPOLEON,—We should have been charmed to have you here with Clotilde for a few days, but since your affairs prevent this I will frankly confess that it would be very difficult for me to assign a particular day for you to come here because the weather makes hunting and taking drives very uncertain for us. Besides, as we are returning soon to Paris, the Empress and I will be happy to see you again shortly.

With, etc.,

NAPOLEON.

27th November, 1862.

MY DEAR COUSIN,—I will make a point of giving a categorical reply to your letter. I will do this to-day or to-morrow as I am much occupied.

With my sincere regard, nevertheless !

NAPOLEON.

CHAPTER XIII

The Polish insurrection—Prince Napoleon makes a violent speech in the Senate in favour of Poland and attacking Russia; its bad effect; the Emperor reprimands his cousin—The correspondence of Napoleon I—The Polish refugees—The National Archives.

A GRAVE question was agitating the nations and disturbing the chancelleries of Europe at this period. Poland was in revolt. After long years of methodical and implacable oppression, after many sanguinary repressions by which Russia had endeavoured to stamp out any hankerings after independence, persecution, far from weakening the national sentiment, had excited it to a high pitch. A strong wind of revolt had at last blown over this nation which hitherto had been so resigned. A final provocation produced an explosion.

One night in January 1863 the police in Varsovie and the chief towns laid hands on the young men belonging to the well-to-do classes who had been conspicuous by the ardour of their patriotism. They were imprisoned, or forced to join the Russian army. Some escaped by means of organised raids, others took to their heels. They collected in bands in the country districts, and took refuge in the woods, at that time deep in snow. Their numbers soon increased. They armed themselves with anything they could find, waiting until they were strong enough to lay hands on rifles. In spite of certain checks, the insurrection spread throughout the whole country.

Europe was not insensible to the appeals made by the insurgents. Inasmuch as public opinion in England, Austria, and France especially, took their side, the Governments themselves felt the necessity of intervening. Prussia alone showed a reserve which amounted to approval. She wished to spare the susceptibilities of the Tsar, whose benevolent neutrality, to put it at the lowest, would be necessary for her on the day when she should play her own part on her western frontiers. The other countries, at the risk of wounding the Muscovite colossus by a pin-prick of no great force, prepared to address a collective remonstrance, which produced no effect, as is the case when the power of the bayonet is not ready to back up diplomatic notes.

Napoleon III and Prince Napoleon, both so deeply imbued with the principle of nationality and the independence of the people, were unable to keep out of this movement which produced so vibrating an echo amongst us. The Prince, all the bolder from having none of the responsibilities attaching to power, thought that the moment had come for us to intervene. On the 20th February, 1863, he sent to his cousin a long note in which he unfolded a plan of joint action for the reconstruction of the kingdom of Poland and the remaking of the map of Europe.[1] Two days afterwards Napoleon III recommended prudence to him in the following letter:

The Emperor to Prince Napoleon

22nd January, 1863.

MY DEAR NAPOLEON,—I have listened with keen interest to the reading aloud of the memorandum you have communicated to me, and have reflected over it. What you propose is a dream, as you say, but a dream which might be possible of realisation one day. But the very greatest prudence and the greatest skilfulness is required to reach a good result. It is natural that you should take a real interest in what you see indistinctly is capable of realisation. That is why I am going to beg you to do nothing in what concerns the line of action I

[1] See Appendix, Note III, p. 264.

intend to follow. I have to deal with powers who are very touchy, and the moment they have any reason to see ambitious views on my part they will reject any kind of alliance. On the other hand, if the Press determines to make me go faster than I think is wise, I shall be compelled to make declarations which will interfere with my policy. I want neither manifestations nor provocations, which always force one to make compromising declarations. For example, the news published in the *Opinion Nationale* on the telegram in favour of Poland is inaccurate in the first place, and is also inopportune. To-day we are on moving ground, and it will be possible only by the exercise of great prudence for me to render firm the soil on which I must rest my policy if events are favourable to me. In any case, I count upon you to aid me instead of embarrassing me, and I implore you not to *marcher plus vite que les violons.*

  With, etc.,   Napoleon.
I send you a police report.

It was not long before the Polish Question was brought up in the Senate. On the 17th March, 1863 a debate, provoked by petitions in favour of Poland, was begun in the Assembly. Several Senators came forward as advocates of the petitioners. On the following day Prince Napoleon spoke. In energetic and original language full of lively sallies, he pleaded warmly on behalf of the Poles. Unfortunately, carried away by his generous sentiments and violent temperament, he made an attack on the Emperor of Russia, to whom for years past Napoleon III had not ceased to make advances. Billault, the Minister of State, considered his words all the more imprudent from the fact of their emanating from a personage so highly placed. He made a protest, and endeavoured to make clear what were the real views of the sovereign. The Prince at once turned on him and bitterly reproached him for having voted for General Cavaignac and not for Prince Louis (the Emperor) in 1848.

The Emperor feared that the declarations of his cousin might compromise him. In a letter published in the *Moniteur* on the 22nd March he congratulated Billault on having faithfully interpreted his views. "Your words," he said, "were conformable with my sentiments on every point, and I repudiate any other interpretation."

The Prince and everyone else understood the allusion, and he showed his wounded feelings. The three following letters[1] passed between him and his cousin in this connection:

Prince Napoleon to the Emperor
Paris, Palais Royal,
Thursday, 26th March, 1863.

SIRE,—I have been treated personally as badly as possible by Your Majesty both in public and private. Should behaviour such as this impose upon me respectful and complete silence? *Yes*, if I only consult my tastes and my interests. *No*, if I believe I have a good idea to submit to you, and can serve the cause of the Empire, of nationality, and of liberty in Europe.

The Emperor will judge of this. If I am blamed past hope of recall you will give me no reply, and I shall understand. If, while you blame you do not altogether repudiate me, you will summon me to your presence and will hear me.

You have shown great contempt for me, Sire, in not taking into account that I remained silent during the debate on the Address, and in saying that the Senate

---

[1] Emile Ollivier has published them in the *Empire Libéral*, Vol. VI, pp. 174-82.

voted the Address *unanimously*, notwithstanding my vote, which possesses, possibly, as much weight and value as those of MM. Boissy, Rochejaquelin and company.

You have sided with those who desired a debate in the Senate on Poland as against me who was anxious for silence, as I had some confidence in you. You have not been willing to receive me after the debate, nor to permit me to explain to you what happened. I, your relative, your friend in your days of exile and misfortune, have not even had an opportunity of exculpating myself before the face of enemies of yesterday and devoted servants of to-morrow, that is to say, since you obtained the upper hand.

Lastly, your published letter has visited me with public blame and gave approval to M. Billault, who agreed with M. de la Rochejaquelin and praised up Russia, and said that anyone who voted against the Order of the Day was your enemy. All this has wounded me deeply, but has not discouraged me. What does my person matter and what is it in comparison with the great interests at stake? In spite of everything, the memories of my Cousin Louis, of Arenenburg, and of London, dominate in my heart over those of the Emperor in the Tuileries who, possibly, *has his reasons* for acting as he has.

I have, therefore, continued to study and reflect, and have drawn up a political and military plan adapted to present circumstances, which are no longer what they were a month ago.

Is it worth your while to waste an hour of your time in listening to this plan? I think so, because I have drawn it up. It remains to be seen whether the Emperor agrees with me, or whether his displeasure over my speech overrules everything.

May it please you, etc.,

NAPOLEON (JEROME).

The Emperor to Prince Napoleon[1]

Paris, 29th March, 1863.

MY DEAR COUSIN,—I have delayed answering your letter, for it pains me to enter into a discussion which can only lead to recriminations over the past. I will confess I was surprised to see how little justice you render to my conduct towards you during the past twelve years, and how greatly you misconceive your own. The memories of our boyhood are as dear to me as they are to you, but they have nothing to do with the questions which are occupying us to-day.

From the very day after I was elected President of the Republic you have never ceased to be hostile in your words and actions to my policy, whether during my Presidency, on the 2nd of December,[2] or since the restoration of the Empire. How have I taken my revenge for this conduct? By seeking on every occasion to bring you forward, by making a position for you worthy of your rank, and by opening out to you a field for your brilliant qualities. Your command in the Crimea, your marriage, your allowance, your appointment as Minister for Algeria, your appointment to command an army corps in Italy, your admission to the Senate and to the Council of State, are patent proofs of my regard for you. Need I remind you how you have responded to them? In the East (the Crimea) your discouragement made you lose the fruits of a campaign which you had begun well. Your marriage was a great impediment to an independent policy on my part by tending to make M. de Cavour believe (a thing entirely contrary to my intentions) that your marriage to the daughter of the King of Sardinia

---

[1] Note in pencil, in the handwriting of the Prince: " Strange, but very hard. The Empress is bound to have a minute of this, I know." As a matter of fact, the handwriting in this letter, entirely in the hand of Napoleon, is far less bold than in the other letters, and one rather has the impression that it is a re-copy and not a first effusion.

[2] The date of his manifesto, which resulted in Louis Napoleon being elected President of the Republic on the 10th December, 1848. See p. 52.

The Second Empire and Its Downfall

was a condition *sine qua non* to my treaty with him. And your portfolio of Algeria? You handed it back to me one fine day because of an article in the *Moniteur*. Your allowance? One has every right to be astonished that you never receive, and that your name never appears connected with any work of charity.

With regard to your speeches in the Senate they have always been a serious embarrassment to my Government. Do you complain of my conduct towards you? People are far more amazed that I have for so long tolerated in a member of my family an opposition which alarms and induces hesitation among the partisans of the same cause. *The Times* recently said, when talking of you, that if an English Prince were to follow in England the same line of conduct as you, he would be disclaimed by public opinion. Make certain that the same thing applies in France, and that, with the exception of a few flatterers without any influence, people disapprove of an attitude which bears all the external marks of rivalry. Have I, notwithstanding, any claim to demand that your words should be the faithful echo of my intentions and my views? No; but what I have the right to require from a Prince of my family is that when making a speech before the first Assembly in the State he should at least conceal divergencies of opinion under suitable forms when they exist.

I will never admit that it is an advantage to anyone to speak in the Senate as though at a club, casting insulting words at the heads of everybody, and expressing oneself without any reserve, just as though your own past were without reproach, and as though your own future did not require careful handling.

In your last speech you violated all decencies. By quoting from what I have written you had the appearance of wishing to place my actions in contradiction with my words. By attacking the Emperor of Russia, even over his good-will shown towards me, you placed me in the position that supposing to-morrow the Russian Ambassador were to commit an act of impoliteness towards you, I should have no right to make a complaint to his Government. Lastly, by attacking my Minister personally you showed a want of tact and an animosity which it is difficult to excuse. And after that you find in my letter to Billault an affront to yourself! It was indeed, however, the gentlest and most polite method of reply that one could have chosen!

Now that I have told you all that I thought, there are no longer any but two lines of conduct for you to follow. 1. Either be, what you ought to be, a help and support to my Government, and in that case I shall be happy to continue to give you tangible evidence of my former regard. 2. Or else take a separate course apart by giving free play to the violence of your opinions, and in that case it will be necessary that my behaviour to you shall testify publicly to my displeasure, for it is impossible for people to understand that I can receive as a friend in the evening one who has made an attack on me in the morning. It is for you to choose. I should regret it keenly if your good sense and your good heart do not get the better of your fiery spirit.

With, etc., NAPOLEON.

Prince Napoleon to the Emperor

Paris, 31st March, 1863.

SIRE,—The purpose of Your Majesty's letter is too clear for me not to understand it. What good would it do me to reply at length to the numerous reproaches Your Majesty has brought against me? I feel it would be useless and would have no influence on your mind to tell you that you reprimanded me when I was your

Ambassador,[1] in 1849, in a very harsh letter which there was nothing in my conduct to justify, and that I do not know what there is you could reproach me for in regard to the 2nd December. As the event took me by surprise, and as I knew nothing about what was happening, I was altogether passive in my conduct.

Your reproach on the subject of my marriage in connection with the treaty with M. Cavour I also do not understand, so extraordinary does it seem to me. My father-in-law, Marshal Niel and M. Nigra are the witnesses of my conduct in this matter, which up till now the Emperor has always approved. As regards my first speech in the Senate, on Italy, you wrote to congratulate me. Your Minister of the Interior, M. de Persigny, was much more enthusiastic over it than even my own friends. As to my last speech, it was preceded by the statement made by the Minister of State, who himself congratulated me upon what I had said. And God knows I did all I could to avoid a debate! It was M. Billault who wanted one, as he mistrusted you and wished to bind you down by what he said. As to personalities directed against the Minister, that is true: I was wrong to remind M. Billault that he had voted for General Cavaignac, that if all Frenchmen had followed his example you would not be Emperor, and that he had served you with honour and fidelity only since you had obtained the upper hand; but I made these interruptions on the day after my speech, and they were wrung from me by the Minister when he said that I appeared to be threatening the Emperor with a revolution, and that a manifestation was taking place in the street, and that to vote against the Order of the Day was to show myself an enemy of the Emperor!

I ask Your Majesty's pardon for making this explanation,

[1] See pp. 54–6.

which I would have given to you verbally in your presence if I had seen you. Now you are good enough to end your letter, Sire, by two very vague and not clearly formulated alternatives. The first is an encouragement, the second a threat: I think of anticipating your wishes by absenting myself: it is the only course left to me. In this way I am proving that I will never be an obstacle or cause of embarrassment to you, and that I know how to sacrifice myself when necessary.

I will therefore ask the Emperor for his approval for me to go to Egypt with my wife. If you will be kind enough, Sire, to give your consent, our departure shall take place very shortly, and I shall be happy if by being far away I can remove every pretext for the recriminations, reproaches, and prejudices to which I give rise.

I ought not to allude to politics which Your Majesty has so carefully avoided in your letter. You will quite understand, however, if, without wishing to pry into the secrets of your future conduct in the Polish Question, I venture to express one wish; and that is that the Emperor will consider giving me a Command if war takes place, for, by not doing so, this would prove to me that there is no longer any place for me in the Empire.

May it please you, etc.,

NAPOLEON (JEROME).

The Emperor to Prince Napoleon

1st April, 1863.

MY DEAR COUSIN,—I will receive you with pleasure this evening at 6 o'clock, if that will suit you.

With, etc., NAPOLEON.

26th April, 1863.

MY DEAR COUSIN,—I see no objection to your going to Italy if that is agreeable to you.

Give the King many messages from me, and with all good wishes for your journey, etc., NAPOLEON.

The Prince and Princess left for Italy that same day, after which they visited Egypt and then Syria. They did not return to France until the 6th July.

The Emperor to Prince Napoleon
Vichy, 10th July, 1863.

MY DEAR NAPOLEON,—I have learnt of your return and Clotilde's with pleasure. I am amazed and delighted that she was able to bear the fatigue of the journey. I see no objection to your fresh projects. I am awaiting impatiently the answers from St. Petersburg, for it will be necessary then to take up a line.

With, etc., NAPOLEON.

I am happy to know that your son is in good health. It will be necessary to think about having him baptised.[1]

By decree of the 7th September, 1854, a Commission, under the Presidency of Marshal Vaillant, had been appointed to publish the correspondence of Napoleon I. It continued to act until the last days of 1863, and issued the first fifteen volumes of this remarkable collection. Actuated by a very broad spirit it published practically all the documents which it could find, making a general rule of suppressing only matters of slight interest or what was unnecessary or mere repetition. Prince Napoleon, a man who always advocated the liberty of the Press, even thought that the matter included was sometimes too undiscriminating. It appears that he placed the cult of Napoleon above his passion for liberty. By surrendering certain letters to the curiosity of the public he feared that the criticisms therein directed

[1] The solemn baptism of Prince Victor never took place; the church would not recognise his godmother, Queen Sophie, who was a Protestant.

against members of the family, or the measures that circumstances had imposed, might attach some discredit even to the memory of the Emperor. He opened his mind to his cousin, and in a note which he sent him on the 11th November, 1863 (Appendix, Note iv., pp. 268–71), he unfolded his ideas on the matter. As a result of these conversations Napoleon III, who was glad to find a field in which the ever wakeful activity of the Prince might exert itself, decided to dissolve the former Commission, and to appoint a second, on the 3rd February, 1864, the Presidency of which he entrusted to Prince Napoleon. We need not quote here the more or less official reports drawn up by the latter, but allusion is made to this work on several occasions in the correspondence of the two cousins.

The Emperor to Prince Napoleon[1]

Vichy, 20th July, 1863.

MY DEAR NAPOLEON,—I think, with you, that perhaps too many personalities have been allowed to appear in the *Correspondance de l'Empereur*. However, there are certain letters which ought not to be suppressed in spite of the blame they throw upon members of our family. For example, I did not wish that they should exclude the one addressed by the Emperor to my father, although he censured his conduct, because these letters are a great honour to the Emperor. The same should hold good in the case of those you send me. We should cut out everything that is wounding, and irrelevant from a historical point of view, but we must include everything that shows the military genius and the patriotic sentiments of the Emperor. I shall write to Marshal Vaillant in this sense. I ask nothing better than that you should be a member of the Commission.

With, etc., NAPOLEON.

[1] Marginal note in the Prince's handwriting: "Meet Marshal Vaillant at 12.30 p.m., Friday, 24th, at his Ministry. Take the entire *dossier* of the Emperor."

Biarritz, 22nd September, 1863.

MY DEAR COUSIN,[1]—I see with pleasure that you are taking an interest in agriculture, and I approve of your journey to England. I, too, should like to be able to give you some occupation more suited to your abilities, but one must wait till opportunities arise.

The Empress sends you a thousand kind messages.
With, etc.,
NAPOLEON.

Compiègne, 16*th December,* 1863.

MY DEAR NAPOLEON,[2]—You are aware that I have dissolved the commission charged with the publication of *La Correspondance de l'Empereur.* We must now set about reconstituting it. I think of appointing you as President, with the addition of four persons to work with you. These would be: Marshal Vaillant, M. de Flahaut, M. de Laborde, and General Frossard, without counting the secretaries.

I send you General de Flahaut's and Marshal Vaillant's observations on the note you delivered to me. I shall not adopt all their ideas, but nevertheless I am quite decided to continue the publication in the same chronological order.

I am returning to Paris on Saturday. We will discuss together the new arrangements.
With, etc.,
NAPOLEON.

Notwithstanding this new occupation, which he took up, however, with ardour, Prince Napoleon did not find therein sufficient food for his always insatiable energy. He was restless. He would have liked to play a part

---

[1] Prince Napoleon received this letter at Meudon on the 23rd September.

[2] This letter was dictated, and was only signed by the Emperor. Two notes are attached to it, one by Marshal Vaillant, the President of the Commission, and the other by General de Flahaut, giving their views of the way in which it seemed to them suitable to continue the work. M. de Laborde was at that time Director of the Archives of the Empire.

which was closed to him by circumstances. He gave vent to the unrest working in his mind in the following letter to his cousin:

Prince Napoleon to the Emperor
Palais Royal, 8th May, 1864.

SIRE,—I beg the Emperor will allow me to have a conversation with him, and to indicate when His Majesty can receive me. It is not a matter of politics in general; I see that you do not care to talk about them with me, and I will respect your reserve. It is not a question of money: thank God I have no request to make in this connection. It concerns some advice which I wish to ask you as to what I should do for my future. I am forty-two years old, and my health is not good; I am growing old. I have one child, and soon I shall be having a second. With my name, my position, and possibly with what little ability nature has endowed me I must endeavour to render service to my country in a reasonable sphere, and leave behind some traces of my life—in a word, I must find out what is my duty and do it. I wish to ask your advice, which will depend upon your intentions. There arrives a period of life in which one must cease to live a day-to-day existence. Before choosing a form of life which is to decide my whole future, it is my duty—I will almost say my right—to consult you, because you are the Emperor and head of my family. I am sufficiently a philosopher to accept everything resulting from what I may decide upon, and I have enough strength of will to bend my character to attain the end I should like to reach! I am very much afraid of wearying you, and this has held me back up to now. But I must, nevertheless, come to a decision as regards my future, and resolve to follow some course with continued perseverance. I have an ambition which is neither open to blame nor unreasonable, and all will depend on what you shall say to me. Having nothing to hide from you, my frankness, therefore, shall be complete. I did not wish to use an intermediary between us; I thought that between you and me, Sire, there was no need, and I come to you to say, " Give me one hour in order that by arriving at a right judgment I may choose some definite line of conduct." I await Your Majesty's commands to come and see you.

May it please, etc.,   N. J.

Princess Clotilde was shortly to give birth to another child—Prince Louis, who was born at the Palais Royal on the 16th July, 1864. Louis I, the King of Portugal, was his godfather, and his godmother was Princess Mathilde. The Queen of Portugal, Marie Pie, was the daughter of the King of Italy, and, consequently, the sister of Princess Mathilde.

Prince Napoleon to the Emperor
24th June, 1864.

SIRE,—I returned from the country a few days ago, and wish to leave for Havre and other points on the coast where I can have some sea bathing, which has been recommended by the doctors.

As I shall not be able to be here on the return of Your Majesty from Fontainebleau, I desire to give expression to my respectful homage by letter, and to discuss with you the birth of the child which I am expecting to take place towards the end of July.

My intention is to have it baptised privately, quite simply, as was done in the case of the eldest, and to wait for the public ceremonial baptism until there shall be some fresh regulation, and this proceeding will entail no drawbacks from the religious point of view, and will avoid a very wearisome ceremony. If this intention be carried out (and I hope Your Majesty will give your consent), there would be no need to choose a godfather or godmother, but Clotilde has expressed her wish to-day that these should be chosen.

I therefore propose as godfather the reigning King of Portugal, and my sister as godmother.

If the child is a boy it will receive the names Napoleon *Louis* Joseph Jerome, and if a girl, *Mathilde* Eugénie Catherine.

When the King of Portugal shall have consented to become godfather, I think it will be suitable to ask his representative in Paris to be present at the birth.

I await the Emperor's approval to take the necessary steps.

  May it please, etc.,   Napoleon (Jerome).

The Emperor to Prince Napoleon
25th June, 1864.

My dear Napoleon,—I have no objections to make as concerning the second child which Clotilde is shortly to present to you, and approve of your choice of godfather and godmother.

I hope the sea-bathing will do you good, and on your return we will discuss the Privy Council, in which I think you will be able to render great services to France and to me.[1]

I will appoint General Daumas with pleasure to the Luxembourg, if, however, it is not the part of the Senate to make the appointment.

I regret the death of the King of Wurtemberg.[2]

  With, etc.,   Napoleon.

[1] A few months later the Emperor increased the prerogatives of the Privy Council and appointed Prince Napoleon to be its Vice-President. The Decree was signed on the 24th November, 1864, and appeared in the *Journal Official* on the 3rd January, 1865.

[2] William I, King of Wurtemberg, died on the 25th June, 1864. He was the brother of Catherine of Wurtemberg, the mother of Prince Napoleon.

The Emperor to Prince Napoleon
Fontainebleau, 6th July, 1864.

MY DEAR COUSIN,—I have informed Marshal Vaillant that I authorise the Commission for the water-supply of Meudon as you have proposed, merely adding one additional member.

I send you the authorisation you ask for, and, etc.,
NAPOLEON.

Fontainebleau, 5th July, 1864.

I authorise Prince Napoleon, my Cousin, to examine or cause to be examined, the sheets in the Imperial Archives containing the papers referring to my Father, the former King of Holland.   NAPOLEON.

The insurrection in Poland had been gradually extinguished—crushed out pitilessly. Deportations had succeeded the massacres. Poland became dumb again; as in former times "order reigned in Varsovie" once more. In order to escape vengeance, very large numbers of patriots had taken refuge abroad, especially in France, in whom they had placed all their trust. Their lot was an appalling one, all the more because the majority belonged to families who had been well-to-do formerly, and knew none of those manual callings which, failing anything else, can assure the earning of daily bread anywhere.

How could such distress as this be alleviated? Prince Napoleon, who formerly had warmly pleaded the cause of the insurgents, did not abandon them now that they had been conquered.

Prince Napoleon to the Emperor
Paris, Palais Royal,
Saturday, 23rd July, 1864.

SIRE,—Your Majesty knows my keen sympathy with the Polish cause. Those who fought for the independence and liberty of their country are arriving in France in large numbers: their misery is appalling; they are literally dying of hunger. Their position is all the more painful because those arriving among us are educated people for the most part, who had possessed means and a high position at home. During the last few days I have known three who *killed themselves* to escape from their necessities. I know a young Lithuanian who can barely keep himself alive on three *sous* a day. The little I have been able to do for these brave souls, and my well-known sentiments, make them often appeal to me. What can I do alone? Just give them some succour, insignificant as compared with their needs, but quite a heavy call upon me, and be often exposed to the danger of bestowing my alms on the wrong people as I know nothing about those to whom I give. It is the same case with many charitable and patriotic persons.

The subsidies given by the Minister of the Interior are a mere nothing. All he gives is fifteen to twenty-five francs a month; the preliminary enquiries are lengthy, and the formalities are complicated. The existing Franco-Polish Committee has no more money; its principal source of revenue came from public lectures which have been suppressed by the Government; in addition, it is composed of avowed opponents to the Government, MM. d'Harcourt, Odilon Barrot, Lafayette, etc. It receives no money from the public; we are unable to enter into relations with it. Under these circumstances we thought of starting a Relief Committee, and I will agree to become its President and leave to it its real character, one exclusively of benevolence; we should like to admit men of all shades of opinion, Frenchmen only, and even ladies. In order that it may act upon the public and draw in subscriptions, it is necessary to have men of some position upon it. We shall hope to obtain money from our large financial houses. To achieve this end and to have any chance of success, we must have the sanction and the active support of the Emperor.

A word from you is enough as regards *the sanction*. And for *active support*, if you would be willing to subscribe even the smallest sum, and the Empress too, its success would be very certain! I think that the first persons to figure in the relief committee for the poor Poles might be as follows: Prince Napoleon, Count Walewski, Duruy the Minister, General Mellinet, the Archbishop of Paris, a few of the Councillors of State, Senators, and Deputies, the Editors of the *Débats*, the *Siècle* and *Opinion*, and any other people who might wish, and who might bring in subscriptions.

The committee would take in hand charitable gifts, lotteries, concerts, and would then distribute relief.

I have not spoken about my scheme to any of the people whose names I am mentioning to Your Majesty, before knowing whether you approve of it.

I will ask the Emperor to give me an answer as soon as possible, because their poverty is decimating these poor Poles day by day.

I am going to make an expedition to Havre for the regatta, and shall be back in Paris to-morrow.

My wife and young child are going on well.

May it please, etc.,

NAPOLEON (JEROME).

The Emperor to Prince Napoleon
Vichy, 24th July, 1864.

MY DEAR COUSIN,—In spite of my desire to help the Polish refugees I can take no decision without consulting the Ministers, which I will do. You know I have made an increase in the budget of 300,000 francs under the heading of assistance for the Poles.

With, etc., NAPOLEON.

Prince Napoleon to the Emperor

Havre, July 1864.

SIRE,—Your Majesty has charged me with the publication of the correspondence of our Uncle. I have nothing but praise for the help I am receiving from all the members of the Commission, with the exception of M. de Laborde, Director of Archives. This official, offended probably on account of his not being able to act just as he did under the former Commission, has taken up a bad attitude towards me; I should not have wished to discuss the matter with Your Majesty had not a letter I have just received *forced* me to do so; I am sending it to the Emperor, who will form his own judgment on it.

In order to place Your Majesty in a position to appreciate this matter, I send you a copy of all the correspondence I have had in order to obtain facilities for *taking cognisance* of papers which are necessary to me.

I asked for an examination to be made, and to go *myself* with an *employé of the Archives*, for the purpose of taking cognisance of the papers of my Uncle Louis. M. de Laborde refuses permission *in any case*, that is to say, even though the Emperor ordered it, to allow M. Judenne,[1] one of my assistants, to enter, and as for me, he refuses to receive me *without an order from Marshal Vaillant*. It is not correct, what the Director says: those whose business it is to make researches are always authorised to go themselves or to send to the Archives. This has been the case with M. Ducasse[2] and many

---

[1] The former archivist of ancient manuscripts.

[2] Baron Ducasse, a former aide-de-camp to King Jerome, wrote many books on history and strategy. He was commissioned also to put in order and to publish the *Mémoires of King Jerome*.

others. In my own case it seems to me that the Emperor's decree charging me with the publication gives me a title which proves that I have not only the right, but the duty to make researches in the Archives which I deem to be useful. How am I to direct this publication when I am unable to collect the facts? M. de Laborde knows that Her Majesty the Empress was good enough to send me by the hands of Madame Cornu the originals of the letters of the Emperor Napoleon to his brother Louis, and he refuses me what Your Majesty has shown such eagerness to send me.

I ask Your Majesty to send me an order authorising me once and for all to make, or to cause to be made, any researches and copies which I deem to be useful, in the presence of an employé at the Archives. It cannot be otherwise, and this is only common sense. How can an employé at the Archives divine and choose intelligently the documents likely to interest an author if the person who is doing the work does not indicate what seems to be useful for his purpose? Everywhere, in France and abroad, in all the Archives of the world, matters are thus arranged, and permission is given to anyone to make researches. This is the case at the office of Foreign Affairs, at the War Office, and at all the institutions where I am making researches.

It is painful for me to be compelled to bother you over such a simple thing, but what can I do? I have been actually obliged to apply to Your Majesty to send me an authorisation which will enable me to accomplish the Mission with which you have been good enough to charge me, and which I accepted with gratitude.

NAPOLEON (JEROME).

I beg the Emperor to have an answer sent to me.

CHAPTER XIV

Prince Napoleon's indiscreet speech at Ajaccio, entailing a public rebuke by the Emperor, published in the *Moniteur* by his command ; the Prince's reply, and his resignation from the Privy Council—Subsequent reconciliation between the Emperor and the Prince—Proposals by the Emperor of a form of Government on more liberal lines.

THE friendship existing between the two cousins was to undergo yet another critical phase, but one that was not of long duration, although the circumstances were made public.

On the 1st May, 1865, the Emperor embarked at Marseilles to go to Algeria, where important questions connected with the organisation of the country demanded his presence. His absence lasted for some weeks. Before his departure he handed over the Regency to the Empress, who was to preside over the Council of Ministers and the Privy Council, of which it will be remembered Prince Napoleon was Vice-President.

The unveiling of a monument at Ajaccio to the memory of Napoleon I and his four brothers was to take place in the course of this month. Prince Napoleon went to take part in this ceremony, and on the 15th May made a speech which on many points was a masterly one. Unfortunately, in the midst of a series of historical pictures vigorously sketched, the orator was unable to refrain from ungracious remarks about the policy followed by our Government. Basing himself on the actions and words of Napoleon I, he advanced a plea for the most absolute liberty and, returning to his favourite idea, attacked from top to bottom the Temporal Power of the Pope which had our diplomatic support.

When the Emperor received the text of this speech at

Algiers he showed very great dissatisfaction. "As severe with his pen as he was gentle in his words," he dictated to his secretary, Francheschini Pietri, a very stern letter, which he sent to Paris. At the same time as Captain Le Gallifet handed it to Prince Napoleon, the Empress received a copy, with instructions to have it inserted in the *Moniteur*. It appeared on the morning of the 27th May. The Prince replied to it on the same day, and sent in his resignation as Vice-President of the Privy Council and President of the Commission of the *Exposition Universelle* of 1867, so that the evening papers published in the same issue both the Emperor's letter and the Prince's reply thereto.

His resignations were accepted. The Emperor returned to Paris on the 8th June. The Prince did not present himself at the Tuileries. He sent his principal Aide-de-camp, General de Franconière. The Emperor talked with him for a long time, and charged him to tell the Prince to come and see him on the following day. Unfortunately that same afternoon the Prince met with a carriage accident. He was somewhat seriously bruised, and was unable to leave Meudon before the 18th June ; he informed the Emperor, who made an appointment with him for the following day.

The Prince wrote a very curious account of this interview, which lasted between one and two and a half hours. It will be found in the Appendix, Note v., pp. 272–6.

The Emperor to Prince Napoleon
Paris, 27th April, 1865.

MY DEAR NAPOLEON,—I am leaving on Saturday for Africa, where I expect to remain for three weeks or a month. I hope to see you before my departure, but if you have not returned by then I should like to tell you that I should be very happy if you will kindly remain in

Paris during my absence and add to the moral authority of the Empress by your presence.

Tell me what projects you have in view, and with, etc.,

NAPOLEON.

The Emperor to Prince Napoleon[1]

Algiers, 23rd May, 1865.

Monsieur et très cher Cousin,—I am unable to refrain from putting on record the painful impression the reading of your speech delivered at Ajaccio has given me.

When leaving you with the Empress and my son during my absence as Vice-President of the Privy Council, I wished to give you a proof of my regard and trust, and was hoping that your presence, your conduct, and your words would show the unity reigning in our family. The political programme which you place under the *ægis* of the Emperor can only serve the enemies of my Government. To views which I cannot admit, you add sentiments of hatred and animosity which are no longer suitable in these days. In order to be able to apply the ideas held by the Emperor to present times, it is requisite to have passed through the hard school of responsibility and power. Besides, can we, pygmies that we are, really appreciate at its true value the grand historic figure of Napoleon! As though we were standing in front of some colossal statue, we are powerless to take in the whole of it at one and the same moment. We never see more than the side which meets our view; hence arises the inadequacy of the impression produced, and differences of opinion.

But what is clear to the eyes of everybody is that with a view to keep down the spirit of anarchy—that formidable enemy of real liberty—the Emperor established first in his own family and then in his Government a severe

---

[1] Published in the *Moniteur.*

discipline which admitted of the will and action of one only. I shall be unable henceforth to separate myself from the same rule of conduct.

With these words, *Monsieur et très cher Cousin*, I pray that God may have you in His holy keeping.

NAPOLEON.

Prince Napoleon to the Emperor
Palais Royal, 27th May, 1865.

SIRE,—Following the letter of Your Majesty of the 23rd May, and its publication in the *Moniteur*, I send in my resignation as Vice-President of the Privy Council and President of the Commission of the *Exposition Universelle* of 1867.

Veuillez agréer, Sire, l'hommage du profond et respectueux attachement avec lequel je suis.

De Votre Majesté,
Le trés dévoué Cousin,
NAPOLEON (JÉRÔME).

Two letters, all that we possess for the end of the year 1865, prove that if, as a consequence of this affair, the relations between the two cousins officially remained strained, the misunderstanding was less serious in reality than the public believed.

The first was written by the Emperor to the Prince; the second by the Prince to the Empress, who had just met with an accident at Neuchâtel, the consequences of which might have been serious.

The Emperor to Prince Napoleon
Fontainebleau, 29th August, 1865.

MY DEAR COUSIN,—I have received the volume of the *Correspondance* which you sent me. We might be able to increase the subsidy allotted for the impression if Marshal

Vaillant can see his way to make a contribution from his own department. I will discuss this with him on my return.

I have no objections to make to the journeys you tell me about, and with, etc.,

NAPOLEON.

Prince Napoleon to the Empress
Prangins, 12th October, 1865.

I was very happy to learn direct from Your Majesty that the accident at Neuchâtel will not leave any traces on my Cousin's pretty face. What you say about Arenenberg awakens tender memories of the past. As for the future nothing can be more precious to me than Your Majesty's counsel, and the reflections, so nobly expressed, on the *rôle de la jeunesse*. I am living peacefully in the country with all my small family until the bad weather comes to drive us away. We take pretty drives in the neighbourhood, and really, I am beginning to think that my true vocation is that of an agriculturist who is a bit of a philosopher.

Taking advantage of the permission the Emperor gave me when writing to me in August, I have promised Clotilde to take her to Italy to see her sister the Queen of Portugal. We do not yet know the date of their arrival, as punctuality is not one of the qualities of the young Portuguese couple, but there are many others like them.

Veuillez agréer, Madame, etc.,

NAPOLEON (JEROME).

Nevertheless a coldness undoubtedly existed between the two cousins. For a year the Prince kept himself at a distance, maintained silence, and lived for the greater part of the time outside Paris, in the country, or travelling. But towards the end of the spring of 1866 events did not allow him to remain any longer in retreat. The situation between Prussia and Austria was becoming more and more strained. They were practically on the eve of a war which, whatever the results might be, might entail the immediate consequence of dragging us also into the dispute.

On the 19th June the Prince went to discuss the question with the Emperor. In order to give a clear definition of events he handed to him a note which will be found in the Appendix, Note vi., pp. 276-7. He reminded him that it had been mooted a few months before to make him President of the exhibition which was in preparation for 1867. This idea had not been capable of realisation. Now that possibilities of war were appearing he insisted on having a provisional appointment, while they were waiting, such as the Command of the Guard, to be exchanged for a more active appointment in the event of war.

On the following day the Emperor wrote:

The Emperor to Prince Napoleon
Paris, 21st June, 1866.

MY DEAR COUSIN,—I have given mature reflection to the request you made to me two days ago, and I will explain all that is in my mind. Since what happened last year a divergence of opinion has existed between us. The questions will now be: 1. To put an end to this divergence in the eyes of the world; 2. To find some position for you which will testify to our good understanding.

I will put aside this second question for the moment, as it presents difficulties in the actual state of affairs, but what I am anxious to do is to draw to your attention the fact that during my sojourn in Africa it was the Empress who was called upon by me to manifest my disapproval to you, and therefore I think it would be suitable that the reconciliation should also come through her hands. It amounts to this, that if I make it up with you without her intervention she might say rightly that I charge her with the disagreeable commissions and leave the others on one side.

Up till now I have spoken to no one about our conversation, and I think it would be a nice thing for you to empower the Empress to speak to me of your wish, and even to communicate it later to Rouher, for it is only right that those who have compromised themselves with you in carrying out my intentions should be the agents in putting matters right again between us.

I hope you will regard these reflections as representing only my desire to restore harmony between us.

With, etc.,

NAPOLEON.

Next day the two cousins had another conversation at the Tuileries, of which the Prince kept an analysis. He showed himself quite disposed to ask the Empress to intervene, but refused the interference in his affairs of M. Rouher, against whom he harboured complaints in connection with the 1867 exhibition. He insisted especially on receiving a military appointment. The Emperor feared that the taking of this step here and now would alarm public opinion, which was in a very nervous state already, and would make people believe that our entry into war was imminent. As a set-off he undertook to give a military command to the Prince if war eventuated. On his promising this it was agreed that the situation between them should remain provisionally in its then state, and that the Prince should go to Havre, for a sea voyage, or to Switzerland, but that his absences

[1] The Minister of State.

should always be of short duration, and that when passing through Paris he should go and see the Emperor.

A good understanding was thus restored between them, and this is proved by the mission the Emperor entrusted to the Prince in July 1866 when he sent him to Italy in order to make the King sign an armistice with Austria.[1]

Although the following letter from the Prince to the Emperor presents an official character, we think it should be included on account of the interest of the subject. It shows the spirit in which the Prince directed the work of the Commission charged with the publication of the correspondence of Napoleon I.

Prince Napoleon to the Emperor
Paris, the   January, 1867.

SIRE,—In conformity with the Decree of the 3rd February, 1864, we have the honour to render an account to Your Majesty of the present state of our labours in the publication of the correspondence of the Emperor, Napoleon I.

In our last report we submitted to Your Majesty the principles which were to guide us; experience has shown us that they were good.

We have wished to avoid too numerous repetitions of the same idea, often reproduced almost identically the same in several documents. Those who have made a study of the methods of the Emperor are aware that when Napoleon I gave an order he saw to its execution himself, especially when it was a question of military operations. He wrote reminders one after the other, even to secondary agents. Is there any need to bring into prominence a repetition of details such as these, which might serve no good purpose and might be wearisome?

Our invariable principle has been never to modify

[1] The account of this mission will form the subject of a volume shortly.

or mutilate any of the documents published : we are giving the text with scrupulous and even minute fidelity. We are making a point of bearing this in mind so as to render all misunderstanding impossible.

Will Your Majesty be pleased to note well the proofs to which we are submitting the memory of Napoleon I. We are exhibiting in the full light of day all the actions of his Government, we are laying bare[1] the secrets of his most intimate thoughts. What Government in the world has been unveiled to history with such complete frankness? No other Government in France has acted with the same absolute openness, and confidence in the judgment of posterity: far from allowing their State papers to be published[2] some have taken measures of precaution against the possibility of compromising publications: large numbers of very important documents have disappeared from our archives.

We hardly find more than one single Government abroad, of any reigning dynasty, which has made public the letters written by its founder, but the whole of his political correspondence has been excluded from the edition of the works of Frederic II of Prussia, as is indicated in the preface.

We have faith in the good sense of the public. We feel that the light of justice should permeate every work on Napoleon, and we wait for time and enlightened men to appreciate this loyal publication at its full importance.

We have issued volumes 16, 17, 18, 19, and 20 since the year 1864, when the new Commission began to function. If our labours have not gone forward more quickly the reason is that we thought we ought to make researches in the different offices of archives in Germany, England, Spain, Italy, and Portugal. However limited in expenditure these researches have been, they have diminished

---

[1] Marginal correction : " *livrons.*"   [2] Marginal correction : " *connaître.*"

the funds at our disposal, and we find ourselves unable to meet the expense of issuing a larger number of volumes without exceeding the limits assigned to us. In order to avoid in the future a similar inconvenience, we have requested the Ministry of the Emperor's Household and of Beaux Arts to transfer this allocation from the ordinary to the extraordinary budget. This transference secures for a credit which is temporary by its nature the place it ought to occupy in the non-permanent expenditure.

We have utilised what time the smallness of our resources has allowed us in examining documents which go far beyond the period reached by the publication. It was a method of diminishing our general expenses and of hastening the end of our labours.

To-day we can anticipate with some certainty that the correspondence from 1811 to 1815 will require six volumes, that from 1815 to 1821 the writings of Napoleon will not form more than three or four volumes, and that these nine or ten volumes can be finished in two years.

May it please you, Sire, etc.,
The Prince-President of the Commission,
NAPOLEON (JEROME).

At this same the Prince experienced a great joy. In face of the crevices which were beginning to appear in the imperial edifice in no uncertain fashion, Napoleon III, in a return to his former ideas, felt that liberty alone could consolidate his power, and that the hour had come to take a further step in the direction of a constitutional *régime*. On the 19th January, 1867, he requested the resignation of his Ministers in a letter to them unfolding his new reforms, which was inserted in the *Moniteur* on the following day. These were too much in conformity with the principles of Prince Napoleon for him not to congratulate him at once.

Prince Napoleon to the Emperor
Paris, Sunday, 20th January, 1867.

SIRE,—Yesterday, the moment I learnt of the great events which are in preparation, I presented myself at Your Majesty's, who was unable, and possibly unwilling, to receive me. I only went, however, for the purpose of shaking you cordially by the hand, of congratulating you, and of expressing to you the joy with which your new policy was inspiring me. Your *acte additionnel* in favour of liberty is an immense act. It is good for you, Sire, for your son, and for France. It will cause an immense sensation in Europe, where it will make us again take up a position of great prestige if it is loyally and skilfully applied.

The French people have always understood you when you trusted them.

Coming at a good time and on your own initiative, a wise law concerning the Press and on the right to hold meetings will be useful and glorious reforms, and not concessions torn from you and a source of weakness. For my part, you know my old convictions; partly brought up by you I have only had two passions—glory, and the liberty of our country brought about by the Napoleons. Persevere. Do not allow yourself to be stopped by egotistic and narrow-minded people, especially those of little education, and when the time comes for history to be able to say that after re-establishing order and giving to France a real glory you have been capable of initiating real and practical liberty—oh! you will have little cause to envy the greatest sovereigns.

This is the first cry from my heart which I take leave to send straight to your own.

May it please, etc.,

NAPOLEON (JEROME).

The Emperor to Prince Napoleon[1]
Paris, 19th January, 1867.

MY DEAR COUSIN,—I did not receive you yesterday because I was engaged in writing the letter which appeared to-day. I am much touched with the way in which you regard the new phase on which we are entering, and with, etc.,

NAPOLEON.

Prince Napoleon to the Emperor[2]
Paris, 24th January, 1867.

SIRE,—I thank Your Majesty for your last short note. It is very precious to me since it is a mark of your regard.

As Your Majesty appears to wish that I should not come and discuss the grave political events taking place, I will keep away. I feel, however, that the duties resulting from my position and the memories of our old friendship make it incumbent on me to communicate to Your Majesty information which may render the new policy fruitful.

The publication of your liberal programme produced at first an effect of satisfaction all the more real because it was unexpected. The newspapers enjoying a monopoly, the majority of which are hostile, had some difficulty in concealing their embarrassment beneath a show of reticence, and objections as to small details. Our enemies were put out of countenance.

A striking effect was in preparation. The appointment of your new Ministry[3] has suddenly altered these

---
[1] This letter is dated the 19th in error; it was written on the 20th.
[2] Emile Ollivier knew of this letter, which he reproduced in his *Empire Libéral* (Vol. IX., p. 219), but his text is slightly different from that which we give here.
[3] Rouher: Minister of State and Finance; De la Valette: Minister of the Interior; Marshal Niel: War; Moustier: Foreign Affairs; Baroche: Justice; Admiral Rigault de Genouilly: Marine; Duruy: Public Instruction; Forçade de la Roquette: Public Works; Marshal Vaillant: the Emperor's Household. Rouher, Baroche, and De la Valette had belonged to the previous Cabinet.

dispositions, and one hears these words spoken everywhere, "It is not seriously meant." M. Thiers exclaimed, "It is a take in; but we shall know how to profit by it."

People repeat on all sides that it is intended, by skilful editing and the pitfalls lurking under the new arrangements, to take away the benefits of the principles so explicitly conceded by the Emperor; mistrust is general. If this impression continues a hostile and formidable turning round in public opinion will take place, and your generous initiative will have weakened instead of strengthening you.

How could it be otherwise?

You change the Ministers of the special departments, and keep the political Ministers. You even keep those who have no voice and cannot go to the Chamber.

People appear to think, Sire, that M. Rouher is too omnipotent as a Minister of State, the only really important instrument of the Government: in addition you give him the Ministry of Finance, you leave him his relations, and swell the number of his creatures. M. Rouher is a man of great talent and of real value; he has, besides, rendered too many services for Your Majesty to part with him, and the idea of appointing him to the Finance Ministry appears excellent to me. But if he is necessary and suitably placed in an administrative department, ought he to retain the task of representing and defending your new internal policy? A new order of things requires new men. Remember, Sire, our Uncle in 1815 chose the support of Benjamin Constant, Sismondi, and appointed Carnot, the member of the committee of Public Safety, to be Minister of the Interior. What confidence will be inspired by the words of a Minister who will be led to praise that which a year ago he condemned as seditious? If he says the time was not suitable then, people will reply that, as the Government was stronger a year ago than it is to-day, your concessions are only an act springing from weakness.

If the sovereign adapts himself to the circumstances and regulates his conduct in accordance with them, the country will be grateful to him, for, inasmuch as he cannot be removed, he must be in a position to make changes. But Ministers do not possess the immunity of a sovereign: if they are self-respecting they should serve the Emperor with their ideas and fall with them. They can only enjoy consideration and be serviceable on this condition. The evil of our times, Sire, consists in the instability and the lack of backbone in men's characters, and the weakening of conscience; and the spectacle of Ministers being ready to uphold, without making any transition from one day to the next the policy they have combated, or remaining at their post with a view to bring it to grief by intriguing against it, is not calculated to raise the *morale* of a nation. May Your Majesty be persuaded that no spirit of barren criticism has decided me to write to you. My sole motive is my desire to see the success assured of a policy of which I ardently approve, and which I see with grief is being compromised by the weaknesses and uncertainties with which it is being put into execution.

Accept my observations with kindness, and do not see in them anything but the expression of my deep devotion to you and to your son.

Agréez, Sire, l'hommage, etc.,

NAPOLEON (JEROME).

The Emperor to Prince Napoleon
Paris, 28th January, 1867.[1]

MY DEAR COUSIN,—I do not refuse by any means to have a talk with you, and if you had come and dined

---

[1] By a slip of the pen this letter bears the date 28*th July,* whereas it should, incontestably, be 28*th January,* and is a reply to Prince Napoleon's letter of the 24th January.

last Monday I could have wished for nothing better than to have discussed the affairs of the day with you. Your observations would be just if my Government was a government by Parliament, like that of Louis Philippe. In his day, when Ministers were changed, the entire policy was changed. The responsible Ministers who went out bore with them the entire responsibility for the past. It cannot be like that to-day. Up to a certain point I am responsible for all that Ministers have said or done, and if I take the initiative in making reforms this does not condemn the past in any way. Besides, in the present circumstances, as I did not possess any man either at the Ministry of the Interior or at the Foreign Office who was capable of any skilfulness in language, it was absolutely necessary to retain M. Rouher in his quality as a Minister of State, so that he might be authorised to deal with all questions.

Lastly, I could not abandon the greater part of the *corps législatif,* who have always shown towards me absolute devotion, by taking on new men who are complete strangers to what has occurred.

I am very glad, my dear Cousin, to give you these explanations, and with, etc., NAPOLEON.

The Emperor to Prince Napoleon[1]
Palais des Tuileries, 30th June, 1867.

MY DEAR COUSIN,—I had a request sent to you to come to the Tuileries for the reception of the Sultan,[2] but I think it will be more suitable that you should come with me to the railway station. I therefore beg you will come to the Tuileries at half-past three. We can go together to the Gare de Lyon.

With, etc., NAPOLEON.

---
[1] This letter was dictated, and only signed by the Emperor.
[2] The Sultan Abd-ul-Azis came to Paris to visit the Exhibition.

CHAPTER XV

The last years of the Empire—The Pope's appeal to France for support against the threats of the forces of Garibaldi—Defeat of the Garibaldians at Mentana, and the second occupation of Rome by French troops—Incidents of the Elections of May 1869.

WHILE he was continuing the publication of the *Correspondance de Napoleon I*, Prince Napoleon had been in a position to see what was taking place at the office of the Archives of the Empire. He had spoken about it to the Emperor, and on the 24th September, 1867, he wrote to him another note on the subject. In his opinion too little restraint was exercised in communicating State Papers. "Never before have there been published," he said, "so many works hostile to the Empire taken from the documents at the Archives." He concluded by proposing to modify the rules of the Archives, to go back to the former State Secretariat, and to replace the Director, M. de Laborde, by someone else. He also asked to be given special authority to consult and, when necessary, to take away with him, certain papers relating to the Imperial family from 1815 to 1848. We shall see that the Emperor refused to remove M. de Laborde. It was not until April in the following year that he withdrew him from his post and entrusted it to M. Maury. He appointed the former a Senator in compensation.

The Emperor to Prince Napoleon[1]

Biarritz, 5th October, 1867.

MY DEAR COUSIN,—I have received your letter relative to the Archives of the Empire. I share your

[1] This letter was dictated, and only signed by the Emperor.

views completely, and if I have not yet replaced M. de Laborde, it is because I have been trying to give something in compensation to a man who comes of an honourable family, and who has just been struck down in his dearest affections. As for the papers connected with our family, I myself desire to run through them as soon as I return to Paris, and I will afterwards hasten to send them to you.
With, etc.,
NAPOLEON.

On the 23rd October, 1867, the Emperor of Austria arrived in Paris. Napoleon III and Prince Napoleon received him at the railway station, and the population gave him a very warm welcome. A few days afterwards he sent the Prince the decoration of the Order of Saint Etienne.

The Emperor to Prince Napoleon
Paris, 29th October, 1867.

MY DEAR COUSIN,—I authorise you with great pleasure to accept the decoration of Saint Etienne which the Emperor of Austria has sent you.

I should have been very glad to give you the sporting rights of Sénart, but this is what happened. At the time of the re-establishment of the Empire sporting rights everywhere were already let. I was obliged to indemnify the holders, giving 50,000 francs to one, and 60,000 francs to another. The sporting rights at Fontainebleau belonged to a joint membership consisting of Fould, Caumont La Force, etc. They would not entertain the idea of an indemnity, and gave up their rights to me on condition that I made over to them another forest. As the Duc de la Force and M. Adolphe Fould are still in possession of the forest of Sénart I can hardly turn them out.

I regret not being able to render you this small service, and with, etc.,

NAPOLEON.

This matter was quite a secondary one. Another important affair was occupying the mind of the Prince. Public attention was being directed again towards Rome. On the 2nd December, 1866, the French flag had ceased to float on the castle of St. Angelo, and our occupying force had returned to France. After a few months of tranquillity, the Pope, who now had only his own troops to rely upon, found himself being threatened by the armed bands of Garibaldi at the beginning of the autumn of 1867. According to the terms which had been agreed upon, the Italian troops scattered through his States should undoubtedly have offered opposition to any violation of his territory, but through secret connivance they allowed the invaders to filter through little by little. Rome was being threatened. In his distress the Pope applied to Napoleon III who, on the 17th October, informed him that he might count upon the assistance of France. This was an announcement of an approaching relief expedition.

On the same day Prince Napoleon wrote to the Emperor, who had just returned to St. Cloud after a fairly long stay at Biarritz:

Prince Napoleon to the Emperor
Palais Royal, 17th October, 1867, 1 p.m.

SIRE,—I have just this moment received the following telegram from my father-in-law:

"Florence, 17th October, 10.30 a.m.

"I learn that the Emperor has decided to send troops to Rome. You can understand the effect this will produce in Italy. The consequences will be terrible for both nations. Do what you can to prevent this misfortune and reply to me at once."

This is the first news I have received from Italy about these matters, as my father-in-law has not written to me for over three months. I am replying to the King in the following telegram which, I hope, will have the approval of Your Majesty:

"I am absolutely without knowledge of what is taking place concerning a French intervention at Rome. I am a perfect stranger to everything, not having seen the Emperor for a long time. Your Majesty can guess what I feel about such an event."

May it please you, Sire, etc.,

NAPOLEON (JEROME).

The overthrow of the followers of Garibaldi at Mentana (3rd November), and the occupation anew of the Holy City by our troops, put back to a subsequent date the realisation of the dream of making Rome the capital of Italy. Prince Napoleon, very hostile to an intervention on our part, did not conceal his chagrin. He retired to Prangins, making known his desire to prolong his stay there in order to avoid the New Year receptions in Paris. Nevertheless, yielding to the wishes expressed by the Emperor, he thought better of this decision, and returned to the Palais Royal. But he showed his intention forthwith of publishing his opinions in the newspapers. He drew up a protest against the Temporal Power which he proposed to issue. It required the intervention of the Emperor to prevent his giving effect to this design. The Prince yielded.

The Emperor to Prince Napoleon
St. Cloud, 10th November, 1867.

MY DEAR COUSIN,—I give you permission to go to Prangins, and with, etc.,
NAPOLEON.

Prince Napoleon to the Emperor
Paris, December, 1867.

SIRE,—As soon as I was informed that Your Majesty feels it to be more suitable for me to be here for the 1st January, I left the country. I begged M. Rouher, who came twice to see me, to ask you, and Her Majesty, the Empress, to allow me to give you a few explanations verbally on what I have heard concerning the bad interpretation which has been given to my conduct. I explained to the Minister of State how much I desired that the Emperor would be kind enough to approve of the conduct I feel is incumbent on me, in order to avoid any possible future breach. But to bring this about it was necessary to see Your Majesty, as what I have to say, by force of circumstances would require a long and detailed interview. M. Rouher told me yesterday that the Emperor was too much occupied at St. Cloud to receive me, and that he would give me notice as soon as you returned to Paris. I therefore await Your Majesty's commands; but what I did not tell the Minister, reserving to myself to do so directly, is that there is a personal matter on which I should have liked to consult Your Majesty. If I am not able to do this I trust the Emperor will thoroughly realise that that is not on account of any wish of mine.

May it please you, Sire, etc.,
NAPOLEON (JEROME).

The Emperor to Prince Napoleon
10*th January*, 1868.

MY DEAR COUSIN,—The more I ponder over our conversation the more I experience the wish to prove to you how greatly to be regretted it would be if you have the appearance of separating yourself from me. In ordinary times it is always vexatious to exhibit in public any division which exists in a family, but under the present circumstances any publication in opposition to my policy would appear a bad act on your part. In reality the circumstances are grave. I am being attacked on all sides, and your opposition would only look like an act springing from weakness. In spite of the sentiments of friendship I have for you, I feel bound to tell you again that if, notwithstanding my formally expressed wish, you are determined to take a separate course, I shall be compelled to give public notice of a sensational rupture between us, which would cause me much pain and would not save you.

With, etc., NAPOLEON.

Prince Napoleon to the Emperor
Palais Royal, 14th *January*, 1868.

SIRE,—I have received Your Majesty's letter and have stopped the publication which one of my friends was going to issue. I did not reply sooner because I had certain arrangements to make, the setting-up having been completed and the proofs already printed.

I am deeply pained over your letter, and at seeing how greatly Your Majesty has changed towards me since our conversation. I have neither to accept nor to refuse; I must submit to the complete abstention you impose upon me, which creates so sad a situation for me by taking away from me the rights possessed by the least

citizen, and which places me in the position of a suspect and a pariah in my own country! May you see, Sire, in the sacrifice I am making to your wishes the greatest testimony of deference and devotion that I can give you! May it please you, Sire, etc.,
NAPOLEON (JEROME).

On the 29th February Prince Napoleon left for North Germany, whence he returned on the 22nd March, after having had some very interesting conversations with Bismarck in Berlin. On the 31st May he set out again, this time for South Germany, which he visited as a tourist, as well as Austria, Hungary, and Roumania. He returned to France on the 27th July.

The Emperor to Prince Napoleon[1]
Plombières, 3rd August, 1868.

MY DEAR COUSIN,—I learn of your arrival in Paris with pleasure. I have followed your travels with interest, and from all I hear they have been accomplished under the best auspices.

I imagine you will require a rest, and hope the sea-bathing will do you good.

Give Clotilde many kind messages from me, and with, etc., NAPOLEON.

Fontainebleau, 12th August, 1868.

MY DEAR COUSIN,[2]—I am expecting to hold a review in the Champs Élysées on the 14th at 3 o'clock. I shall be charmed if you will accompany me, but, in any case, if you care to come to the Tuileries at 1 o'clock we could have a chat together.

With, etc., NAPOLEON.

[1] The Prince received this letter in Paris on the 4th August.
[2] The Prince received this letter in Paris on the same day, and kept the appointment.

As a matter of fact for some years past the Prince had kept out of politics and lived in almost complete privacy. At the end of March 1869 he deemed the situation of France to be so uncertain abroad, and so dangerous within, that at first he conceived the idea of speaking out openly to the country from the tribune in the Senate in connection with the debate on the budget. On further reflection he feared to " *ébranler au lieu de remédier,*" as he wrote, and chose rather to give expression to the manner in which he regarded things in a long memorandum addressed to the Emperor in the form of a letter (31st March, 1869).

The Emperor to Prince Napoleon
4th April, 1869.

MY DEAR COUSIN,—I must first thank you for the memorandum you have sent me, for I much prefer this kind of communication to a speech in the Senate, which would place the public in the secret of our differences of view. I should have to write several pages to give a reply to the statement of your opinions. I will confine myself to telling you that while I fully appreciate the motives which have dictated your memorandum, I cannot share your way of looking at things.

To-day firmness is required within. Abroad, we must wait on events without trying to precipitate them. Be assured that I shall always receive with pleasure the expression of your reflections, and with, etc.,

NAPOLEON.

In May 1869 elections took place. The Prince interpreted their results in a note which he sent to the Emperor on the 28th May (Appendix, Note vii., pp. 277–82).

At these same elections Ernest Renan was a candidate for the Seine-et-Marne Department, together with M. de

The Second Empire and Its Downfall

Jeaucourt, and M. de Jouvencel, who had been in disgrace in connection with the events of the 2nd December. A report having been circulated that the Prince was advising Renan to retire in favour of M. de Jouvencel, the Emperor wrote to him the following short note:

The Emperor to Prince Napoleon
Paris, 28th May, 1869.

MY DEAR COUSIN,—People have written to the Minister of the Interior that you are making M. Renan hand over his votes to M. Jouvencel—a dangerous and a very hostile man. I hope this is not true, for it is very important for us to unite our efforts against our common enemies. I beg you will tell me how the case stands.

With, etc., NAPOLEON.

We may add that at the second scrutiny (6–7 June) M. de Jouvencel was elected by 10,454 votes against M. de Jeaucourt's 9,165, and Renan's 8,866. The Prince was in close relations with Renan. This we have seen in the correspondence which passed between them, recently reproduced in the *Revue de Deux Mondes*. This intimacy is confirmed by the following undated letter, of which we have neither a minute nor the original. We quote it from the *Papiers et Correspondance de la Famille Impériale.* These papers were found in the Tuileries in 1870.

Prince Napoleon to the Emperor
Undated.

SIRE,—You will be astonished, perhaps, to receive this letter, especially when you see that it mentions nothing about politics, personal affairs, or requests. M. Renan is my friend: he is a very superior *esprit*; I see him often, and we discuss philosophy. He is publishing a collection of various articles, and I have made him promise to add a preface to it which I am sending you, and for which I ask you to spare half an hour. I do not share *all* the ideas of M. Renan, but a great part. I do not think you will regret reading this. Permit me to hope that it will afford you a few moments of interest and lofty reflections—my sole end. I am addressing the man, the thinker, far more than the sovereign : after all, beneath the purple mantle there must remain a heart, and beneath the crown, a head ; I am very sure of this, and I have been unable to resist the desire to make you read these lines. If they bore you, forgive me, and above all do not mistake the very simple motive which has caused me to make you this communication.

May it please you, Sire, etc.,

NAPOLEON (JEROME).

The two short notes which follow show the good relations existing at this time between the cousins, notwithstanding their political differences.

The Emperor to Prince Napoleon
2nd November, 1869.

MY DEAR COUSIN,—I will see you with pleasure on Thursday at Compiègne for dinner.

With, etc., NAPOLEON.

Prince Napoleon to the Emperor
(Telegram to Compiègne)

Paris, 6th November, 1869, 12.15 A.M.

Since yesterday morning Clotilde and I have been receiving very grave news concerning the health of the King of Italy. My wife, who is much disturbed, wishes to leave for San Rossore, near Pisa, where her father is. I have requested the Italian Minister to write to the President of the Council to sound him concerning our

journey. The train does not leave Paris until the evening.
The news we may receive will make Clotilde and me wish
to leave at once. I beg leave to request the Emperor to
assent to our departure if necessary. News, direct from
the Aide-de-camp of the King at 10.45 this morning,
bad. Please let me know your wishes at once.
NAPOLEON (JEROME).

The Emperor to Prince Napoleon
(Telegram)
Strongly approve your departure, and deplore the cause
rendering it necessary.
NAPOLEON.

The illness of the King of Italy did not have the fatal
issue which was feared at the moment.

The Commission of the *Correspondance de Napoleon I*
having completed its labours the Prince wrote the following letter to the Emperor and, a few days after, sent him
a note (Appendix, Note viii., pp. 282-84.) relative to the
possibility of collecting in one spot all the letters of
Napoleon.

Prince Napoleon to the Emperor
Paris, 22nd November, 1869.

SIRE,—The *Correspondance de Napoleon I* is finished,
and I am engaged in winding it up. Fifteen hundred
and fifty copies have been printed. As the two first
volumes were given away freely by the former Commission I have only 127 complete collections remaining.
I am sending them to the Minister of the Emperor's
Household and Beaux Arts, but before doing so will
take the commands of Your Majesty on a proposal I wish
to make.

I thought it might be suitable to present each of the members of the Commission who have lent me their assistance a certain number of copies—five at least—*gratis*.

There are also some meritorious employés in the office of the Secretariat who appear to me to be worthy of the same favour.

The following is the list of persons I propose to Your Majesty for this exceptional distribution : they are the members *still living* of the Commission :

MM. Amédée Thierry, General Favé, Alfred Maury.

Those attached to the Secretariat :

MM. Rapetti (secretary), Judenne, Lacroix, Gallet de Kulture, Blandeau.

May it please you, Sire, etc.,

NAPOLEON (JEROME).

Approved.[1]

The members[2] of the Commission have zealously given their time and labour and will only possess as a mark of your satisfaction these copies which I beg you will authorise me to transmit to them. Your Majesty, in case of approval, need only mark it at the bottom of this letter.

The Emperor to Prince Napoleon
26th November, 1869.

MY DEAR COUSIN,—I have commissioned Bourbaki to examine the invention of the Polish General. I shall be very glad to see the apparatus one morning. I shall be receiving a few people on Saturday, and shall be very glad if Clotilde and you will care to come to the *soirée* (9.30).

I will see what I can do for your two *protégés*.

With, etc., NAPOLEON.

[1] Added by the Emperor in the margin.
[2] The postscript is in the hand of the Prince, while the rest of the letter, with the exception of the signature, is written by a secretary.

25th January, 1870.

MY DEAR COUSIN,—I have just signed the appointment of General Franconière as *Grand Officier*.
I am very glad to tell you this.
With, etc., NAPOLEON.

4th March, 1870.

MY DEAR COUSIN,—I have read carefully the note you have sent me.[1] I regret to tell you that I am not of your opinion. The ideas set forth in your memorandum are diametrically, radically, opposed to my own. It would be superfluous, therefore, to listen to a further development of the idea. I shall sink, perhaps, but standing upright, and not cankered at the roots.
With, etc.,

NAPOLEON.

21st March, 1870.

MY DEAR COUSIN,—I will receive to-morrow, Tuesday, at 10.30, the Commission of the *Correspondance de l'Empereur Napoleon I*, and shall have great pleasure in congratulating them on the accomplishment of their task, as also their President.
With, etc., NAPOLEON.

3rd June, 1870.

MY DEAR COUSIN,—I have no objection whatever to the voyage you contemplate.[2]
With, etc.,

NAPOLEON.

---

[1] This refers to a note drawn up by the Prince on the 18th January, 1870, on the suggestion of a *plébiscite* for a new constitution. (Appendix, Note IX, pp. 285-8.)
[2] A voyage to the North Cape.

CHAPTER XVI

The Franco-German War of 1870—Prince Napoleon sent on a Mission to the King of Italy to endeavour to gain his active support for France—The disaster at Sedan of General MacMahon's army on 1st September, and the capitulation of the Emperor; the Emperor a captive at Wilhelmshohe—The Empress Eugénie at Chislehurst—Stormy interviews between The Empress and Prince Napoleon—The Emperor at Chislehurst—The forthcoming Elections in France—Death of the Emperor at Chislehurst, 9th January, 1873.

A CALM often precedes the storm. This was the case in 1870 before the war. At the beginning of July so little apprehended were complications near at hand that "Ministers and Diplomatists almost everywhere were going to their summer residences in the country." Thus Prince Napoleon in the company of some friends left on July 2nd for a cruise to the North Cape.

Warned during the voyage of the gravity which events had suddenly assumed, he hastened to return to France. He was back in Paris on the 24th July. At first it was proposed to give him the command of a landing party destined to operate on the shores of the Baltic. Then this idea was given up. For the moment he was attached to the Emperor's staff, without any special command.

After our first reverses on the morning of the 19th of August the Emperor decided to send the Prince to King Victor Emmanuel with a view to endeavouring to draw Italy and even Austria to come to our assistance. The Prince hesitated to accept a mission the uselessness of which he foresaw. He asked to be allowed to share the lot of our soldiers to the end. The Emperor appealed to his devotion in terms that there was no resisting. He left for Florence. The telegrams that passed between them tell us how these negotiations fared.

The Emperor to Prince Napoleon
25*th July*, 1870.

MY DEAR COUSIN,—We have spoken at the Council of what concerns you. This is what has been decided : Prince Napoleon will be Commander-in-Chief of the troops landed and of the Allied troops of Denmark. The Navy will act independently under the orders of Admiral Bouet, who will, however, be instructed to concert all operations in agreement with the Prince.

From now until then you can come with me. I am counting on leaving on Wednesday or Thursday.

With, etc.,

NAPOLEON.

His Imperial Highness, Prince Napoleon, having been charged by the Emperor with a Mission to Italy, all authorities are required to give him aid and assistance should the need arise.

Given at the Imperial Headquarters at the Camp at Châlons.

19th August, 1870.   NAPOLEON.[1]

Prince Napoleon to the Emperor
(Cipher telegram addressed to the Emperor at Châlons by way of Paris)

Florence, 21st August, 1870. *Noon.*

Arrived this morning. Saw King and Ministers. Italy well disposed, but powerless in a military sense for a month. Politically will do what you wish. In military sense nothing without Austria, who will have to declare herself shortly. If you have any wishes regarding Italy's political action tell me ; she will act.

NAPOLEON (JEROME).

---

[1] Emile Ollivier gives the text of this order in *l'Empire Libéral* (Vol. XVII., p. 294) as having been signed by Marshal MacMahon. The original distinctly bears the Emperor's signature.

His Imperial Highness, Prince Napoleon, Florence
(Telegram partly in cipher)
Imperial Headquarters, 22nd August, 1870.

Thank you for your telegram. Am pleased with the good dispositions of the King. Vimercati,[1] who is here, thinks the King might be able to send us some troops; I doubt it. In any case the time for negotiations has not yet arrived. We have good news from Bazaine. I hope things will go better.

NAPOLEON.

Prince Napoleon to the Emperor
(Telegram in cipher to the Imperial Headquarters, *viâ* Paris)
Florence, 23rd August, 1870.

Your Majesty's telegram received. Did not write, knowing the King had done so. I am pressing them here as much as I can. Ministers very ill-disposed. Generals favourable. Chamber divided. They have waited three days for a reply from Vienna, where King and Ministers have written three times sharply. If news not too bad at home have not lost hope of drawing Italy to go to war, but not certain. Be assured am neglecting nothing. Meanwhile not arming sufficiently here.

NAPOLEON (JEROME).

Prince Napoleon to the Emperor
(Telegram in cipher to the Imperial Headquarters, *viâ* Paris)
Florence, 25th August, 1870.

King received first reply from Austria. Not favourable to military action. Speaks of diplomatic action with Russia. Still waiting for positive reply. Italy not ready, sending an envoy to Vienna. Italy will not do much

---

[1] An Italian of the Diplomatic Service.

by herself. Ministry opposed to participating in the war; to-day is much alarmed. If our army had a success it might change things.

NAPOLEON (JEROME).

Prince Napoleon to the Emperor
(Cipher telegram addressed to Imperial Headquarters)
Florence, 27th August, 1870.

I do not think I can make Italy decide on war before fresh events happen. Has refused all discussion on diplomatic intervention. Have had no reply to two last telegrams sent to Your Majesty. People write me from Paris that they are attacking my mission, that they will make an interpellation in the Chamber, and that the Ministry will not defend me. In this situation my duty is to obey only the Emperor, not recognising and not being willing to serve any other chief. Only three things possible :

1. Remain here to pursue negotiations.
2. To rejoin you as best I can ; it will be difficult not to pass through Paris.
3. To give me liberty of action if you think cannot be any use near you.

Await your commands. Beg you will formulate them clearly.

NAPOLEON (JEROME).

The Emperor to Prince Napoleon
(Telegram in cipher)
27th August, 1870.

Received your telegrams. Nothing new here. I beg you will remain where you are to pursue negotiations. I will write to Paris to defend you if they are attacking you.

NAPOLEON.

On the 1st September MacMahon's army sustained the disaster of Sedan, and on the following day the Emperor capitulated. As soon as he learnt this appalling news Prince Napoleon wrote the two following letters which he sent to Visconti Venosta, Minister for Foreign Affairs of the Kingdom of Italy, with the request to forward them to the Emperor:

Prince Napoleon to the Emperor
Florence, 4th September, 1870.

SIRE,—I learn the news of battles lost and of your captivity. My devotion and my duty dictate my conduct. I ask to rejoin you, more especially to-day when all hope of defending my country is impossible after the events that have happened in Paris.

Whatever be the conditions placed upon me, I will submit to them in advance in order to be near you. Misfortune can only bind closer the bonds which have held me to you since my boyhood. I beg Your Majesty to accede to my request, which I am addressing to the King of Prussia.

May it please you, Sire, to accept, etc.,

NAPOLEON (JEROME).

Prince Napoleon to the King of Prussia
Florence, 4th September, 1870.

SIRE,—I beg Your Majesty will allow me to rejoin the Head of my Dynasty, the unfortunate Sovereign who is your prisoner of war.

Your Majesty will understand the sentiment which inspires my request.

May it please you, Sire, to accept the homage of my profound respect,

NAPOLEON (JEROME).

The Second Empire and Its Downfall

After the overthrow of the Empire the Mission of the Prince came to an end. He left Italy, and, having no longer any place in France, took refuge at Prangins in Switzerland.

The Emperor to Prince Napoleon[1]
Wilhelmshohe, 17th September, 1870.

MY DEAR COUSIN,—I have been much touched by your offer to share my captivity, but I wish to remain alone with the few persons who have followed me, and have even requested the Empress not to come and join me.

I hope that we may see each other again some day under more happy circumstances. Meanwhile, with, etc.,

NAPOLEON.

While the Emperor was in captivity at Wilhelmshohe the Empress had taken refuge in England with the Prince Imperial, and was living at Chislehurst, near London. At the beginning of October Prince Napoleon went to see her there in the hope of being of use to his young cousin. Leaving Prangins on the 2nd October he arrived at Brussels on the 5th, and was in London on the evening of the 6th. On the 7th he went to see the Empress. After placing themselves each *au courant* with their situation, they talked of any advantage it might be to know exactly the conditions which Bismarck seemed disposed to grant if the Empress were to treat with Prussia in place of the Government in Paris.

On the evening of the 11th October there was another interview. M. de Persigny accompanied the Prince. The Empress, to whom a kind of *questionnaire* had been sent, related the approaches which had been made to her by Bourbaki and Regnier, but she was nervous,

---

[1] This letter, which the Prince received at Prangins, is quoted by Emile Ollivier (*Empire Libéral*, Vol. XVII., p. 565).

and gave vent to her dissatisfaction over the past, her
hesitation concerning the future, and her animosity
against the Prince. A third interview took place next
day. It was a stormy one, and ended up, if not in an
open quarrel, at least in a marked coldness.[1]

A fortnight later there appeared in the *Daily News*
of the 26th October a note, inspired by the Empress,
saying that she had taken no part in any of the
negotiations for an armistice or peace, as people were
saying, and containing a disagreeable remark about the
Prince.[2] The Prince immediately raised a protest in
very courteous language in the same newspaper against
these attacks. On the 29th there were further notes
from the Empress. The Prince cut short these polemics.

Prince Napoleon to the Emperor
London, 1st November, 1870.

SIRE,—My wife writes to me that Your Majesty has
commissioned her to propose to her Father that he
should buy certain property you have in Rome. She
wrote to the King at once, but my dear Clotilde, who is
very strong-minded and devoted, knows nothing about
business. If, therefore, Your Majesty should wish to
give me particulars I will undertake the matter.

I came to London on my personal affairs, and to see
if I could be of any use to your son. In accordance
with what you wrote to me I did not pass through
Cassel. My first visit was to the Empress, who received
me coldly. I went there a second time with MM. de
Persigny and Duperré, and, lastly, the Empress *begged*

---

[1] The Prince kept an account of these interviews.

[2] "Le Prince Napoléon, était-il-dit, qui avait fait cause commune avec ceux qui eussent voulu induire l'Impératrice à faire un acte impolitique, en est pour ses peines, tandis que ses violentes récriminations contre la politique de l'Empire ont eu pour résultat de lui faire quitter Chislehurst un peu soudainement, aprés une réception glaciale et sans autre résultat que de s'entendre dire quelques dures verités par son illustre cousine."

me to return with MM. Rouher, Chevreau, etc. At this Council the Empress, without my having given any provocation, allowed herself to give vent to unheard-of violence of language against me. I was able to preserve the utmost calmness, but thought it best to withdraw without deigning to reply to senseless accusations of treason! I will not give you the details, Sire, although I have written down all that took place, because it would only give you pain and would be useless at the present time. One day the whole truth will be known. I embraced your son on leaving Chislehurst whither I had come at the sole call of my devotion.

I am living a very retired life here. I am revisiting the memories of our early days! I am not receiving again any one from the *entourage* of your wife. Doctor Conneau has not come to see me. This will explain why I have not written to you sooner.

A few days ago the Empress thought well *to give an account of my conduct in public*. I am sending you the newspapers containing the articles *dictated* by her. The first one drew from me a reply in very moderate language which I signed.

I wished, Sire, to give you these quite private explanations in order that you should not think that our disasters have changed my sentiments towards you, but after the insults of the Empress, which she has made public, I can have nothing more to do with her. I have nothing to reproach myself for, but each one must bear the responsibility for his actions. I deplore what has taken place.

May it please you, Sire, etc.,

NAPOLEON (JEROME).

My address is: Comte de Moncalieri, Claridge's Hotel, Brook Street, London.

Q_E

The Emperor to Prince Napoleon
Wilhelmshohe, 8th November, 1870.

My dear Cousin,—I have received the letter you wrote me, and have learnt with pain all that passed at Chislehurst, but I must also confess that your language to the Empress was rather unseemly, as much on your account as on mine.

Misfortune embitters characters, and creates divisions, instead of bringing together those who have the same interests.

I had written to Clotilde to make an offer to the King that he should buy the Palace of the Cæsars in Rome, but as she did not wish to undertake the matter I have written to Arese[1] about it.

With, etc.,   Napoleon.

The Emperor to Prince Napoleon[2]
W., 25th November, 1870.

My dear Cousin,—I have received the account of your stay in England together with your letter. I read it with profound grief and if you wish me to tell you the truth, you have been wanting in tact, and the Empress in *sang-froid*. In the position we are now in it is very sad to see dissensions in the family.

For the moment there is nothing we can do. A reaction in our favour will come of itself, for the anarchy reigning in France cannot last.

I thank you for the services you offer with your father-in-law, but Arese has been commissioned to make the negotiations.

With, etc.,   Napoleon.

My tender regards to Clotilde and your children.

---

[1] Marquis Arese, for long in close relations with the Emperor.
[2] The Prince received this letter at Prangins on the 28th November.

Prince Napoleon to the Emperor
Prangins, 23rd December, 1870.

SIRE,—Would you permit me to come on the occasion of the New Year to express to you all my good wishes? The situation is sad for us, and appalling for France, and God knows what the future has yet in store. I have received Your Majesty's letter of the 25th November. If I have not replied to it, it is because it seems to me I can add nothing to the account I have already sent you. I am just as pained at what has passed, Sire, as you are. I hope you will do me justice. On my side I remain what I always have been to you, and it is not ill-fortune that can change me.

I see sometimes MM. Pietri and Fleury. I have received good news of Your Majesty through M. Levert.[1]

My wife and children present their respectful homage to you and the Prince Imperial.

May it please you, Sire, etc.,　　　　N. J.

The Emperor to Prince Napoleon[2]
Wilhelmshohe, 31st December, 1870.

MY DEAR COUSIN,—I thank you for your letter and for the good wishes you send me for the New Year. We have much need for the New Year to bring us some compensation for all we have suffered. Remember me to Clotilde and your children, and with, etc.,

NAPOLEON.

The Emperor to Prince Napoleon
Wilhelmshohe, 22nd February, 1871.

MY DEAR COUSIN,—I was very glad to learn from your letter that you approve of my Proclamation. It appears certain that there will be a *plébiscite* within a month from

---
[1] A former Prefect, and afterwards a Deputy.
[2] Received at Prangins 3rd January, 1871.

now. We must therefore prepare ourselves for it, and each one must do all he can in his power.

The news I am receiving from the provinces is good, but public opinion in Paris is detestable. I am obliged to send my letter to Mathilde. I was careless enough to burn yours before taking down your address.

With, etc.,

NAPOLEON.

Prince Napoleon to the Emperor
London, 22nd April, 1871.

SIRE,—I have seen in the English newspapers that Your Majesty has not been well. On the 10th April I made M. Villot[1] write to M. Pietri, your secretary, expressing my wish to see you : *no reply.*

About the 15th or 16th April I sent M. Villot to Chislehurst with a request to see you. M. Davillier replied to M. Villot that you were not well, and that you would give me notice when you could receive me. *No reply* since then.

Four days ago my cousin Joachim Murat came to see me, and I begged him to ask you when I can see you. *No reply.*

This significant silence pains, without astonishing, me. It can only arise from an influence it is easy to guess. In wishing to see you from time to time my only intention was to show you *personal* devotion, which our misfortunes cannot change.

May it please you, Sire, etc.,

NAPOLEON (JEROME).

Comte de Moncalieri, London, Claridge's Hotel, 49 Brook Street, 22nd April, 1871.

[1] A Captain of Hussars, and Orderly Officer to the Prince.

The Emperor to Prince Napoleon[1]

Chislehurst, 21st July, 1871.

MY DEAR COUSIN,—I have had long talks with Fleury without our conversations resulting in anything definite. I have commissioned R.[2] to prepare, as far as this can be done, the lists of candidates for the forthcoming elections, and he has promised to gather round him devoted and energetic men. I think I shall stay definitely in England, especially if the Empress is successful in selling her diamonds well. We are passing through a period of transition during which we must have patience and organise.

I keenly regret the unreasonable outbursts of J. David.[3] I keep on saying, " May God keep me from my friends ; I will undertake my enemies ! "

E. Ollivier ought to know well that I do not approve of his impolitic diatribes, and that I shall not conceal it from the authors. It is ridiculous in a sovereign degree to wish to get rid of the responsibility between ourselves which falls upon us. In 1870 three authorities were equally responsible—the Sovereign, the Ministry and the *corps législatif*. If the Sovereign had blamed the policy of the Ministry he would have thrown it out. If the latter had disagreed with the Sovereign it would have resigned. And if the *corps législatif* had blamed the conduct of the Government it would have overthrown the Ministry. The three authorities were therefore agreed, and each one ought to bear their share of responsibility.

The Empress and I beg to be remembered to Clotilde, and I renew to you the assurance of my old and sincere regard.

NAPOLEON.

---

[1] Received at Prangins, 24th July. The Prince replied on the 14th August.
[2] Rouher.
[3] Baron David, the former President of the *corps législatif*.

The Emperor to Prince Napoleon[1]

Chislehurst, 21st August, 1871.

MY DEAR COUSIN,—I have received your letter of the 14th. You will give me pleasure if you will send me your ideas on a plan of organisation. But everything does not rest on organisation. Men must be found of sufficient importance to group others around them and to have the power of directing. I am very glad at what you say about E. O.[2] I always preserve for him a large share of my affections. I imagine there might be a certain advantage in being nominated for the Council-General of Corsica. However, to accept or to canvass for votes at this moment would be to recognise a Government which I hold to be unlawful, and I should regret that anyone bearing my name should have the appearance of recognising all the illegal things that are being done to-day. I send you a passage from a circular by a former Senator. If he thinks it beneath his dignity to compete for the position of a Councillor-General, how much more a member of my family. I made the same reply to Napoleon Charles[3] who is here, and wished to offer himself also. If you want an opportunity to speak, you could be nominated, and when refusing say what you have to say.

The Empress and my son wish to be remembered to you and Clotilde.

With, etc., N.

The Emperor to Prince Napoleon[4]

Ch., 29th August, 1871.

MY DEAR COUSIN,—I have received your letter and reply at once. I think your *brochure* is perfect.[5] I have

[1] The Prince, who was absent momentarily from Prangins, received this letter on the 29th. He replied on the 2nd September. He was thinking of offering himself to the Council-General of Corsica.
[2] Emile Ollivier.
[3] The grandson of Lucien, and son of Charles, Prince of Canino.
[4] Received at Prangins on the 1st September; answered on the 3rd.
[5] A *brochure* written by the Prince entitled *La Vérité à mes Calomniateurs*.

only three observations to make : 1. As the language is very guarded, the sentence I have marked seems to me to require cutting down. 2. " My cause " strikes me as being too pretentious. 3. I have added a sentence on page 3, in order that we shall not have the appearance of disposing of Denmark's troops as though they belonged to us.

The news we are receiving from Paris is very favourable to us.

With, etc., NAPOLEON.

The Emperor to Prince Napoleon[1]
Torquay, 15th October, 1871.

MY DEAR COUSIN,—It is true I have not written to you since receiving your memorandum. It is because I should have had to enter into many explanations which I feel to be useless for the moment. The news from France is good, but it is a further reason for acting with great prudence, and not spoiling a good position. If you do not receive a passport I am of opinion that you should not go notwithstanding that, for it could not have any good result. On the contrary, a refusal will place you in a better position, for people are always in favour of the oppressed.

I have had no other *brochure* printed than the one you know of concerning the organisation of Prussia, but I am engaged in writing the account of the campaign of 1870.

I am returning to Chislehurst on Thursday. The Empress will not return till about the middle of November, always supposing that her affairs are settled by that time.

My kind remembrances to Clotilde, and with, etc.,

NAPOLEON.

[1] The Prince, who was absent, found this letter at Prangins on the 31st October. He answered it on the 12th November.

The Emperor to Prince Napoleon[1]
Camden Place, 16th February, 1872.

MY DEAR COUSIN,—You will have learnt of Rouher's being elected, and of the death of poor Conti.[2] It is well said that we cannot have a joy without some admixture. I am receiving several letters from Paris where, they tell me, several candidates already are coming forward, and that I must decide between the Duke of Padua, Pietri, etc. In any other circumstance I should have made no reply before having your opinion, but after what passed several months ago, I did not hesitate to say that justice demanded that they should nominate Charles Abbattucci in order to recompense him for his act of self-abnegation in retiring to make room for Rouher in the Chamber. There would really be a sovereign injustice in not taking his disinterestedness into account. I hope you approve this decision.

I have prepared a manifesto, but I shall not issue it before the occasion. Things are going well, and we must take great care not to compromise the good position which events have created.

Many kind messages to Clotilde, and with, etc., N.

Prince Napoleon to the Emperor[3]
Chalet de Prangins, près de Nyon ; Canton de Vaud (Suisse), 19th February, 1872.

SIRE,—As soon as I had heard of the death of poor Conti, which was so unexpected, I summoned a person who is engaged on my affairs in Paris to come here. Foreseeing the difficulties of another election I was anxious, without losing an hour, to do all possible to avoid misunderstandings.

---
[1] Received at Prangins on the 19th February. The Prince replied on the same day.
[2] A senator. He died in Paris on the 13th February, 1872.
[3] The letter is addressed : " À. S. M. l'Empereur, à Camden Place, Chislehurst, sous le couvert du Comte de Pierrefonds, par M. Baring, Banquier à Londres, Angleterre, 8 Bishop's Gate Within, City."

M. Rouher, with whom my secretary was closeted before his departure, has written me a long letter, telling me that he quite understood we must act *together*, and asking me if it suited me to pose as a candidate. He did not give me his opinion. I received from the same source news of Duvernois and several of our friends. Pietri wrote to me from Marseilles on landing. I have answered M. Rouher by my secretary, telling him in substance that I had not yet decided, but that it seemed indispensable to have a meeting with the Emperor before settling on anything. I proposed to him that I should go to Brussels, which is only six hours from Paris, and from there to London, fully prepared to subordinate my personal affairs to the necessity of having a serious discussion with the Emperor. I have no doubt that M. Rouher has sent you my letter. He has not yet answered me, but he told my secretary that he recognised the need of an understanding, but that, under present circumstances he would have to consider a re-arrangement, and that he was reserving himself to reply to me at length. M. Duvernois, I know, was anxious to be nominated. Your Majesty will see, therefore, that I have not lost a minute, not in coming to a decision, but in placing you in a position, together with all of us, to study the matter and decide with full knowledge of everything.

This morning I received Your Majesty's letter of the 16th, and you appear to have decided that it is necessary to put forward M. Ch. Abbattucci. Permit me, Sire, not to discuss the different candidates. As regards Charles Abbattucci, whom I am very fond of, you seem to be confusing him with his brother, Séverin, when you say that justice demands that he should be recompensed for his act of self-abnegation. It was not he, but his brother, who withdrew to make room for the election of M. Rouher. Further, Abbattucci has not been able to secure his nomination as Councillor-General in his own canton. His standing as a Député would create great difficulties, and has little chance of success. But allow me to say, the choice of a candidate is of secondary importance to-day. It seems to me that we ought to consider especially whether a public manifestation given by Corsica in favour of my name would not be useful to the party, and of a nature to strike public opinion. I quite see the objections which this might arouse, and, personally, I am very little drawn to enter the lists, but I think it is a course which at least requires to be well weighed and discussed before coming to a decision. Your Majesty, by saying nothing to me on the subject, appears not to have thought of it.

But there is no need for hurry. The election will not take place as soon as all that, and since Conti's death, with a view to avoiding just this precipitate nomination before coming to an understanding I have written to my friends, and in particular to the newspaper I own in Ajaccio, not to rush forward anything, and this newspaper is going to publish one or two articles saying that the question remains open and that no premature pledge must be entered into.

I think this is really the only wise course to follow. Without having decided upon anything, as I have told you, and being quite prepared to bow to your opinion and that of properly qualified advisers, after seriously examining matters which can only be done *vivâ voce*, you will permit me to hold myself in reserve until I have had an opportunity of discussing them with Your Majesty. The events which may take place during the time between now and the election, probably six months (and in any case we shall be advised long before by the writ convoking the electors), will give ample latitude to decide whether my candidature is opportune or not ; we shall have to see.

As my projected journey to go and see you at once is no longer urgent after what you have written to me, and the difficulties arising from replacing M. Rouher, and, to repeat, as a decision is not pressing, I am going away for two or three weeks to Italy, to my father-in-law, with whom there are certain family matters I have to discuss, and some useful information to obtain. I shall also see in two days, when I shall be in Italy (if it is undesirable that I should go to Corsica), how to judge of the position for myself.

Allow me, Sire, to beg of you not to commit yourself in the case of M. Abbattucci or other persons, a thing which might really entail difficulties and cause vexatious discord, for I do not think anyone can put up a fight against me in Corsica. If the Emperor will reply to me at Prangins, where I am leaving my family, my letters will be forwarded without delay. In any case, I intend to go to London in April.

Accept, etc.,

NAPOLEON (JEROME).

P.S. My wife thanks Your Majesty for your kind remembrances, and presents to Her Majesty the Empress and to the Prince Imperial her respectful homage. My eldest son is completely recovered from his illness.

N.

The Emperor to Prince Napoleon[1]
Camden Place (Chislehurst), 5th April, 1872.

MY DEAR COUSIN,—I have not written to you for a long time because I knew you were in Italy. I am glad to hear of your return, and shall be very happy to have a talk with you when you come to England. I have told Rouher to write to you when he will be coming here.

I agree with you that it will be better to wait before

---

[1] Received at Prangins on the 8th.

choosing a candidate for Corsica. Besides, I have told Casabianca that I did not wish to be mixed up in it, and that it is for the Corsican Committee in Paris to decide the matter.

The Empress and my son wish to be remembered to you and Clotilde, and with, etc.,

N.

The Emperor to Prince Napoleon
(Camden Place, Chislehurst), 12th May, 1872.

MY DEAR COUSIN,—I think it would be very impolitic for you to present yourself as a candidate in Corsica at the present time, and that you must wait for a more opportune moment, when by-elections or general elections shall take place. It will be desirable then that all partisans of the Empire should enter the lists. Under such circumstances I will recommend all my friends to support your candidature, not only in Corsica, but in all the Departments wherein you may have a chance of being elected. From now up till that time, while preparing the ground, I desire that you maintain the greatest reserve.

With, etc.,

NAPOLEON.

The Emperor to Prince Napoleon[1]
(Camden Place, Chislehurst), 14th May, 1872.

MY DEAR COUSIN,—I thank you for your letter. Some good points might have been used from your memorandum, but it is now too late. The letter ought by now to have been sent to Paris. I beg you will not forget to send your

---

[1] The Prince received this letter in London on the 15th May, in which was added a subscription list containing fifty-eight names. It is headed as follows :
"The Emperor, 100,000 francs.
"Prince Napoleon,
"The Duc de Cambacérès, 50,000.
"Raimbeaux, 40,000, etc."

quota or subscription to Rouher. There is no need for you to send a large sum, but it is important that your name should figure on the list.

With, etc.,   N.

The Emperor to Prince Napoleon[1]
(Camden Place, Chislehurst), 17th July, 1872.

MY DEAR COUSIN,—Since your departure I have not heard a word from you, and I do not know what you are doing. You will see from the newspapers that matters are becoming more confused daily. Nevertheless, I do not think there will be anything fresh before the autumn. I should much like you not to neglect to keep up good relations with the amiable singer of whom you spoke when here. It would be very important to enter into friendly communications with her.

I am expecting to go to the seaside for salt-water baths at the beginning of August. Tell me your plans, and with, etc.,

                                                        N.

The Emperor to Prince Napoleon[2]
(Camden Place, Chislehurst), 13th October, 1872.

MY DEAR COUSIN,—I have been unable to reply sooner to your letter because at the time of my receiving it I learnt of the difficulties being placed in the way of your staying in France. I have followed with a keen interest all the phases of your journey and, from the political point of view, can only congratulate myself on the result. If, on the other hand, your plan was to remain quietly in France, I think that this last event will place an obstacle in its way. I hope they will make it the subject of an interpellation in the Chamber.

As regards what concerns you in the next General

[1] Received at Prangins on the 20th.
[2] Received at Prangins on the 17th, and answered on the 12th November.

Elections I feel that while acting in conformity with the letter I wrote you, in order to be successful it is important not to noise it abroad. By letting people know beforehand the plans one has formed, one raises a host of opposition and obstacles.

You must choose the Departments where there is a possibility of having a chance, and each Department which shall elect you must think it is the only one.

I tell you all this because I have already learnt that many people blame the multiple system of candidature instead of giving it their support.

I hope that Clotilde will not have taken too much to heart the want of consideration on the part of the Government. The Empress desires me to tell you that she thought her protest very noble and very well made.

With, etc.,

N.

The Emperor died at Chislehurst on the 9th January, 1873.

APPENDIX

NOTE I

" Letter written to the Emperor on the 18th March, 1856 concerning a general amnesty on the occasion of the birth of his son."[1]

Note for the consideration of the Emperor Napoleon

Paris, 18th March, 1856.

Be it known to all :
A Full and Complete Amnesty obliterating the last traces of our civil discords :
A Law abrogating :
1. The Law of the 10th April, 1832.
2. The Order of the 26th May, 1848.
3. The Order of the 27th June, 1848.

Obliterating the last traces of our political proscriptions.

Would the dangers of such a measure be greater, or less, than the advantages ?
This is the question to be examined.
The advantages :
By an amnesty a great blow would be struck at the revolutionary party who rose in insurrection, for it would be reduced to being nothing but a staff with no army, a staff composed of heads completely divided, and therefore each compelled to put himself forward openly, not as a *victim* but as a *pretender*, no longer as one *proscribed*, but as one who *himself proscribes*, or as a *voluntary émigré*. To come back to France through the gateway (of whatever breadth and height it be) of an amnesty without conditions, and without restrictions, is in some sort to recognise the Government : it is an easy matter to write out beforehand the names of all those who will not come back, and, further, one could add the names of those who, following the example of the amnesty accorded to Barbès, and feeling the falsity of their position, would swell still more the number, not of *exiles*, but of *émigrés*. If Barbès, amnestied unconditionally, had not felt it was possible for him to reside in France without losing all *prestige*, renouncing all pretensions and giving up all future prospects, could Blanqui act in any different manner ? If Barbès and Blanqui had continued as *émigrés*, could Ledru Rollin and Louis Blanc return ? Clearly not. By means of an amnesty, therefore, all the exiles become *émigrés*. By means of an amnesty we return in full measure to the rights of universal suffrage

[1] These words were written on the margin of the note in the hand of Prince Napoleon.

after departing from legality by the *coup d'état* of the 2nd December. By means of an amnesty the Emperor shows his confidence, and a boldness which is often prudence; he shows that he has the nation with him, and that he has nothing to fear from insurrection on the part of his chief men. By an amnesty he shows that he has every confidence in the fidelity of the Army, and does not fear that it will be affected by the return of Generals Changarnier, Lamoricière, Bedeau, Le Flô, and Colonel Charras. The return of these officers is the only danger perhaps; nevertheless one feels that he should not hold back this great measure. What greater harm could these four Generals do than General Cavaignac, who was himself President of the executive power? What weight had he? What weight will they have? One soldier only, Colonel Charras, if he came back to France, would enter upon active and secret machinations; but, in the first place, it is doubtful whether he would consent to return by means of an amnesty, and if he did, would it not be an easy thing to catch hold of the thread of his machinations?

Napoleon I said at St. Helena:

"Public opinion is a power invisible and mysterious, which nothing can resist; nothing is more easily moved, more vague, or stronger, and, while wholly capricious, is nevertheless true, reasonable, and just, far, far oftener than one thinks.

"When I was provisional Consul one of the first acts of my administration was the deportation of fifty anarchists. Public opinion, by whom they were held in horror, suddenly turned round in their favour, and forced me to draw back. But shortly afterwards these same anarchists, endeavouring to *plot together*, were brought to naught by this same public opinion, which forthwith came round to me again. Thus at the Restoration, by going the wrong way about it, they managed to render the regicides popular, the very men whom the great mass of the nation had proscribed the moment before." *Memorial de Sainte Hélène*, 18th November, 1815.

The return of the four Generals would not offer any great danger, but if not entirely exempt, this consideration should do away with it: if they do not return to-day, they never will; and how will History regard the *banishment in perpetuity* of four Generals who have served their country gloriously, who served her in grave and difficult circumstances, and were banished without being condemned, without being judged? Posterity is a tribunal whose decrees should possess a great weight, and the Emperor cannot and should not place himself above them. Was not the condemnation of Marshal Ney, and is it not still, the condemnation of the Restoration and of the Bourbon dynasty of the elder branch? Can we put in the same balance the weight of actions such as these and the weight of temporary difficulties or insignificant dangers? The Emperor should take History into account and concern himself with the future at least as much as with the present, with posterity as least as much as with present tranquillity!

In a letter of Napoleon I to Prince Jerome we find: "*Ayez des périls j'y consens, mais avec de la gloire.*" Are not *les perils avec la gloire* of greater value, especially when one can affirm that the perils attaching to the return of certain exiles are more imaginary than real? On the contrary, if these perils appear to exist they will only give greater distinction, greater force, greater re-echo, and greater grandeur to a measure of amnesty against which one looks in vain for any serious objection or one which is not commonplace.

By the abrogation of the three Laws or Orders of proscription, one would mark the difference between the reigns—between the reign of Napoleon III doing away with the Law of the 10th April, 1832, and the reign of Louis XVIII proscribing the Bonapartes; between the reign of Napoleon III doing away with the Law of the 26th May, 1848, and the reign of Louis Philippe proscribing the Bourbons of his family and the Bonapartes; between the Republic giving birth to the Order of the 27th June, 1848, and the Empire not fearing to repeal it. Lastly, by this abrogation, after having changed all the *exiles* into *émigrés* by an amnesty, one would change the *pretenders* into *citizens*. There are no more Pretenders; there is only one heir of Napoleon III.

It is clear the Bourbons will not come back.

This great measure has a *cachet* which seems to bewilder one by its grandeur! All the small-minded, and men of routine, will oppose it, because they will not understand it: the people, the masses who have the instinct of great thoughts, will approve! It would be a magnificent appendage to the signature of peace; but a large, complete, all-embracing and unrestrictive measure is required to give it its true character. Any restriction would be *unavailing* against danger, and *mean* in its effect. When the sun shines a veil in front of it does not shelter it effectually, but it produces a shadow which destroys all its brilliancy.

Enough said. Here we have one of those actions which the Emperor alone is in a position to appreciate; they are difficult of discussion with people who cannot sense them!

NOTE II

Note for the consideration of the Emperor on the Defence of France.

Paris, 1st May, 1859.

Right up to the last moment, ministers, diplomatists, and officials denied that war with Austria was possible. The most circumstantial and formal warnings were not able to draw them out of their incredulity and apathy. We are bearing to-day the penalty for these deplorable illusions which, possibly, are not combined with any calculated ill-intentions. From the military point of view we find ourselves behindhand in every prevision demanded by the most ordinary prudence. Material, men, horses—everything is lacking, or, at least, everything has to be improvised and, what is strange, the Emperor, who was the first to foresee the war, has been taken unawares.

This is not the time for recrimination, but at least let the past serve as a lesson for the future. We are hopeful that by a display of activity we may repair by the war in Italy the deplorable mistakes of the last

RE

six months, but other events are in preparation, more terrible and more menacing, than those of which Italy is the theatre. Do not let us allow ourselves to be taken by surprise a second time.

In a few weeks Germany will have armed more than four hundred thousand men. A Prussian army of two hundred thousand men could in fifteen days be transferred by rail to our northern frontier, which is open on every side. For our part our conviction is that a German war will be difficult to avoid. The over-excited state of German passions will drive their Governments towards a conflict with France. May the illusions we held regarding Austria not be repeated in the case of Prussia. The second mistake would be still graver than the first. We are at the mercy—I must say it—of the decision of Prussia; she is assembling her army to-day for a defensive purpose; to-morrow she has it in her power to give this concentration an offensive character, to oppose which we should possess far less than the disorganised France of 1792 found to offer resistance to the Duke of Brunswick.

The Emperor and his Dynasty may doubtless succumb, but they should not fall without having done their duty by France and the cause they represent. To allow France to be invaded and dismembered through apathy, through puerile optimism, through fear of looking dangers in the face to their full extent, would be dishonour to the name of the Napoleons, and a hundred times worse than even the loss of the Empire.

The line of conduct the Government ought to follow is to make the greatest military preparations, but of such a character as not to alarm Germany, nor to give her a pretext of turning against us. They should, therefore, in the highest degree and exclusively, represent a formidable system of national defence. If we meet with reverses in Italy these preparations will serve as against Austria; if we have success—and in that case the intervention of Germany will become all the more likely—we ought to make provision against this aggression.

Not only ought these military measures to have a defensive character, but it would even be well to proclaim this aloud with a certain amount of ostentation. If anything can conjure away or put off the storm preparing on the other side of the Rhine, it would be the spectacle offered to Europe of a country concentrating all her forces upon the defence of her territory, and thereby having the appearance of renouncing any offensive obnoxious to her neighbours.

It should be our purpose to embrace all the strength of the people in a great system of military defence. With them rests the strength of the dynasty and of France. The people alone have it in their power to save the one and the other, and it is to them we must address our appeal. The policy of the Emperor at the present time should be to turn the people into soldiers for the purpose of defending our territory, and it is urgent that it should assume a most active form. It is necessary to demonstrate to all that the Imperial Government is not disheartened, and that it has faith in the popular masses, whence it arose. Failing this energetic action, patriots, seeing themselves betrayed, will lose heart and abandon the direction of the public mind to the malevolent passions of the *bourgeois* classes, whose unbridled fury against the Emperor surpasses all conception!

Appendix 259

It is necessary before everything that the determination of the Emperor to defend himself, his belongings, his throne, and France should manifest itself in a decisive manner; that an energetic directorship should preside over everything, that an end should be put to all half-hearted measures, and that a clean line of separation should be made between those who are his friends and his enemies. If the lack of uniformity of view in the counsels of the Government, if the absence of one united policy accepted and adopted by all the emperor's instruments, have already proved so fatal in the first operations of a campaign of limited extent, how will it be when the person of the Sovereign shall be at a distance, exposing himself to all the chances of war? Only the concentration of all the live forces of the people in one great homogeneity of patriotic measures, both military and defensive, can counterbalance the baleful influence which the absence of the Emperor must exert necessarily on the leadership of the Government.

Guided by these considerations we propose that the following measures should be adopted without delay, and *before the departure of the Emperor* :

1. The increase of the *cadres* of the Army by the creation of twenty-five fresh line regiments.

2. The organisation of *extra-ordinary* operations in all the arsenals so as to complete the material required within the shortest delay.

3. The purchase of horses for the artillery and cavalry from every quarter and on a large scale. We do not think we are in a position to complete the number of horses necessary for our cavalry and artillery from our interior resources.

4. Dismount a quarter, at least, of the strength of our mounted gendarmes. By this means we should obtain immediately four thousand horses fully trained and ready to enter the ranks. The dismounted gendarmes could be remounted with fresh horses which they would have time to train, or, better still, from local resources, none of which can escape them on account of their perfect knowledge of the country.

5. The organisation of bodies of volunteers in the large cities,—Parisian volunteers, Lyons, Lille, Strasbourg, Bordeaux, Toulouse, the Alpes, Corsica, etc. The men entering these Legions would enter into an engagement solely for the whole duration of the war. The pay and allowance would be the same as for the infantry regiments of the Army. The officers up to the rank of captain inclusive would be chosen by the Emperor from among the volunteers. Their position would be the same as that of the officers of the Foreign Legion, on a *foreign footing*, that is to say, that at the expiration of the war they could be returned to their homes. The duties of battalion commanders and adjutants would be reserved for officers of the Army.

The creation of Volunteer Legions would correspond with one of the social conditions created by war, to which the organisation of the regular army lends itself only imperfectly. In reality there would be no question of going about obtaining soldiers in the country districts; they form the nursery of the regular Army and at the present time we should have to leave out those following agricultural pursuits. We must therefore look to the towns and great manufacturing centres for the enrolling for the common defence of the mass of artisans, workmen, *outcasts*, and the sons of people of respectable families whom the war stirs to excitement, or reduces to poverty and, as a result, to discontented passions owing to the closing of the workshops. Many men, urged by the existing poverty, or caught up by the general enthusiasm, and having no idea of entering a military career, will be willing to go and serve for the duration of the war, and will volunteer of their own accord, bringing in their friends and neighbours as well. This mutual example, in addition to a general spirit of rivalry, should bring about the organisation in city after city of Volunteer Legions. And this formation, while responding to an absolute present need and giving a great impetus to public spirit, would possess the advantage of not engaging the future, of not increasing the normal *cadres*, of not creating any claim on the Treasury or one to the detriment of the officers of the Army, or of placing any limit to the sacrifices required in war-time.

6. To make provision for the immediate armament and the thorough victualling of our fortresses in the north and east.

7. To organise strong companies of gunners and marksmen from the National Guard in these fortresses, in order that the population may be in a position to take part in the defence of the towns in a practical and adequate manner.

8. Placing Paris in a state of defence. Supplying the outlying forts with a complete armament, and the *enceinte* of the fortifications with guns to defend them, to the number of five for each bastion.

Of all the measures we are proposing the armament of Paris is the most serious and important. It should have for effect the giving of a great patriotic impetus to men's minds, and should be a proof that the Government is not blind to the peril, that it realises the gravity of the situation, and that it is contemplating it seriously, and without discouragement. It would testify to the firm determination of the Emperor to defend the country to the utmost extremity.

The arming of Paris could not be regarded as a threat to Europe. On the contrary, the distinctly defensive character of this measure would define the attitude of France as being determined on concentrating her efforts on Austria and as being far from wishing to cause anxiety to her neighbours. Besides, it would only be doing in France, not alone what Austria is doing, but also Prussia, the entire Confederation (of Switzerland), and England as well, who is arming her coasts as though she were expecting a descent on them any day.

Placing Paris in a state of defence would have, therefore, considerable weight, not only on military policy, but also on the political attitude of Europe.

As we possess these immense defensive works all ready constructed round Paris we ought to utilise them. If Paris were placed in security against foreign invasion it would give us an immense advantage; it would render the interior of the country safe, keep Europe out, and give entire liberty to the movements of our armies operating on our frontiers or beyond.

Without this base of national defence nothing is secure to-day, we repeat, in the present condition of our forces, and the safety of the Emperor, and of France, depends on the will of Prussia and of Germany.

Those who believed, against all evidence to the contrary and even right up to the last moment, in the success of diplomacy, may possibly be possessed of a similar blindness as regards Germany as that which has just been dispelled with difficulty. But seriously-minded men who take into consideration the lessons from history and things as they really are, have no illusions on the second phase which is going to open before us. It is one of the utmost gravity; the road to Paris lies open, and more than two hundred thousand Prussians are in a position to set out within a fortnight. Such is the situation.

It is necessary to combine with the measures I am proposing an entire system of administrative direction without which they will come to nothing. The orders must be clear, precise, and be executed with great promptness and absolute goodwill. Each of these great measures of national defence must be watched over by officers or special commissioners delegated by the Emperor, and charged with the duty of rendering an account to him of the way in which the instructions he has laid down have been carried out, and of the conformity of their administration with his commands.

If we could infuse into the mind of the Emperor the profound conviction which animates us in regard to the important questions we are raising, we should have no fear for the future, or at least should feel conscious of having done our duty. If the Emperor approves of this line of conduct it will rest with him to consider who are the instruments possessing the capacity to pursue it together with him. It is beyond doubt that hearts and minds able to rise to the height of a quite exceptional situation will be required. It is a question for personal consideration and confidence, the solving of which belongs to the Emperor alone.

NOTE III

Note for the consideration of the Emperor on Affairs in Poland

Paris, 20th February, 1863.

For the third time since the last division of Poland in 1794 events are bringing back to France the possibility of pursuing a policy, the success of which would lead to the full, normal, and definite development of her interior strength.

In 1807 and 1808 the implacable hostility of England, and the immediate necessity of creating a counterpoise in the Russian Alliance prevented Napoleon I from restoring on sufficiently broad and entirely independent bases the Polish nation, the scattered elements of which victory had placed in his hands.

Twenty-three years later, the personal feebleness of Louis Philippe and his throne, and the cowardice of his advisers, paralysed the national impulse which urged France to go to the succour of Poland on the morrow of the July revolution. The popular instincts, deceived and trampled under foot, have never pardoned the House of Orleans for the disappointment of which they were made victims. The recollections of this historic phase, put an end to by the famous sentence "*l'ordre règne à Varsovie,*" pressed heavily on the reign of Louis Philippe. They were the first to greet him on the barricades in February.

In entering on to a consideration of the present state of Europe resulting from the wars in the Crimea and Italy, and from the triumph of modern ideas, the immense preponderance of France and the character of depth and progressive initiative which has signalised the conduct of Napoleon III as regards internal affairs, we think we can clearly see in this concurrence of exceptional circumstances the approaching realisation of a conception which has been treated up till recently as chimerical. It seems impossible that the man who founded the greatness of Imperial France on a policy of nationality just as Richelieu founded that of the France of the Bourbons on the lowering of the House of Austria, can abandon this policy at the very moment when it is able to lead him to its supreme achievement without putting forth great efforts, and with the applause of the whole world. If we pass over the period of putting it into execution and imagine to ourselves the question settled, if we bring before our eyes a kingdom of Poland with a population of twelve or fifteen million people governed in accordance with modern principles and recognised by Europe, there is no need to insist upon the advantageous and great position such a result would give to France. The end we have in view is, therefore, a good one.

The restoration of Poland is an axiom of our policy. All discussion on this subject would be superfluous. We have been able to discuss in more or less good faith the suitability there was for France to create a united Italy or only to assure her independence; as concerning Poland the most narrow political egoism and the most belated diplomacy are in agreement with the most generous, the most unreflecting popular aspirations in recognising in her reconstruction the ideal of French policy.

The Triple Alliance, the origin and foundation of the Holy Alliance of 1815, broken up by the rupture of the tie which held it together; Slav nationality coming to life in its true form—the Polish and European form —instead of in the Russian and Asiatic form under which it offers something hostile and repulsive to civilisation; Germany deprived of the chief elements of her material strength by the loss of her Slav dependents, and shut in between France and a nation brought up to hate her German oppressors even more than her Russian oppressors; an ambitious ally, warlike and heroic, always under the protecting hand of France, brought near to her by her interests and passions, but separated from her by her frontiers; lastly, the number of Continental Powers augmented, and the Polish element playing permanently the part of separating the three Northern Powers—here we have the simple picture, arresting and true, which the idea of a resurrected Poland suggests to the minds of everyone, to the good sense of the man of the people, to the imagination of the writer, and to the experience o the statesman.

The present circumstances are such that the action of France can be developed in Europe under easy and unfettered conditions which probably will not occur again. Of these present conditions some are internal and others external. To appreciate the former at their true value we must go back in our minds to the recent war in Italy, to which an intervention on the part of France in favour of Poland presents an evident analogy. At that time we had the singular spectacle of a nation taken unawares by the initiative of its head, at first astonished and hesitating, and then drawn on little by little by the grandeur of the conception, and finally rushing forward with unheard-of ardour and limitless confidence towards the goal that was offered. Who could deny that the success of this memorable war, which opens up a new era of the rights of peoples and of modern international policy, was not due as much to the incredible stirring of the mind of the public in France as to the victories of Magenta and Solferino? And yet this impulse of opinion towards Italy which carried along and decided everything was fought against by egoists and enemies before, during, and after the war. Resistance to the Emperor's policy was very keen on the part of the Legitimists on account of their dethroned princes, and on the part of the clericals on account of the menace to the Temporal Power! Taken as a whole the upper classes, not very liberal by nature, and of aristocratic leanings, treated the Italian war as a revolutionary war, and predicted a letting loose of demagogic passions and the ruin of every monarchical and religious institution. Their outcry was swollen by those proceeding from men still in the grooves of a superannuated policy, holding opinions, we are willing to believe, independent of the influence of former parties, but still little enlightened. To hear them talk it was impolitic to allow the substitution of a united nation at our gates, susceptible of creating difficulties and possibly danger, for an agglomeration of small states, with no mutual understanding and no effective strength.

Well, intervention on behalf of Poland will be exposed to no opposition in any of the above quarters. The Polish clergy is openly on the side of the insurrection; it is as much a war of religion as of race; so much for the Catholics. The memories of Polish nationality are mingled with those of the old French monarchy. They are a tradition; so much for the Legitimists. No one of aristocratic pretensions affected by rich Parisian Society to-day and by high Government circles is unfavourable to Poland. Seeing the example given by the brilliant Polish nobility and these heroic priests, a war on behalf of Poland will seem almost like a crusade in the eyes of our upper *bourgeoisie*, reactionary from a feeling of good taste, and religious-minded from vanity, whose evil influence on the *personnel* of the Government cannot be disputed. As for the masses and the people, a surer and truer instinct will lead them towards this great cause, which for them is one concerning liberty and independence. If at the moment the nation appears to be somewhat lukewarm it is because it has no confidence. The revolutions have not affected our people; they have caused them to mature; they remain cold under vain declamation, under noisy and ineffective demonstrations; they no longer rise to enthusiasm except for the purpose of action, and in doing.

Let the Emperor say: " The restoration of Poland is no longer a dream; she is about to come to life again. Before speaking I have acted. I have my allies, and I know my enemies. I know what to expect from the former, and to fear from the latter. Everything has been foreseen, the end and the means. Let us march forward, and, made strong by the assent of the nation, I am going to realise the greatest conception, and repair the greatest crime of modern times."

Let the Emperor give forth these words, and they will arouse an enthusiasm the like of which has not been seen. The question is the same in 1863 as it was in 1831. There is now, in addition, the heroism of a nation running unarmed to face death, and in front of the crushing preponderance of France created by the wars in the Crimea and Italy over a humbled Russia and Germany. As regards the facilities from inside, which a French intervention might expect to encounter in Europe, these will depend on the diplomatic skill we display, upon the plan adopted, the dispositions taken towards each Power by France, and the equilibrium between so many diverse and profoundly disturbed interests which she will seek to preserve.

We may perhaps at the outset lay down the principle that the territorial re-arrangement must not be a partial one. Not only must we leave none of the former Polish provinces, whoever their present oppressors may be, outside a reconstituted Poland, but it is necessary to consider the question of Venice and also of the Orient (Constantinople) in solving the general situation. The design of French diplomacy will be to direct European policy in such a way that each of the Powers, while thinking they are only obeying their own inspirations, will be really following the course marked out in the general plan which the Emperor has decided upon on his own initiative, and in which he will continue to be the guiding spirit, if he is quite clear about what he means to do. Below is a suggestion of what this plan might be, conceived from an almost ideal point of view, and capable of being modified by force of circumstances:

1. The kingdom of Poland, the former Polish provinces now incorporated in the Russian Empire, Posnania and Galicia, shall form an independent State.
2. Venetia shall be handed over to the kingdom of Italy.
3. Servia, Bosnia, Bulgaria, part of Roumania, Albania, and, speaking generally, the Slav provinces in the Ottoman Empire shall become a State, or a Confederation of States.
4. Wallachia, Moldavia, and Bessarabia shall be made into an independent State.
5. Constantinople shall be made a free city.
6. Greece shall receive as an addition to her territory Epirus, Macedonia, and Thessaly.
7. Austria shall receive large compensations in Germany in return for giving up Venetia and Galicia.
8. France shall have the lands possessed by Bavaria, Hesse, and Prussia on the left bank of the Rhine, while Belgium shall be respected.
9. Sweden shall have Finland and, possibly, Denmark.

If France adopts this plan and proceeds to carry it out there will be, as a necessary result, a partition of the different European interests, which we will now indicate:

Italy will be our active ally, without any restrictions. All her material and moral resources will be placed at our disposal.

Sweden will have no difficulty in securing the anti-Russian opinion of the public on our side; the character of the King makes this certain.

Appendix

England can be brought to regard the territorial re-arrangements in a light favourable to her interests.

By the restoration of Poland, of the Slav Confederacy, and the kingdom of Roumania, the great stumbling-block in the way of English policy would disappear, that is to say, the danger of seeing the Russians in Constantinople. England would thus find a way out of the *impasse* in which she is placed of having to uphold at all costs an Empire which is condemned, from the fear of seeing it become the prey of a formidable rival. On the other hand, there exists in that country (England) a background of sincere liberalism which is having greater weight every day on her traditional policy, and is modifying it. Would the England of 1863 dare to take the side of this work of iniquity and spoliation against which the conscience of all people is protesting, as she did in 1815 ? The road travelled by public opinion since the latter date is immense. The old Toryism of forty years ago would not have hesitated to march to the aid of Austria and of the Treaties threatened by France. In 1859 the public sense of uprightness, political prudence, and the sentiment of the justice of the Italian cause stayed the hand of the English Government. It is quite certain that any initiative on a large scale promoted by France is bound to arouse a certain amount of distrust and animosity in England. But four years ago we had proof of how little such feelings weighed as against the humanitarian spirit animating the great mass of the nation and a few of its most highly considered statesmen. If the Emperor reassures the English in regard to the aggressive *arrière-pensées* with which they credit him, if he represents to them the intervention of 1863 as the corollary and the complement of the intervention begun in 1854 transferred to another theatre, but destined, when all is said and done (like the latter intervention), to save the shores of the Straits and the Black Sea from Russian domination, it will not be difficult to secure on their part not only a benevolent neutrality but moral support. If France shows herself determined to pursue this generous design, cost what it may, England will probably decide to co-operate so as not to leave to her all the honour, when she sees moreover that her dearest interests are involved in its success. What will be asked from her will be her moral co-operation and simple diplomatic engagements which, while giving her every opportunity as an ally to watch closely over her own interests, will not draw her into any of those costly armaments and chances of war which are as repugnant to her as they are exciting to the genius of the French.

Austria is the real pivot of our plan, and seems to be the Power most difficult to attract and to preserve in a state of benevolent neutrality. By a political foresight which does the greatest honour to her statesmen she is almost anticipating the position France has in reserve for her. Either the present conduct of Austria during the past month since the beginning of the (Polish) insurrection is completely lacking in sense and an unqualified imprudence, or else it is the result of careful reflection in face of the grave events in Poland. It is clear that she could have no right to be astonished by any overtures on the part of France, since by favouring the insurrection she is lending a hand in a revolution, the success of which must infallibly cost her at least one province. She must already have contemplated in her mind the sacrifice of Galicia; she must think of what compensations she can take. Only to see the freedom of her movements and the newness of her attitude one might imagine that her policy is bringing about at this moment, not a partial, but a radical evolution, and that by the same stroke she is dreaming of freeing herself from everything in her heritage from the past which constituted her weakness and proved her ruin. We will speak of Venetia. If we suppose the Austrian statesmen to be deeply penetrated by the real conditions of the existence and greatness of their country, we must credit them with the following line of reasoning : " Sooner or later we shall have to give up our dominion over Galicia and Venetia. The Polish question offers us a unique occasion to cede honourably what will one day be taken from us, and to place our alliance and our neutrality at a sufficiently high price to enable us to obtain the equivalent of what we are going to lose." Such is the line of thought the French Government should develop, and such the inclination it should exploit in its relations with Austria. As a secondary consideration it will not fail to make much of the territorial advantage Austria will extract from the restoration of Poland. She (Austria) will find herself separated by a powerful barrier from a formidable neighbour, now become odious to her as much on account of her ill-will in 1859 as of her services in 1849.

It would be narrow policy to bargain with Austria for the price to be paid for her sacrifices. Besides, it is not France who will pay her this price, but Germany. We have indicated the possibility of re-arranging the territorial distribution of that country, by causing the disappearance of certain secondary States, such as Bavaria and perhaps Saxony. Here we have, we must allow, one of the most delicate portions of the plan proposed. The natural march of events equally with diplomacy, will help in developing this conception, in causing it to be accepted, and in bringing it to maturity. Let us say only that anything that can contribute to make Germany into two sharply defined sections, and to constitute the whole of her into two great states, is to the advantage of France. When there shall no longer be on German soil any but Austrians and Prussians the idea of a unified Germany will be dead. There remain, lastly, Russia and Prussia. Here we have our enemies, and our only ones, whom we must beat, and who, in short, will bear all the burden of this great " general post " in Europe as a penalty for their former violation of the rights of nations, and of their present unworthy conduct.

There now remains only to indicate the diplomatic point whereby France will be enabled to enter into the Polish question.

The treaty of intervention between Prussia and Russia opens out a quite natural and highly legitimate way. This treaty, designed to combine them in common action for the suppression of the Polish element, is an act conceived directly in the spirit of the Holy Alliance—the spirit of 1815. As such, France refuses to recognise it; she tears it up.

Such is the plan we should like to see adopted by the Emperor, for it is not one to be entrusted entirely to diplomatists for its execution. If it be destined to influence the mind of the Emperor, it is not even necessary that it should be communicated to the Ministers who carry out his will. We should like to feel that this plan might form a sort of *critérium* to which the Emperor in his meditations would refer all the successive developments of his policy. History contains a memorable example of a comprehensive design as vast as the one we are proposing. This was the famous plan of the complete re-grouping of Europe conceived by Henri IV, of which Sully alone had cognisance. The practical means by which a commencement of putting into execution the plan proposed may be divided into overt and secret measures.

Secret Measures : The immediate despatch to Vienna of a personal agent of the Emperor, bearing a letter to Francis Joseph. This might be just a letter of authorisation given to the agent for the purpose of accrediting him. The person chosen should be a diplomatist of sufficient experience and sufficiently sure for the Emperor to leave to him the liberty to develop his proposals either more or less in accordance with the reception accorded to him.

After a reply has been received proceedings would be taken in Italy and Sweden.

Overt measures : Issue an official notice, arresting and immediate, coincident with the departure of the agent to Vienna so as to give Poland a testimony of French sympathy. Make a proposal to England to associate herself with it. This public demonstration is necessary in order to sustain and encourage the insurrection, the whole plan being based on its duration. The Poles, in expectation of being assisted, must manage to hold out at all costs for a month and a half, up to the time when it shall be possible to pass from diplomatic to military action.

This document, in the form of a Note, should be drawn up in a manner capable of allowing it to remain as a mere protest, or to serve as the point of departure of a rupture according to the nature of the reply from Austria.

If this reply be favourable, that is, if it promises her support or only her benevolent neutrality in a written engagement, France will present an ultimatum to Prussia insisting on her ceasing her intervention, and on her breaking her treaty with Russia ; this high-handed proposal will naturally be rejected, and will be followed immediately by war.

This ultimatum would be communicated to England together with an invitation to her to associate herself with it. As we should then no longer hide from the English Cabinet that war would follow immediately after the threat, we should allow her to occupy Antwerp with a fleet as a pledge assuring her of the moderation of our designs.

In order to give us the necessary freedom of action, and to avoid scattering our forces, we should have to instruct General Forey to treat with the Government of Juarez[1] immediately after our entry into Mexico, or even at Puebla, and to re-embark his troops without delay for France.

The Emperor will base the rapidity of his action on the news from Vienna, but the military preparations should begin from to-day.

If Austria's reply be wholly unfavourable, that is, if she declares that she will take up arms in defence of the Federal Territory, there would be no occasion to push to extremities an enterprise which would have arrayed against it the three great military Powers of Central Europe. All that will remain of the initiative taken by France will be the first Note sent to

[1] President of the Republic of Mexico during the French expedition.

Prussia, which will be merely an honourable protest in favour of the rights of a nation, and a heavy responsibility resting less upon Austria than upon England, whose co-operation if it were as whole-hearted as that of France would be able to make up for all the other alliances.

If the attitude of Austria permit, the chief elements of military action would be:

The first part of the war would consist in the invasion of the German provinces on the left bank of the Rhine, Belgian neutrality being respected.

When our base of operations shall have been established on the Rhine our first objective will be Berlin, and the second, Varsovie.

The principal army, set apart to march upon the Rhine and Prussia, will number 300,000 men. Its point of concentration will be Metz.

A second army of 100,000 men will be assembled at Strasbourg, destined to hold the small States of the German Confederation and prevent them from sending their contingents to Prussia from fear of the invasion of their own territory.

A corps of 60,000 men concentrated at Cherbourg will be set apart to be transported to the Baltic in order to operate on the coasts with Vilna as their objective, in this way cutting the Russian line of operations. The armoured fleet would act against Cronstadt. At Toulouse 30,000 men from the depots would be concentrated, to watch the Spanish frontier.

The Italian contingent would act with the great army, that of Sweden with the troops which have been embarked.

We have therefore a total of 490,000 effectives which France should send to the front. By deducting 70,000 Italians and 20,000 Swedes, that would represent the effective strength we should have to feed and maintain. We do not think we should be very far from the truth in taking the figure of 800,000 to represent the number of men it would be wise to call up so as always to have 400,000 ready to fight.

NOTE IV

Note relative to the publication of the correspondence of Napoleon I sent to the Emperor at Compiègne on the 11th November, 1863.

The Purpose of the publication:

A collection for posterity of all interesting documents from the hand of the Emperor Napoleon I is a grand conception which ought to be carried out in the reign of Napoleon III.

It is the erecting of a monument to the glory of the Emperor; it should be a most complete *répertoire* for the enlightenment of history.

To enable this work to be done well, much tact and much care is requisite, and it should be inspired by pious admiration and great devotion to the memory of the great Emperor.

Appendix

Everything appearing in a publication of this kind, carried out under the directions of his nephew and successor, the Emperor Napoleon III, possesses the greatest importance.

This purpose cannot be attained unless a simple, but very clearly defined programme, be adopted.

Our ideas on the subject are as follows :

1. The erecting of a monument for the glorification of the Emperor, which should endeavour to make him known under his most favourable aspects.

2. To insert nothing which is contrary to the truth, for one has no right to falsify history, even through enthusiasm for the Emperor.

3. To show the Emperor in his true light to posterity, but only to publish letters likely to be favourable to him.

4. To avoid everything which may do harm to individuals without bringing any advantage to the Emperor.

Let us quote an example :

Any letter written by the Emperor has an evident interest, and possesses a value of its own, but it may do harm to the person to whom it is addressed. We understand its being published in consideration of its value and the good it may do to the Emperor. It is evidently this sentiment which decided the present Emperor to allow the publication of letters injurious to his own father.

We are not of opinion that because some harmful document has been published already in some obscure and little-known collection, there is not grave inconvenience in letting it appear in the great work in question.

The present publication is a historical work of high importance, which will place on record the most complete and the most authentic collection, concerning the history of the Emperor, and will be lasting, and the publicity which will be given to it cannot be compared to anything which may often be ephemeral and soon forgotten.

5. To suppress every document which in the opinion of the Emperor was not written to be made public, but was written by him for some special and personal purpose, and not to serve the general ends of history.

6. To suppress all documents possessing no interest, and which can only render this publication long and diffuse.

Character of the publication as it has been carried out hitherto :

The work, as now proceeding, does not correspond to the purpose which should be kept in view. It is not properly divided ; as chronological order by itself is not enough, it is often tiresome and long, and it is impossible to make ready research into it ; in making a study of it one has the feeling that no clear principles have guided the choice of the documents ; we feel it is possible to discern that this work has not been done in a sufficiently profound sentiment of admiration and devotion. If this continues it will do the Emperor more harm than good. His enemies will discover therein weapons for use against his memory. We think there is a certain lack of order reigning in the interior organisation of the work of the Commission.

There is no guarantee that documents are safeguarded from being taken away, and some have been read by indiscreet persons. From the financial point of view this publication is costing a great deal, and yet it does not proceed sufficiently quickly; the employés are badly paid; editors are permitted the right of reproduction without paying anything for it. The credits allowed might be put to a better use.

With the allocation inscribed on the budget for this year, five or six volumes could be published without difficulty, instead of three or four. The quicker this publication advances, the more closely will it correspond to its purpose, and be more economical, inasmuch as the general expenses, and especially those for the *personnel*, are the same every year whether one more or one less volume appear.

An example of the bad use the funds are put to is contained in the case of a gentleman[1] who came to grief over agricultural insurance, and is duly inscribed as a member of the Commission, who attends very seldom and yet draws a salary of 8,000 francs per annum—the highest of all—while there are poor employés who do a great deal of work and only draw 2,400 francs and some even 2,000 francs.

The following were appointed members of the Commission by decree of the 7th September, 1854:

Marshal Vaillant.

M. Ch. Dupin, Vice-President (he never comes and takes no interest in it at all).

General Aupick, dead.

General de Flahaut, who, although absent, follows the work with care, devotion, and intelligence. He always opposes the insertion of documents which might harm the Emperor.

M. Henri Boulay de la Meurthe, dead.

M. Prosper Mérimée.

M. de Chabrier, who resigned because he did not wish to associate his name with a publication which he considered was being badly carried out.

M. Armand Lefèvre, prevented from taking part in the work through illness.

M. Chassériau.

M. Perron, who draws a salary which is completely thrown away and who, although a duly inscribed member of the Commission, has been charged with the direction of the Secretariat and takes no concern in it.

Other decrees appointed:

General Petit, dead.

M. Cucheval Clarigny.

M. Paul de Champagny, a Deputy.

M. de Laborde, Director of the Archives, replaced M. de Chabrier in 1858.

M. Goschler, secretary to M. Thiers, and appointed through his influence in 1863 for the sole purpose of watching this publication in order that it may not be at variance with his *Histoire du Consulat et de l'Empire*.

[1] The Prince first wrote the name of M. Perron and then scratched it out.

Appendix

At the present time, therefore, the Commission consists of :
Marshal Vaillant, President.
M. Ch. Dupin, Vice-President.
General de Flahaut.
M. Chassériau.
M. Paul de Champagny.
M. Cucheval Clarigny.
M. de Laborde.
M. Perron.
M. Goschler.

Changes to be introduced in this publication:

The Commission should be composed at the very most of five or six members.

The Emperor's family has a right to be represented on it, and the interests of his dynasty and family, which might be found in any simple publication written by a private individual, ought not to be excluded.

A secretary ought to be appointed to act under this Commission, with the qualified title as such, its prerogatives and salary.

A special officer for military matters.

Another employé for civil matters.

A certain number of additional employés at a suitable remuneration, a dozen in all, who would cost no more than the present employés.

Basing itself on the programme unfolded above, the publication should be divided into four chief categories, as follows :

1. Politics in general.
2. Military matters.
3. Government and interior administration.
4. Private affairs and various.

Nothing could be easier in the future than this new division which would possess many advantages ; as regards the past it would be necessary to recast the thirteen volumes already issued ; the work of doing this would not take more than six months ; it would not mean the loss of a considerable sum of money, inasmuch as 1,500 copies are being printed, of which 1,000 are distributed, and a large portion of the work already done would be available again.

If the Emperor adopts these ideas, it would be necessary, in order to carry them out, to issue an Order, which would not appear in the *Moniteur*, and which, while thanking the present Commission for the work it has accomplished, would enact that H.M., wishing to adopt a new classification, appoints a new Commission composed of MM. —— with an allocation of —— from the permanent budget.

A letter from the Emperor to the President would indicate very concisely the programme to be followed by the Commission.

The President would be responsible to the Emperor. He would consult the Commission, would appoint the employés, and would work only with them so as to make sure of their discretion.

The present funds would suffice without any increase.

NOTE V

Note on a conversation between the Emperor Napoleon and myself which took place on the 19th June, 1865, at the Tuileries.[1]

On the 15th May, 1865, I inaugurated at Ajaccio in Corsica a monument to the Emperor Napoleon I and his four brothers. I made a speech and sent notes of it to the Emperor, who was travelling in Algeria, by M. ——, the captain of the armoured frigate *Gloire*, who left Ajaccio on the 17th May. The Emperor was very dissatisfied with my speech. He wrote to me from Algiers on the 23rd May a very severe letter, and sent orders to the Empress, in whose hands he had left the Regency, to publish it in the *Moniteur*, which was done on the 27th May. I replied on the 27th sending in my resignation as Vice-President of the Privy Council and President of the Commission of the *Exposition Universelle* of 1867. My letter was inserted in the newspapers in the evening at the same time as that of the Emperor. The Ministers were very much up in arms against me, especially M. Lavalette, the Minister of the Interior. The Empress preserved apparent calmness. I know she is delighted over this censure and this rupture with the Emperor. On the evening of the 6th June she wrote to me at Meudon, where I was staying with my wife, stating that the Emperor had sent her an order to publish in the *Moniteur* of next day a notice that my resignations had been accepted. On the 8th June the Emperor arrived in Paris; I did not present myself at the Tuileries, but sent General Franconière, my chief Aide-de-Camp, to inform the Emperor that after his letter I did not feel it to be my duty to present myself without an express order. The Emperor had a long talk with Franconière and gave him a message for me to go and see him next morning, Sunday, at 9.30, in his private study. While this was taking place on Saturday I had gone to pay a call in Paris in an American buggy drawn by one horse. My horse bolted and threw me from the vehicle in front of the Hippodrome, near the Arc de l'Étoile. I sustained rather severe contusions which kept me in bed and confined to my room at Meudon until the 18th June. When I was feeling better I informed the Emperor through Franconière that as I was now recovering I was able to go and see him; he made an appointment for next day, the 19th, at 1 p.m. On arriving at the Tuileries at the entrance beneath the clock I found on duty there General de Goyon, A.D.C. in uniform, and Walsch, the Chamberlain, who announced me. M. Benedetti was to have had an audience and was waiting in the Salon des Drapeaux. The Emperor at once received me in the Council Chamber, which is just before you come to his private study, where he receives me habitually. We were both in morning dress. The following conversation took place and lasted until 2.30:

The Emperor, with an air of embarrassment, giving me his hand: "I hope you are better; your accident might have been very serious."

Myself: "Yes, but I am getting over that, Sire," and added a few details.

---

[1] In margin: "Very interesting conversation, one of the frankest and the most animated I have had with my cousin the Emperor. Throws light on many things."

Appendix

The Emperor: " I did not think it had been so serious. Sit down."
We seated ourselves at the round table on two chairs. He lighted a cigarette.
The Emperor: " I am *désolé* over what has happened, but I was obliged to do it. I am not angry with you personally, but for a long time past I have been annoyed at the trouble you cause me; I will not have people think that I have two policies, one official and one hidden, of which you are the instrument. I wrote my letter specially to put an end to it, and to show that I disapprove of what you said. It was to free myself of any kind of responsibility that I did it."
Myself: " While admitting that His Majesty might wish to free himself from responsibility and not allow himself to be compromised, he could have done it in a less wounding form. I was quite prepared to send in my resignation from the Privy Council; I had offered His Majesty to do so two months ago, and I only remained at his earnest wish."
The Emperor: " You exaggerate the violence of my letter; its terms do not say what you see in it."
Myself: " I do not think there is any instance of a similar publication. Our uncle used to write harshly. He had reason to be annoyed, both with your father when he gave up the throne of Holland, and with Murat when he betrayed him. Well, the *Moniteur* never appeared on the scenes; he never published anything like it. I am deeply wounded and quite understand the whole drift of it. After all, for what have you to reproach me? My ideas of a liberal Empire? I have held them since reaching the age of reason; you have developed them in your writings; it has been the theme of the entire Bonapartist and Liberal party from 1815 to 1848. Knowing that I should have to make a speech at Ajaccio you ought to have understood well that I could not make one in any other spirit. I gave you notice through M. Conti, the head of your Private Office. You could have asked me to inform you of its purport, or to discuss it with you before your departure."
The Emperor: " I did not think of it, to tell you the truth, but that makes no difference. I will be equally frank; there is no need to find fault with such and such a passage in your speech; it was the whole gist as I read it; the beginning struck me as very good, and I was almost provoked at the end, where I read into it a programme, and that was what gave the motive to my letter. No one must make out a programme in my government, even a good one, apart from me. There cannot be two heads under one hat; that cannot and must not be; you cannot hold an opinion differing from that actuating my policy; I will not permit it."
Myself: " How is it that you have not found my previous speeches distasteful, or have not, at least, requested me formally not to make any more? Why invite me to the Privy Council when you were aware of my opinions and conduct?"
The Emperor: " Yes, I did not attach importance to it, but in reality I am not annoyed at what has happened; I am very glad; this was bound to arise any time during the past five or six years, and your speech was as much a pretext as a reason. I am very glad I was not in Paris; if I had been I might possibly not have written, or, at least, published, my letter,

from weak motives ; you would have come to me ; we should have talked together as we are doing to-day ; I should have reproached you and the matter would have rested there ; as it is, I wrote to you and caused my letter to be published. This was better, and there is no occasion to go back to it. I do not discuss my policy ; it is an easy thing to blame it when you are not in power. Already the country has too much liberty. You say I am despotic, while I can do nothing without the Council of State, the Ministers, or God knows who ! I can do nothing."

Myself : " Apart from you the citizens can do nothing, can write nothing ; there is no liberty of any kind. I do not think that will suit France in the long run. Our great uncle understood that. That your Government is badly organised and full of friction I know well ; you have not even the power to do good, but the country is oppressed. You are aware I have thought this always. From 1852 to 1859 you let me say that I was out of touch with public opinion, but since 1859 the awakening of public spirit and its liberal leanings have made you annoyed that I was the expression of that public spirit. You do not care for me any more ; you only appointed me Vice-President of the Privy Council at the solicitation of MM. Walewski, Magne and Persigny, who were anxious to justify their 100,000 francs by setting up the Privy Council again, and to make people believe in its usefulness. You have repented of it."

The Emperor : " Do not let us talk sentiment ; politics do not include it. Napoleon at St. Helena was no longer in power."

Myself : " Our uncle's greatest enemies say what your Majesty is saying. On the day when it shall be proved that the Empire and liberty are incompatible, our Dynasty will be in a very bad way. My sentiments have never varied. In Switzerland, in England when we were in exile together, and after my return to France, my two convictions have been the raising yet higher of the name of Napoleon, and the establishment of liberty. You must at least, as I said to the Empress, recognise my sincerity and my conviction, for what good does it do me to uphold these ideas ? I could have been influential, rich, and an object of adulation ; I am nothing of the sort ; I am in disgrace with your Government, persecuted, and well-nigh insulted, but I have my conscience and the dream of my life—the Empire establishing securely the glory and liberty of France. I shall never change, and I accept even persecution. If you do not regret your letter, I do not regret my speech."

The Emperor : " Well, well, s be it. But take into careful consideration that revolutions like that of 1830 do not always succeed." Looking at me, and feeling that he had gone too far, after a moment's silence, " Have you nothing to say ? "

Myself : " I acknowledge, Sire, that I have reflected deeply in the past over the revolution of 1830, but that I had never considered any hypothesis of the kind for the future. It is not a revolution like that of 1830 that will take place, but another. I am profoundly amazed at what you have just said."

The Emperor : " It was not said to wound you ; it is a simple argument."

Myself : " I am not a conspirator. I have the defects of the opposite ; you know well what I think ; you are well up in what I do and say ; I

Appendix

speak my mind too openly; people do not conspire or intrigue in that way. I have never seen that kind of thing at close quarters except when I was with you in England. *You* could not bring yourself to believe what people say about me in this respect."

The Emperor: " No, clearly, I do not say I do believe it, but your conduct lends itself to such suppositions. You see all the enemies of my Government. You talk, people make you talk; things cannot go on in this way."

Myself: " True, I never disown my former friends. Many of them are not enemies of your Government. I see very few people, and very few of those you call your enemies; there is never a word said in my house that you might not hear."

The Emperor: " But, *mon Dieu*! It is the force of circumstances! Look at Morny—people believed I regretted his death. It is very trying for him, for this would not have been said six months ago, because when President of the Chamber he wanted to play the liberal and make himself popular."

Myself: " I am not comparing myself to M. de Morny, who owed his influence to a question of birth, of which I will not remind you in support of the belief that you could refuse him nothing, that he was all-powerful, and used his influence to fill his pockets. *I* am an honourable man."

The Emperor: " I will not wound you by making this comparison; I know there is no comparison between you and Morny and all his underhand dealing; but it affords an example to prove that I will not admit of two directives in my Government. I should have ended by telling Morny, ' Play the " popular " *rôle* in the Chamber, but I will not appoint you again to be its President; you can clear out of my counsels.' What I am saying is to show you clearly that my action against you is part of my system, and has nothing personal in it."

Myself: " Your Majesty has a very great contempt for men. True, your Ministers have no strong convictions as a rule."

The Emperor: " As a matter of fact I believe these gentlemen would be quite ready to follow a different policy if I wished it, and that I should not have great difficulty in inducing them to do so."

Myself: " Like M. Drouyn de Lhuys in the convention with Italy on the 15th September."

The Emperor: " What does it matter? That sort of thing is bound to happen; I cannot make men."

Myself: " Look at M. Rouher, who was just as much opposed to the Temporal Power of the Pope as I am, and made two speeches in his favour more violent than mine, wherein he recognised the right of the Catholics to Rome—a thing which M. Billault never did, and would not have done."

The Emperor: " Oh! that's quite true; M. Rouher went too far; that was absurd."

Myself: " If I quarrelled with Rouher it was over the law relating to gratuitous and obligatory public education, to which you had driven me, and on account of his silence when, on two occasions, he did not defend me, in spite of his promises and my observations—me, a member of the Government, and not in a position to defend myself."

The Emperor : " Yes ; there you are perfectly right. Rouher behaved badly, but what would you have had me do in the matter ? It was too late, and at that time I had need of him. And then lawyers—they will plead for any cause you like. However, what is done is done."

Myself, getting up : " I find I must go to Switzerland with my family, and also to the seaside for salt-water baths, as my position in Paris is becoming difficult. I hope Your Majesty sees no objection ? "

The Emperor : " None whatever; do as you wish. Your plans seem quite natural to me."

Myself : " Then, Sire, allow me to take leave of Your Majesty, and to say good-bye."

The Emperor, shaking me by the hand : " Adieu, a pleasant journey, a thousand kind messages to Clotilde." And coming with me to the door : " By the way, will you not take leave of the Empress before your departure ? "

Myself : " I fear, Sire, the Empress will be unable to see me again at present. Later on, certainly ; we will see. Adieu, Sire."

The conversation, of which the above is a *résumé*, lasted an hour and a half. On leaving the *salon* at about 2.30 I found waiting in the first room M. Benedetti, M. Schneider, Vice-President of the Chamber, and M. Petetin, Director of the Imperial Printing Press.

The Emperor was embarrassed during the first half-hour. Once he began talking freely he was at his ease. I was very cold at the beginning, but became animated as the conversation went on. Conclusions are not difficult to draw. The Emperor does not know how to talk ; he has no defence when speaking ; he is either silent and says nothing, or if he speaks he tells one everything in his mind, or one can easily guess it ; hence the cynicism of his words.

NOTE VI

Petition of Prince Napoleon to the Emperor to be given an acting military appointment in the event of war breaking out in 1866.

To His Majesty the Emperor
(Presented personally to the Emperor, 19th June.)
Paris, 19th June, 1866.

The Emperor will recollect his letter to Prince Napoleon, and the difficult position its publication has created for his Cousin during the past year. The silence and abstention on the part of the Prince have been complete ; he has passed almost the whole of this period in the country or in travelling. Some months ago His Majesty had thought of making Prince Napoleon President of the Exhibition ; this idea has not been possible of realisation. To-day, now that grave events are preparing in Europe, Prince Napoleon has expressed to His Majesty his keen desire to be appointed to active service should war break out; he has begged the Emperor to think of him either in the position of Major-General of the chief army, should His Majesty take the command, or as Commander of the naval forces conjointly with that of the troops to be disembarked for action in the Adriatic. His Majesty has received kindly the desire of his Cousin. A few days ago the attitude of France had not been decided; to-day, in the letter read to the Legislative Assembly, it is defined thus: A watchful neutrality for the moment. This attitude is capable of leading France to war if the balance of power in Europe should be changed, or if Italy be defeated; hence arises a great chance of war within a few months. What ought the position of the Prince to be during the present period of waiting?

1. Prince Napoleon can remain as he is, that is to say, quite outside all public matters.

2. The Prince can request to be allowed to go on the Staff of his father-in-law in Italy, as supernumerary. Will the Emperor give his permission? Would the King be pleased to accede to this? Will the position of the Prince as a mere interested spectator, with no official position, without authority or a mission from the Emperor, be agreeable or possible? Will it not be irksome for him, and for Italy, and compromising for the Emperor, the Prince before everything else being determined to remain what he is— a French Prince?

3. The Prince can ask the Emperor for a position dating from to-day. This would be of political advantage to the Emperor, and would benefit the Prince in leaving his present position. *What position can this be?*

Political? No; that would suit neither the Emperor nor the Prince.

Civil? No; that would not suit the Prince.

Remains a military position which might be a provisional one. If war breaks out it could be exchanged for one of the two Commands indicated above.

If war does not break out within a few months the Prince could relinquish his command. This would have in any case the great advantage of blotting out the Emperor's disfavour, which still weighs upon the Prince, and of placing him again in a normal position.

What waiting position could he have to-day?

Either the command of the Guard, or the Higher Command of the French Squadrons.

It is for the Emperor to decide upon the different points submitted to him in this Note.

NOTE VII

Note on the General Elections of 1869.[1]

Paris, 28th May, 1869.

Every great electoral movement possesses a meaning and brings its own lesson. The chart of the May elections, 1869, presents clearly marked lines, easy to recognise, and showing a political photograph of the country.

[1] In the margin in the Prince's handwriting: "Delivered to the Emperor. Very important."

TE

The 292 elections which have just taken place may be classified as nearly as possible as follows :

For the Government, about 200.
For the Third Party, from 30 to 40.
For the Opposition aiming at an overthrow, from 30 to 35.
Purely Clerical (Clerical before Governmental), 7 or 8.
Orleanists and pure Legitimists, scarcely 4 or 5.

These electoral statistics represent fairly accurately the state of public opinion in the country. We may say that in the large towns the elections have been free, the Government having no real means at its disposal of exerting pressure in the populous centres. In the small towns and in the country administrative pressure has made itself felt very strongly ; nevertheless this has not notably affected the results. In fact if the Government has influenced fifty elections which cannot be regarded as either the spontaneous or real expression of public opinion, it cannot be disputed that, owing to its mischievous manœuvres, it has converted a considerable number of electors in several constituencies to favour candidates representing the extreme Opposition, thereby playing into the hands of the latter while trying to thwart them.

The Empire, therefore, together with the name of Napoleon, has been confirmed by a large majority.

Out of all the parties who desire its overthrow one only is of any considerable proportions, and is compact—that of the Social Republic. Its partisans are in agreement as to what they wish to destroy, but they have found it impossible to define a system which they would like to raise on the ruins of the existing state of society. In this lies their irremediable weakness ; it is what prevents them from finding among their numbers any leaders of consideration, and brings about that the tail of the party leads it and controls the head, instead of following it.

The Orleanists only represent an infinitesimal minority among the *bourgeoisie*, which is itself a minority within the mass of the electorate. If they number a few men worthy of consideration on account of their ability and social position, it is in a special degree due to their spirit of intrigue that they enjoy a kind of *prestige* which the deciding proof of the electoral urn has just dissipated.

The Legitimists have been powerless to make any act or manifestation for their party in the elections.

As for the clericals, if there has been one striking defeat it is that of their party. From this we can draw a lesson of the antipathy with which they inspire the country, and of the harm any alliance with them would occasion to the Government.

We repeat again that the name of Napoleon still emerges triumphant from this test.

But among the adherents of the Government, what is the dominating spirit ?

Professions of opinion, circulars, the language used by the candidates elected, and the entire spirit resulting from the elections testify in the most striking manner that the great majority of the electors entertain liberal ideas. Personal government is condemned generally ; for a reactionary

Empire the new Chamber contains only a very small number of partisans —barely thirty.

The Emperor, therefore, is once again the arbiter of the destinies of France. His policy will be followed without question by the elected representatives of the country. The principle of his authority being still further confirmed to-day, it is for him to decide in what sense he will make use of this preponderating influence.

If by making a change of men and system he enters upon a constitutional and liberal path, if he is wise enough to sacrifice a portion of his power, more apparent than real, it is not open to doubt that he will be followed in the Chamber, and his popularity in the country will increase. The mistakes of the past will be extenuated ; hostility, without being disarmed, will lose its influence over the masses ; we may say that the Empire will take root.

If, on the contrary, the Emperor makes use of his considerable influence only to favour the reactionary policy of the Clericals ; if he continues to employ the discredited men forming the *personnel* of the existing system of Government, who are out of touch with public opinion, he may command a momentary success, he will dominate the country for a certain time, but he will strengthen the republican, socialist and revolutionary opposition in the future. The power he will have thus given it will show itself in a terrible manner on the day when interior or foreign complications shall arise.

The situation is a complex one in this sense—that, though the Empire possesses great strength, its adherents are scattered, and in the country districts few and far between, while upon certain points its adversaries are a disciplined and compact body in many of the large towns and especially in Paris. To be situated in the centre of an immense capital, the large majority of whose inhabitants are dreaming, up to a certain point, of the overthrow of the existing state of affairs, is one of the most difficult problems for any Government. Insurrection can be put down by force once, twice, thrice, but to hold Paris by force as the normal system is impossible ; it must be brought back into tune, and its hostility disarmed by enlightening it gradually by means of a wise policy.

It seems to us that in these decisive circumstances the choice of the Emperor can only lie between one of the three following courses which are presented to him :

1. *Reaction.*—A policy of this kind would have probably a momentary success, but in the course of time and in very certainty on the death of the Emperor it would fall. The country would then be delivered over to frightful convulsions, and the marvellous strength proceeding from the name of Napoleon—the sole *prestige* still intact in the midst of so many others which have been destroyed—would be compromised if not shattered for the time being.

2. *The maintenance of the status quo, which we will call " The policy of indecision."*—This would be less deplorable than a policy of reaction ; it would carry on some sort of existence, but with no grandeur, no power, and would allow very few hopes of success. It is a slower but certain defeat for the Empire.

3. *Conciliation or initiation.*—This policy would consist in the Emperor placing himself at the head of the liberal movement, in creating a path for it while dominating it with vigour and directing it. This is the sole course which will produce fruit, the only one which will make the Empire lasting. Undoubtedly it is very late already; the past, and the opportunities lost render this action more difficult; but it is the only reasonable one to adopt. This lofty point of view is the only one capable of surmounting the difficulties to which every system of personal government is fatally exposed, and of minimising the faults inherent in all individual human directorship for the future.

Every Government has gone under through blind moral resistance; it is necessary, we believe, to give way to the liberal movement by a reform of the institutions and by resisting with energy to the last if this movement, departing from moral and legal paths, makes an appeal to force. It is just the opposite which every Government has done; they have resisted as far as the laws are concerned, but have yielded in the streets. There remains, it is true, the attempt to create a power capable of organising a material, as vigorously as a moral, reaction; we think that this is quite impossible, especially in regard to the time at our disposal to effect this. When revolution takes shape in men's minds and the time is ripe, there is no resistance in the material order for long; one cannot in the long run base a system on the fear which revolutionaries may inspire. In moments of danger the men who give the most reactionary advice are the first to abandon one; disorder begins by offering resistance, the spirit of revolution filters in everywhere like smoke through an old building; Louis Philippe said a true word, " I quitted, when everyone abandoned me."

It is not everything to be willing to make concessions, and the art of governing in our time, and in France in particular, is no longer the art of resistance; it consists in knowing how to make concessions. It is necessary to make up one's mind, not to be determined to check the movement, but to enclose it within dykes on each side in a bed from which it will not overflow and submerge everything.

We consider the present situation to be indubitably grave; it is clear that the democratic tide is rising. If it does not know what it wants, it knows what it does not want, and that is sufficient to overthrow. Undoubtedly it is already late, and the situation is not so good as it was some time ago. The Empire has not only used up the men who serve it in official positions, but has also to a certain degree affected those who might be able to serve it in the future; through a too prolonged struggle with them it has weakened them in the estimation of their friends, and lowered them in that of their enemies. To-day it is much more difficult and much more laborious to find new men and to initiate a frankly liberal policy than it was a few weeks ago. But the more we go on either in a reactionary groove or in the *status quo*, the more will the difficulties increase.

To determine to withstand the rising tide appears to us to be impossible, and a catastrophe confronts a policy of this kind. We should like to see **not** merely a separation from the men who personify this policy for the country, and liberal concessions; we think also that this should be done with a certain amount of ostentation. In order to save the Emperor, his Dynasty and the Empire, and to disarm his adversaries, it is necessary to offer up a certain number of men as a holocaust. This may be disagreeable, but it is necessary. The more the names of new men shall possess a certain signification the better it will be; the important thing is to choose men devoted to the principle and the maintenance of the Empire, and at the same time courageous men, who in a struggle involving material force do not fear to support you or to compromise themselves.

We are well aware of the arguments which may be brought to bear against the system we advocate; nothing is apparently simpler than to say, " The Revolution is surging over us: we must resist it." But this is a false reasoning, because you cannot resist it in the long run, inasmuch as the mistakes of the past have given too much force to the hostile parties. The true policy consists in giving way morally while resisting materially. We recognise the difficulties of this line of conduct, but no other is possible. Look at what Austria has been obliged to do as regards Hungary, and wisely; in spite of all the difficulties of coming to a compromise with Hungary any other course would have brought about her immediate overthrow.

Two forces alone exist in our country: the Revolution and the name of Napoleon. By fighting against each other they can bring themselves to nothing by alternative victories; but when all is said and done it will be the Revolution that will triumph. If the Emperor is wise enough to take some portion of its force from the Revolution and combine these two elements, success is not in doubt. To give an example: if three or four months ago the Emperor had chosen a Minister of the views of Ollivier, if he had sacrificed some of his own Ministers, the Prefect of the Seine and the stock-jobbers who compromise the morality of his rule, and had abandoned the official candidates, is there any reasonable man who can state that liberals who accept the principle of the Empire would not have been elected in many of the large towns, and even in Paris, in place of revolutionaries?

In spite of its exaggerations the Revolutionary Party possesses much force; but what makes this force ten times greater are the mistakes of the past, and the out-of-date officials. The *Pays* newspaper creates more partisans of the Revolution than the *Réveil* and the *Rappel*. Mexico, the administration of the city of Paris, the support given to the Temporal Power of the Pope, and the badly drawn-up laws concerning the Press and the right to hold meetings have all contributed to add strength to an exaggerated democratic feeling. To wait too long before yielding is the great danger, because then one has the appearance of giving way; you heed those who tell you that your honour is called upon to offer resistance, etc. Examples of the latter kind are contradicted by all the facts in the history of our times, and one exposes oneself once more to having to realise the truth of the words, " too late."

A society in a state of internecine war cannot continue to live. We are far from shrinking from strife, the emotions, and the political agitation necessary to a free country; but we must save the principle of government and of the sovereign.

Anything can be done with bayonets except to sit upon them.

We will define the policy we recommend in the following summary programme :

Call upon new men.

Favourable treatment of all who desire to make for themselves a position in the country.

Develop in a liberal sense the laws relating to the Press by means of the suppression of the enforcement of guarantees and a diminution of the stamp duty, and a mitigation of reforms tending to impair the influence of the Press which already has lost much of it.

Institution of the jury, or everyone's right to plead, together with the doing away of sending to prison, while maintaining severe punishments by fine.

Proceed further with the law relating to the right of meeting, by suppressing the prohibition to enter upon political and religious questions during the period of the elections—a prohibition which is absolutely useless and illusory, as experience has proved.

The repeal of the law concerning public safety, which is wholly useless.

A lessening of centralisation and of administrative oppression.

Introduce ministerial responsibility (say quite frankly that you are abandoning personal government), a mere constitutional figment, which takes away very little from the Emperor's power.

The reform of the Senate, which should become an elective Chamber of two grades—for example, appointed by the Councils-General.

A reduction in large salaries.

Diminish the power and the number of officials; affirm their responsibility by suppressing Art. 75 of the Constitution of the year VIII.

Develop public education on the widest scale.

Introduce a special law relating to the election of a municipal councillor of Paris, which within certain limits should empower the electors to participate in the choice of municipal councillors.

Foreign :

Relative disarmament.

A pacific policy, especially towards Germany.

The evacuation of the Papal States.

NOTE VIII

Note for the consideration of the Emperor relative to the enrolment of the Napoleonic Archives by making a collection of all the letters of Napoleon I.

7th December, 1869.

From the year 1815 to 1848 the letters of the Emperor Napoleon were carefully preserved in the Archives at the Louvre and were not handled by anyone except M. Thiers.

Appendix

In 1848 the Archives at the Louvre were transferred to the National Archives.

Since the date of the decision of His Majesty the Emperor Napoleon III, when he appointed a Commission presided over by Marshal Vaillant to undertake the publication of the correspondence of Napoleon I, the Emperor's letters have been handled, read, and copied, not only those in the Archives, but those in various public offices, the War Office, the Office of Foreign Affairs, the Office of Public Worship, etc.; from this has arisen a waste, a publicity badly supervised, and indiscretions on all sides.

Admitting in principle the necessity, which is realised, of making a collection of all the letters of Napoleon I, and of not having them scattered about among the different public offices, the following is the situation as regards the existing documents, and the method to be pursued in collecting them all together :

All the letters of Napoleon I, from 1808 to 1821, set apart to be withdrawn, were taken possession of by General Favé, with the exception of five letters which the Director of Archives was unable to hand over and which he feared he would not be able to find, and one referring to the King of Westphalia, which the Emperor withdrew personally some years ago.

The documents only consist of a certain number of letters which we have designated *pièces réservées*, of which the following is a brief list :

Archives of the Empire	287
Office of Foreign Affairs	23
	310
War Office	31
Public Worship	1
Finance	1
Public Instruction	1
Marine	2
Library at the Louvre	1
Total	347

A few are in the Registers, as follows :

1. Daily Register of the minutes of letters dictated by the Emperor Napoleon I. Copies made by command of King Louis Philippe, four volumes :

   Vol. I, April and May 1813.
   Vol. II, June 1813.
   Vol. III, July and August 1813.
   Vol. IV, September and October 1813.

2. *Decrees and Decisions*, 1811.
   Second half-year, 1 Vol.

Copy of the Decrees of the Emperor with a few notes in the margin in the handwriting of the Emperor (from the Ministry of Public Worship).

3. *Extract from the Correspondence of Napoleon I.*, Vol. III, 1809 to 1815 (Ministry of Marine and Colonies).

4. *Register of Correspondence and Orders written from the Island of Elba*, 1814 to 1815, dictated by the Emperor Napoleon (Library at the Louvre).

5. *Correspondence of Napoleon I with his Major-General.*
   1810 : Vols. I, IV, V, and VI.
   1811–12 : Vols. VII and VIII.
   1813 : Vols. VIII and XII.
   (War Office.)

6. *Letters and Orders of Napoleon.*
Copies and originals.
1810, 1811, 1812, 1813, 1814, 1815 (Office of Foreign Affairs).
The letters to be collected together are divided into :

1. *Originals* signed by the Emperor, in the Public Offices, and a few at the Archives.
2. *Minutes*, nearly all at the Archives, with few originals.
3. *Copies*, a portion at the Archives.

I. With a view to collect in one spot all the letters of Napoleon, below are the places from which these documents must be withdrawn :

1. A portion, mentioned above, already withdrawn by General Favé, consisting of hastily written letters almost entirely in the form of minutes, and of the registries wherein are the originals.
2. A considerable portion at the Archives—48,000 letters.
3. Foreign Office, fourteen volumes.
4. War Office, twenty volumes.
5. Public Worship.
6. Finance.
7. Public Instruction.
8. Marine, two volumes, I believe.
9. Library at the Louvre.
10. Council of State. Collection of the letters of Napoleon I to M. Bigot de Préameneu, also his memoirs.
11. Personal Archives of the Emperor
12. Private Archives.

As regards Nos. 1 to 11 inclusive it is easy to collect them if the Emperor will give an order to General Favé to withdraw from these different offices all the letters to be found therein without exception.

As to No. 12 this will be impossible, because these documents are in the hands of private individuals ; we only have more or less authentic copies of them, in addition to the minutes at the Archives.

II. To take these documents from the offices indicated above on an order from the Emperor to General Favé, and deposit them in a place to be appointed. Then, having constituted the new Napoleonic Archives, to draw up a report to the Emperor, who shall decide what is to be done.

Nota.—To consult General Favé as to the place wherein to assemble them and as to the method of taking possession of them.

NOTE IX

Project of a Plébiscite.

18th February, 1870.

A right belonging to the public is necessary in every civilised society; it *must* exist, either in the traditions or in a written charter. The most casual reading of the Proclamation of the 14th January, 1852, of the *plébiscite*, of the Constitution, of the decrees of the Senate, and of the laws, prove that these were rendered in a spirit and letter diametrically opposed to the decree of the Senate of the 8th September, 1869 and to the policy promised by the Ministry on the 2nd January, 1870.

The policy of the country is struggling in an inextricable muddle because the public right of the French rests on no foundations. It is absolutely quite impossible to attempt to reform our political order solely by laws and the decisions of the Senate, without recasting the Constitution and the *plébiscite*. It is a task before which the Ministry will fall. It is the same thing as to attempt to construct a building by beginning with the roof and the furniture, instead of beginning by the foundations and the walls.

As universal suffrage is the sole recognised base of the political order in France recourse must be had to it in essential circumstances. It is indispensable. Its legality is not in doubt; it is in the spirit and letter of all that constitutes our political right, the sole undisputed base of which is universal suffrage.

A *plébiscite is necessary for the Emperor, his Dynasty, and public order, and for the establishment of a liberal Empire:*

1. *For the Emperor and his Dynasty, which are the result of a vote cast eighteen years ago following a* coup d'état *and under a compulsion which cannot be disputed.*—The people, who ratified the *plébiscite*, did so under impressions which were opposed to the public opinion of to-day, and in direct opposition to constitutional and Parliamentary notions. The mandate, therefore, has undergone a considerable weakening, and the moral force of the Empire is affected and is conscious of it. There is urgent necessity to re-temper it by the popular suffrage, the sole undisputed power which still has any authority in these days of general anxiety and complete anarchy in which we find ourselves.

If, from another point of view, the form of monarchy existing in the Empire does not permit it to appeal directly to the people requesting a fresh sanction for the Imperial Dynasty, we must take advantage of the circumstances occasioned by the transformation of a despotic Empire into a liberal Empire to ask their indirect confirmation of the Emperor's Dynasty, which will give to it an undisputed force lacking to-day, whereby to surmount the difficulties in the midst of which it is situated.

This is conformable to the traditions of the First Empire, which acted in this way in 1815 by submitting a new act to the suffrage of the French.

The opportunity arises from a necessity acknowledged by public opinion, by the Emperor, by the Ministry, and by the great corporation of the State, of transforming radically the policy in force from 1852 to 1870.

The advantage to the Empire, therefore, cannot be disputed.

2. *For the establishment of a liberal Empire.*—So long as there is no *plébiscite* a liberal Empire can have no basis; the former Constitution no longer exists; we are doing just the contrary of the system it desired to establish; the new Constitution has not been set up; hence arises this deluge of proposals, innumerable modifications, and details on the part of the Government, Deputies, and public opinion; and, admitting that these modifications be secured, so long as the Constitution of 1852 and the *plébiscite* remain unchanged, nothing will be accomplished, or, rather, all that shall have been accomplished can be undone in quite a legal manner within four and twenty hours. The Emperor can dismiss his Ministers; he can prorogue the Legislative Assembly, and even that would not be necessary; the majority very likely will lend themselves to a return to the former policy (more especially after an interval of a few months has intervened), provoked and hastened thereto by the party of disorder and irreconcilable opposition. The Senate will still remain the legal instrument to approve of the return to a despotic Empire; the Army will be at hand to give strength to this reaction; the great mass of the inhabitants of the provinces, made weary by the powerlessness of the new order of things, by its abuses and the consequent disorder in its train, will ratify what the executive power has done in conjunction with the Senate and with the support of the Army, and the great experiment of giving liberty to France will be still-born once again. After this momentary success downfall is inevitable, especially for the Emperor's successor; it is impossible to-day to endeavour to establish a lasting despotism in France: by despotism one can accomplish everything except to make it lasting. It is an axiom in our case.

The idea of a *plébiscite* is so much in the nature of things that though one may desire to put it off it will come about, but only under less favourable circumstances, after the wearied dissatisfaction and disillusionment of public opinion.

The new policy has need of the Emperor; without the support of the Emperor the new *régime* will have against it the organised forces of the country. The Army alone is in the Emperor's hands; the great mass of the country electors will ratify everything the Emperor wishes; in certain towns the majority, working people and revolutionaries, adhere to a republic; a liberal Empire separated from the Emperor will only hold a considerable portion of the *bourgeoisie*, educated people; but these elements, which are indispensable for governing, are also indispensable against a *coup de force*; they are like slow-acting springs which regain their elasticity with time, but which give way under the pressure of a crisis.

With the support of the Emperor, who will bring to it the Army and the peasants, constitutional liberty will establish itself, and will triumph without difficulty over the revolutionary elements; separated from the Emperor liberty cannot count for much; it is a necessary alliance; the Emperor, by himself, can still attempt to govern by force; he cannot make it last. It is therefore necessary to enter upon this great question of a modification of the Constitution.

Having decided the question of the necessity and of the opportunity

Appendix

of a constitutional transformation of the Empire, let us examine the means. Two offer themselves to the mind :

I. To influence public opinion through the Press by opening a discussion on the necessity of a *plébiscite*, the Proclamation of the Emperor to the French people countersigned by the Ministers ; a declaration by Ministers to the Legislative Assembly and to the Senate, requesting the approval of these two bodies ; submitting within the shortest delay the new *plébiscite* to the ratification of the French people.

The *plébiscite* should bear on six points.

The French people desire :

1. A Constitutional and Representative Monarchy based on the principles of the French Revolution, with the Emperor Napoleon III and his Dynasty, in the order established by the decree of the Senate of the 7th November, 1852, and the organic decree of the 18th December, 1852.
2. Ministers who shall be responsible.
3. Two elected Chambers, one indirectly, the other directly, by universal suffrage.
4. The right of the Sovereign, with the approval of the two Chambers, to make open appeal to the people, when any modification is desired in the present form of *plébiscite* ;
5. The loyal application of these fundamental bases shall be carried out by the constituted authority of the Emperor and the two Chambers.

II. The second means would be to draw up here and now, not the bases of a Constitution, but the Constitution itself, which would necessitate twenty to thirty Articles at least.

The Sovereign would have to propose it to the Senate and the Legislative Assembly. This would be a usurpation of constituted authority by the three powers, which is not legal. A Constitution drawn up in the form of a proposition made to the people would be submitted to its ratification. For a *plébiscite* to give its approval to a Constitution completely drawn up is an illusion.

The inconveniences attaching to this method, which, it is true, is within the traditions of the Republic and of the Empire, would be so great that there is hardly need to go into them. The greatest of all would be the time it would necessitate and the distrust which would be felt by public opinion in acknowledging the Senate and the Legislative Assembly, as at present composed, as the constituted authority. This seems to us to be impossible.

With regard to the plan of having a liberal constitution drawn up solely by the Emperor and the Ministry, and submitting it directly to the people without preliminary discussion and approval by the two Chambers, this appears to us to be without sense ; the Emperor no longer possesses the requisite moral force ; people would see in it a return to dictatorial authority. All the serious objections which might be raised to a *plébiscite* to approve a Constitution framed under twenty or thirty Articles are much more considerable than those attaching to a *plébiscite* on five Articles, of which one only is fundamental—a Constitutional Monarchy and the Napoleonic Dynasty—the other four Articles being only a development of these principles. It cannot be gainsaid that the humblest citizen, universal suffrage being admitted, is capable of declaring himself on the question of knowing whether he desires a Monarchy or a Republic, and of stating the dynasty he prefers. If there is one question on which the people is capable of declaring itself, it is this : it is clear-cut, circumscribed, and decided. As universal suffrage is the basis of our political *régime*, it is not open to dispute that it must be admitted that it is able to pronounce upon this principle with its eyes open. And those who disapprove absolutely of the formula of the *plébiscite* as a regular method of government will be able readily to uphold, if they remain logical to themselves, that under exceptional circumstances it is the only means of emerging from the anxiety and anarchy in which we are situated, of re-endowing the Empire with moral force, and of establishing it on sound political bases, which is the only thing it is in our power to do, since the social bases, now profoundly disturbed, are in the moral order and have nothing to do with the laws.

The opportunity no one can dispute ; the *plébiscite* of 1852 is all distorted ; the necessity of making a change of policy was so evident that the act anticipated the legal right. Since, as a fact, we are trying to apply a constitutional *régime*, let us give it a legal basis, without which the difficulties of applying it will go on increasing, and will preclude us from looking for success.

THE END

INDEX

A

Abbattucci, Charles, 33, 248
Abbattucci, Séverin, 249 *et seq.*
Alba, Duke of, 81
Alessandri, 122
Alexander II, Emperor of Russia, 101, 102, 116, 187, 192
Algeria, 88 *et seq.*, 122, 190, 206
Alma, Battle of the, 59, 60, 62, 68, 78, 88
Almanach de Gotha, 29
Almanach Populaire, 29
Archives, National, 201, 204 *et seq.*, 221, 282 *et seq.*
Arenenberg, 17 *et seq.*, 23, 189, 210
Arese, Marquis, 242
Ascot, 46
Augier, Emile, 157
Aumale, Duc d', 168 *et seq.*
Aupick, General, 270
Austria, Emperor of. *See* FRANCIS JOSEPH
Autemarre, General, 135 *et seq.*, 139 *et seq.*, 144

B

Banque Générale Suisse, 179
Barbès, 255
Baroche, 83, 84, 86, 132
Barrot, Odilon, 52, 202
Beauharnais, Hortense de, 17, 21, 25, 29
Beauharnais, Josephine de (Empress Josephine), 25, 27
Beaumont, de, 33, 95
Bedeau, General, 256
Benedetti, 121, 272, 275
Berry, Duc de, 164
Billault, 187 *et seq.*, 192 *et seq.*, 275
Bismarck, 227, 239
Bixio, Jacques Alexandre, 100, 133
Blanc, Louis, 255
Blandeau, 232
Bleschamps, Alexandrine de, 41
Blanqui, 255
Boissy, de, 182, 189
Bonaparte, Charles Lucien (Prince of Canino, 1803-57), 28, 41, 46
Bonaparte, Jerome, King of Westphalia, 21, 24, 25, 31, 32, 37, 40, 42, 43, 44, 45, 49, 50, 63, 68, 69, 81, 83, 84, 86, 153 *et seq.*, 157 *et seq.*, 283
Bonaparte, Jerome Napoleon (brother of Prince Napoleon), 20, 40-1, 42, 43, 45
Bonaparte, Jerome Napoleon (grandson of Jerome, King of Westphalia, by his marriage with Elisabeth Paterson), 68, 158, 162
Bonaparte, Louis Napoleon. *See* NAPOLEON III
Bonaparte, Louis Joseph Jerome (second son of Prince Napoleon), 199 *et seq.*, 203
Bonaparte, Louis, King of Holland, 20, 201, 204 *et seq.*
Bonaparte, Louis Lucien (eldest son of Charles Lucien), 50
Bonaparte, Lucien (Prince of Canino, 1775-1840), 44
Bonaparte, Napoleon. *See* NAPOLEON I
Bonaparte, Napoleon Charles (a grandson of Lucien), 246
Bonaparte, Napoleon Joseph Charles Paul. *See* PRINCE NAPOLEON
Bonaparte, Napoleon Victor Jerome Frederic (eldest son of Prince Napoleon), 183, 195, 198, 251
Bonaparte, Pierre Napoleon, 41
Bonaparte, Princess Mathilde, 153, 157, 199, 244
Bonaparte, The Prince Imperial, 80 *et seq.*, 85, 182, 203, 208, 239, 255
Bosquet, 59, 66
Bourbaki, General, 146, 232, 239
Bouet, Admiral, 235
Bourqueney, Baron de, 150 *et seq.*
Brunswick, Duke of, 258
Buoncampagni, 138
Bure, Pierre Jean François, 34, 36
Burillon, 33
Buzolini, 21

C

Cambacérès, Marie, 33
Cambridge, Duke of, 65
Camerata, Comtesse, 21, 25, 28, 30
Canrobert, 59, 66, 134
Carnot, 218
Carignan, Prince, 107
Casabianca, 252
Cassagnac, Granier de, 126
Cavaignac, General, 47, 50, 52, 188, 193, 256
Cavour, Count, 101, 105, 108 *et seq.*, 112, 122, 124, 126 *et seq.*, 133, 143, 155, 171, 175, 177, 190, 193
Chabrier, de, 270
Champagny, Paul de, 270
Chancourtois, de, 95
Changarnier, General, 256
Charlemagne, 20, 22, 27
Charles X, 164
Charras, Colonel 256
Chasseloup-Loubat, 120, 128
Chassériau, 270
Chevreau, 241

Index

Clarigny, Cucheval, 270
Clotilde, Princess, 106, 149, 151, 156 et seq., 159, 180, 183 et seq., 194 et seq., 199 et seq., 203, 210, 227, 230 et seq., 240, 242, 243, 254, 275
Comandini, Alfredo, 135
Conneau, Dr., 19, 20, 24, 40, 42, 46, 241
Constant, Benjamin, 218
Constantine, Grand Duke, 46
Conti, 248, 250, 273
Cornu, Madame, 29, 205
Courrier, 38
Courtois, 33
Couza, Prince (Prince of Moldavia), 122
Crimean War, 59–70, 72, 74, 75, 77
Cumberland, Duke of, 164

D

Daily News, 240
Daumas, General, 95, 200
David, Baron, 245
Davillier, 244
Débats, 203
Delangle, 89, 132
Demidoff, 24, 27
Desportes, Félix, 33
Desvaux, General, 147
Ducasse, Baron, 204
Duchâtel, Comte, 25, 29, 31 et seq.
Dufour, Colonel, 45
Dumas, Alexandre, 28
Duperré, 240
Dupin, Charles, 270
Duruy, 203
Duvernois, 249

E

Espartero, 44, 68
Espinasse, General, 95, 97
Eugénie, Empress, 64, 67, 68, 70, 80–1, 99, 107, 112, 121, 149, 152, 171, 180, 182 et seq., 197, 205, 207 et seq., 225, 239 et seq., 245, 247, 254, 272, 275
Exposition Universelle, 80, 272

F

Farini, 139
Favé, General, 232, 283 et seq.
Flahaut, de, 197, 270
Fleury, 243
Forey, General, 267
Fortins, 33
Fould, Achille, 81, 83, 86, 95, 109, 131, 153, 155, 222
Francis Joseph, Emperor of Austria, 148, 267
François II, King of Sicily, 155

Franconière, General de, 98, 141, 153, 207, 233, 272
Frossard, General, 232, 283 et seq.

G

Garibaldi, 155, 171, 223 et seq.
Gauthier, 155
Girardin, Emile de, 100, 133
Goschler, 270
Goyen, General de, 272
Gréterin, 91
Gueroult, 104
Guizot, 31, 33, 132
Guzman, Eugénie de. *See* EMPRESS EUGÉNIE

H

Harcourt, d', 202
Hilliers, General Baraguay d', 64
House of Peers, 19, 43

I

Inkerman, 59 et seq., 69, 78
Istrie, Duc d', 35

J

Jeaucourt, de, 229
Joly, 33 et seq.
Josephine, Empress. *See* JOSEPHINE DE BEAUHARNAIS
Jouvencal, de, 229
Judenne, 204, 232

K

Kisseleff, 124
Klapka, General, 72, 122, 179
Kossuth, 151
Kulture, Gallet de, 232

L

Laborde, de, 197, 204 et seq., 221 et seq., 270
Lacroix, Hortense. *See* MADAME CORNU
Lafayette, 202
La Force, Duc de, 222
Laity, 50
Lajatico, Marquis, 136
Lamoricière, General, 256
Lavalette, 272
Larabit, 33
Laurent, 25
Lefèvre, Armand, 270
Le Flô, General, 256
Le Gallifet, Captain, 207
Levert, 243
Lhuys, Drouyn de, 275
Lind, Jenny, 44, 46
Louis Philippe, 31 et seq., 35, 47, 49, 220, 257, 261, 280, 283

Index

Louis XIV, 27, 30
Louis XVIII, 164, 257
Louis I, King of Portugal, 199, *et seq.*
Lucca, Prince of, 46

M

MacMahon, 238
Magnan, 94, 172
Magne, 132, 274
Malakoff, Duc de, 83, 84, 86
Malleville, de, 52 *et seq.*
Maury, Alfred, 232
Mehemet Ali, 64
Mellinet, General, 203
Meurthe, Henri Boulay de la, 270
Mérimée, Prosper, 270
Mocquard, 114
Modène, Duc de, 111
Moldavia, Prince of. *See* PRINCE COUZA
Moniteur, 115, 121, 124, 127, 130, 149, 183, 188, 191, 207, 209, 215, 271, 272, 273
Montesquieu, 129
Montholon, General, 19 *et seq.*, 50
Morlot, Cardinal, 83, 84, 86
Morny, Comte de, 83, 84, 86, 275
Murat, Joachim, 244
Murat, Lucien, 24, 47, 171 *et seq.*, 273

N

Napoleon I, 25, 27, 45, 51, 206, 213, 218, 231, 256, 268 *et seq.*, 272, 273, 282 *et seq.*
Napoleon III, Early friendship with Prince Napoleon, 9; at Arenenberg, 18; the Boulogne failure, 18; captivity at Ham, 19 *et seq.*; financial straits, 24 *et seq.*; endeavour to sell some articles of value, 27; escape from Ham, 43; London, 43–6; arrival in Paris and election as a Deputy, 47; elected President of the Republic, 52; plot against his life at Marseilles, 56 *et seq.*; Crimean War, 59–70; birth of the Prince Imperial, 80 *et seq.*; the Privy Council, 83; the campaign in Italy, 135–151; *affaire Paterson*, 157 *et seq.*; refuses Prince Napoleon permission to go to Italy, 164 *et seq.*; the Italian question, 167 *et seq.*; rebukes the Prince for his speech in the Senate, 180 *et seq.*; letters to the Prince regarding the publication of the *Correspondance de l'Empereur*, 196 *et seq.*; reply to Prince Napoleon regarding Polish refugees, 203; publicly reprimands Prince Napoleon for his speech at Ajaccio, 206; proposes a new Government, 215; the Franco-German War, 234 *et seq.*; capitulates after defeat of Mac Mahon's army, 238; at Chislehurst, 245 *et seq.*; dies at Chislehurst, 254
Napoleon, Prince, Beginning of his friendship with the Emperor, 9; character, 10 *et seq.*; duel with Count de la Roche Pouchin, 23; tries to visit Ham, 31 *et seq.*; elected a deputy, 47; reprimanded by the Emperor, 53; his activity in the Crimean War, 59–70; returns to France, 71; his opinion of the situation in the Crimea, 75 *et seq.*; Ministry of Algeria, 89–100; mission to the Emperor of Russia, 101 *et seq.*; mission to Turin, 106; his stay at Turin and betrothal to Princess Clotilde, 106–12; resignation as Minister for Algiers, 115 *et seq.*; views on the ministers, 130 *et seq.*; issue of proclamation in Tuscany, 137; his part in the Italian Campaign, 139–49; *affaire Paterson*, 157 *et seq.*; his speech on the Italian question and reply by the Duc d'Aumale, 167 *et seq.*; quarrel with Prince Murat, 171 *et seq.*; a violent speech in the Senate and a rebuke by the Emperor, 180 *et seq.*; birth of first son, 183; complaint of the Emperor's treatment of him, 188 *et seq.*; visits Italy with Princess Clotilde, 195; letter regarding Polish refugees, 201 *et seq.*; the *Correspondance de l'Empereur*, 204, *et seq.*: indiscreet speech at Ajaccio, for which he is publicly reprimanded by the Emperor, 206 *et seq.*; resigns from the Privy Council, 209; report of progress in the publication of the *Correspondance de l'Empereur*, 213 *et seq.*; letter regarding the Emperor's proposal of a new Government, 216; views on new policy, 217 *et seq.*; decorated by the Emperor of Austria, 222; mission to Italy to gain her support for France, 234–7; wish to join the Emperor in his captivity, 238; visits the Empress at Chislehurst, 239 *et seq.*
Ney, Marshal, 256
Niel, Marshal, 106, 108 *et seq.*, 193
Nigra, 105, 114, 122, 128, 193
Noel, 20, 30

O

Ollivier, Emile, 245
Omar Pacha, 65 *et seq.*

Index

Opinion Nationale, 187, 203
Orleans, Prince of, 169–70
Ornano, Napoleon d', 26
Orsay, d', 44
Oscar, Prince, 46

P

Padua, Duke of, 238
Paoli, 33
Parma, Duchess of, 139
Paterson, Elisabeth, 68, 157 et seq., 162
Pays, 281
Pelissier. See Duc de Malakoff
Persigny, Duc de, 50, 83 et seq., 86, 88, 121, 173, 193, 239 et seq., 274
Petetin, 276
Petit, General, 270
Peyrat, 96 et seq.
Piedmont, 105, 108, 111, 114, 123 et seq., 151, 155 et seq., 167, 176
Pietri, Franceschini, 207, 243, 244, 248
Pisani, 114
Pope, The, 139, 141, 163 et seq., 167, 172, 176, 179, 206, 223, 275, 281
Préameneu, Bigot de, 284
Prefect of Police, 52, 72, 73, 122, 172 et seq.
Presse, La, 96, 104
Provisional Government, The, 47 et seq.
Prudhon, 25, 27
Prussia, King of, 238

R

Rachel, 44
Raglan, Lord, 65
Ragon, 80
Raguse, Duchesse de, 35
Randon, 92 et seq., 97
Rappel, 281
Rappeti, 232
Rasponi, 139
Rattazi, 176 et seq.
Rayer, Dr., 152
Rechberg, Comte de, 151
Regnier, 239
Reille, Colonel, 144
Reine Hortense, 102, 137
Renan, Ernest, 228 et seq.
Renaud, Colonel, 68, 69
Reschid Pacha, 64
Réveil, 281
Revue de Deux Mondes, 229
Reynault, 99
Ricasoli, 175 et seq.
Richelieu, 123, 262
Rochejaquelin, de la, 167, 180, 189
Rollin, Ledru, 255
Roncière le Noury, La, 102 et seq., 107
Rouher, 94, 97, 212, 218, 220, 225, 241, 245, 248 et seq., 253, 275 et seq.
Russia, Emperor of. See Alexander II

S

Saint Arnaud, Marshal, 59, 64, 66 et seq.
St. Helena, 50
Salvage, Madame, 21, 29
Salvagnoli, 136
Sardinia, King of, 137, 148, 150, 190
Saxe-Weimar, Grand Duke of, 46
Schefer, 84
Schneider, 275
Ségur, de, 180
Sénart, 222
Siècle, 38, 104, 203
Sismondi, 218
Sophie, Queen of Holland, 183
Stolting, de, 30
Sussex, Duke of, 164

T

Thierry, Amédée, 232
Thiers, 32, 218, 270, 282
Tinan, Admiral de, 156
Tour d'Auvergne, Prince de la, 108, 129 et seq.
Trochu, 63
Troplong, 83 et seq., 86
Tuscany, Grand Duke of, 43

U

Uhrich, General, 135 et seq., 147

V

Vaillant, Marshal, 132, 195 et seq., 200, 204, 210, 270, 283
Venosta, Visconti, 238
Vernet, Horace, 25
Victor Emmanuel II, 101, 105, 108, 112, 125, 183, 199, 223, 230, 234, 235, 240, 251, 277
Vieillard, 33, 36, 40 et seq., 44, 47
Vieillard, Madame, 39
Villot, 244
Vimercati, 236
Visconti, 35
Vogt, Charles, 113 et seq., 122
Voisin, Colonel, 34

W

Wagram, Prince, 44
Walewski, Count, 103, 110, 127 et seq., 138, 157, 203, 274
Walsch, 272
Waterloo, 88
Wellington, Duke of, 88
William III, King of Holland, 183
William I of Wurtemburg, 183, 200
Wimpffen, General, 140
Wurtemburg, Frederick of, 18, 141

Y

York, Duke of, 164

Z

Zouaves, 141